Suzanne Catalano is a creative, imaginative thinker. Suzanne enjoys being on the perimeter, watching people in action and inventing back stories for them, based on the slice-of-life snapshot in her mind.

Suzanne's novel, *Sun-Kissed Mountains of Home*, is a tribute to her love of animals and ranch life. Her experience working at a saddle shop in the local community provided fodder for creating a true-to-life story whose characters are compelling and entertaining.

Suzanne combines her love of horses with her creative writing skills to craft novels featuring animals and their bond with humans.

This book is dedicated to Jean Hegland, author of *Into the Forest.* Jean Hegland, who taught my creative writing class, generously offered to read my manuscript in its first draft. My dreams to be an author were put on hold while life happened. The manuscript, with all Jean's editing notes and words of encouragement sat in a filing box in my garage for twenty-plus years.

In retirement, while going through the process of moving, I came across the box of short stories and novels and after relocating to Tucson, AZ, I resurrected my passion for writing and turned it into a hobby.

Taking Jean's notes and advice, I have since redrafted and edited the manuscript many times over. Twenty-five years later, and the book is finished.

Thank you, Jean Hegland. You proved that sage advice never ages.

Suzanne Catalano

Sun-Kissed Mountains of Home

Austin Macauley Publishers™
London * Cambridge * New York * Sharjah

This is a work of fiction. Names, characters, businesses, places, events, locales, and incidents are either the products of the author's imagination or used in a fictitious manner. Any resemblance to actual persons, living or dead, or actual events is purely coincidental.

Ordering Information
Quantity sales: Special discounts are available on quantity purchases by corporations, associations, and others. For details, contact the publisher at the address below.

Publisher's Cataloging-in-Publication data
Catalano, Suzanne
Sun-Kissed Mountains of Home

ISBN 9798889107132 (Paperback)
ISBN 9798889107149 (ePub e-book)

Library of Congress Control Number: 2023921086

www.austinmacauley.com/us

First Published 2024
Austin Macauley Publishers LLC
40 Wall Street, 33rd Floor, Suite 3302
New York, NY 10005
USA

mail-usa@austinmacauley.com
+1 (646) 5125767

Preamble

The fuzzy disturbances in the cosmic energy, unseen by the human eye, leads the heart, with infinite wisdom. The forces that seek to answer the prayers of many are always at work. In matters of the soul, time isn't measured by hours, days, or years. For some souls, it takes many incarnations, and multiple lifetimes, to find wholeness. To be the two souls that complete their evolutions together within the same lifetime is the pinnacle of the meaning of life itself.

Chapter 1

"Hey, Noah," Ethan Baldwin called from his station at the gate in front of the cattle chute. "Cut that one out over there."

The cow boss nodded, turned and dug in his spurs as the little cutting horse sprang into action. Being held steady by two cowboys, the herd became restless and began to move from the pressure of the additional cowboy. Now split in two, the horse and rider pursued the smaller half, separated the one they wanted from the rest and drove the reluctant cow toward the cowboy waiting at the chute. The heifer entered the chute from one side, received a quick vet check and an annual vaccine, then got shooed out the other end.

"Next," called Ethan as the cowhands repeated the process.

In a holding pen next to the cattle chute, a much more dramatic scene was taking place. One man astride a horse was swinging his lasso above the bawling herd of calves. The rope landed around the head of one poor unfortunate creature while the rest scrambled away. As each calf in turn was wrestled and held down by two men on the ground, a third man held a branding iron to his haunch and a fourth man tagged his ear with an identification number.

The boisterous bovine ranting and running, the shouting and whistles from the men, the horses spinning, bolting, stopping hard, it all might seem like an unusually violent event, but in cattle country, it was just another day on the job.

The morning sun's rays penetrated the atmosphere on this day in early May, illuminating the dust rising above the turmoil below, bearing down equally on man and beast. A brief and unexpected gust of wind on this otherwise calm morning blew down the slopes from the peaks above and across the scene. While the other men bowed instinctively, Ethan lifted his face toward it. His hat shuddered slightly but didn't blow off, and then the wind was gone.

Working since before dawn at the Baldwin family cattle ranch were the group of nine men. With the combination of the sun and the exertion, the overheated men had shed clothing layer by layer. Down to the last layer were their thin, cotton shirts smeared with dirt and stained with perspiration made brown by the clinging dust. The shirts were their last shields of defense against the environment. The men's hats were pulled down low on their dirty, sweat glistened foreheads and they wore handkerchiefs tied over their mouths and noses to keep from choking on the swirling clouds.

This wasn't an easy job, but the experienced cowhands made it look so. The men were working hard to keep things moving in an organized fashion. The cows, mooing in protest, resisted being separated from their calves, while in the next pen, the calves were getting handled.

All the other men at gates, or astride horses were moving the cattle along at a good pace. It was important to get the work done efficiently and with minimal stress. Working with a sense of urgency, the cowboys wanted to finish the job so the herd could begin their journey from the ranch at the base of the mountains up to the beautiful valley nestled between high, snow-capped peaks.

The valley high in the mountains was the summer pasture for the Alma Soñada Ranch. A grand expanse of open space just outside the small city of Rambletap Springs, it was just north of Helena, Montana. The ranch, a fifteen thousand acre spread in the majestic Rocky Mountains, had been the home of the Baldwin clan for generations.

While the history of Montana shows the mining brothers, Granville and James Stewart, along with their partner, Reece Anderson, discovered gold first on Grasshopper Creek, on the north side of the capital city, there was another strike. A second group of miners, immigrants from Europe who originally brought their business skills to New York City, had migrated west to Montana to strike it big. They hit a Mother Lode on Wolf Creek. The miners worked their mine, celebrated their good luck, divided their riches, and parted ways.

One miner, Elias Baldwin, took his share of the gold and bought a beautiful piece of land with a river, a tributary of the mighty Missouri, running through it. His friends laughed at the foolishness when they found out he wanted the land to raise cattle. What did a New York City businessman know about raising cattle, anyway? Despite the ridicule, Elias Baldwin found what many discovered over the next century, Montana is what Texas aspires to be. Cattle country.

Ethan Baldwin, the great-great grandson of Elias Baldwin, was born to work on the ranch and wanted no other life. He couldn't imagine a better day than one spent manning the chute as he looked over every cow and calf with scrutiny. It pleased Ethan with the condition of his and his father's herd. He wanted to honor his ancestors by preserving their legacy. Raising a sizable herd of marketable cattle was the key to success.

He lifted his hat off as he swiped his brow with the terry cloth bands around his wrist. His mother had given him the cuffs for Christmas, but it had embarrassed him to accept them. He always thought he had no need for new inventions, large or small. This time his mom, and the athletes who endorsed these silly looking things, were right. The bands were coming in handy. Although Ethan never admitted it out loud, these terry cloth sponges were a big help in sopping the sweat from his forehead and keeping it out of his eyes.

As Ethan settled his hat down to return to work, he saw Paula coming from the house, and across the courtyard. Paula Mariano, Ethan's former fiancée, had been working at the ranch during the roundup preparing meals for the hired hands. Sporting an unpractical dress that looked like nothing to wear on a ranch, Paula waved as she approached the men at work who had yet to notice her. Even from afar, Ethan could see Paula was wearing too much make-up on her face. He stopped working and hurried toward the fence when he realized Paula didn't turn to the mailbox as he'd hoped.

"Hey, Paula. Looking good!" said one of the cowboys who had taken note. Another whistled in agreement, then they all stopped working.

"Hey, Ethan," the cow boss called. "If you get a break, shouldn't we get one, too?" The cow boss, Noah Crawley, who, from his vantage point in the saddle on the little cutting horse, was intensely watching Paula coming toward the corrals. Noah didn't join in with the whooping and whistling.

"Nobody's taking a break. Y'all get back to work," Ethan answered.

"I'll see to it the guys keep working," Noah's twin brother, Tad Crawley, said to Ethan. Through the settling dust, Tad saw Noah's glowering face as his brother continued to watch Ethan approach the oncoming woman at the fence.

"C'mon, Noah, please?" Tad beseeched his brother to resume the work as he himself took Ethan's position at the entrance to the chute. Though best friends since they were boys, Tad knew that with Ethan and Noah, there wasn't a lot of love between them anymore since Paula had become a wedge in their friendship.

Tad, which was short for Thaddeus, was still running a demilitarized zone between his best friend and his brother since the break-up of Ethan's engagement to Paula. Back in high school, when they were just a group of friends, Tad noticed Paula was showing feelings for Ethan after Noah had confessed to his brother he was interested in Paula, too.

With this inside knowledge, Tad had seen the triangle building between Ethan, Paula, and Noah, and had convinced his brother to be realistic. He had explained to Noah that no girl was worth losing a best friend over. Noah had relinquished and it seemed Tad's intervention had solved the problem.

The tension escalated again when Paula and Ethan became serious, but Noah's feelings for Paula hadn't gone away. "They are not right for each other." Noah had expressed concerns to his brother about Paula and Ethan. "Paula needs a man who can give her all his attention, and Ethan is so absorbed with the ranch, he hasn't time for her." Noah thought Ethan wasn't good enough for the girl with whom he himself had been in love since middle school. It all came to a head when, after a few years of dating, Paula and Ethan became engaged.

"I'm going to tell Paula how I feel," Noah confessed but Tad had quieted his brother once more using reason. "We are adults now and Ethan and Paula are engaged." Tad hoped he had gotten his brother to ignore his feelings for Paula for good this time.

With the wedding date approaching, the planning had been a group activity, like everything they had done since they were children. The more time spent together gave Noah's thoughts the opportunity to fester. Tad could only watch as the three people he cared most about were, like a runaway train, heading for a crash.

The night before the wedding, Tad and Noah threw Ethan a bachelor's party and invited all their friends for a night on the town. They met up at the Bronze Spittoon, the only bar in Rambletap Springs. By someone else's design, Paula ended up at the same establishment with her friends. The night club became one big bachelor/bachelorette celebration with dancing, playing pool and darts, and recreational drinking.

The salute to Ethan's bachelorhood ended after midnight. When they gathered for the trip home, only Noah was missing. They began looking for Noah and noticed Paula was missing, too. The consensus was Noah and Paula were last seen dancing together. It was innocent enough, but when Ethan found Paula in Noah's arms in the gazebo out back, they weren't dancing.

The hurt, the betrayal. Ethan was blindsided by two people who should have had his back, not stabbed him in it. Of course, the wedding was called off and Ethan didn't speak to Paula for months. Tad, who understood the dynamics from all sides, also knew he had to get his brother and best friend to somehow bury the hatchet. After several failed attempts to establish terms and negotiate a truce between them, Tad appealed to Ethan and Noah's common sense. "Think about the ranch," Tad said. "You two fighting is not what's best for anyone."

Running the ranch required the two adversaries to be in close proximity. The former best friends agreed to Tad's appeal but things were never the same. Tad was aware of the constant tension between the cowboys that was always exacerbated when Paula was nearby. Tad's compulsion to interfere continued as he buffered the despicable energy around them. It was a daunting job he had given himself.

Funneling his frustration, Tad turned to the group of hired men still gawking at the distracting sight of Paula, and said, "You heard the man. Get back to work. This ain't no break time."

~****~

As Ethan reached the fence where Paula stood, he could tell she enjoyed interrupting the work. She bowed and shimmied as if she was on a stage performing for the men's adorations. The catcalls only encouraged her…

"What is it?" Ethan said, trying not to clinch his jaw. He wished Paula hadn't created such a fuss among the hired hands.

"Don't be so angry. You should be happy to see me."

A petite woman in her twenties, Paula was a blond, but not naturally. She sprayed her hair into a fashionable updo, and her false eyelashes were so thick they made it hard to see into her eyes. Ethan despised Paula for thinking she could still tell him how to be. They weren't together anymore and she had no right.

"What do you need, Paula?"

"Your mom just called. Your father will come home on Sunday."

"Okay, good. Was that it?" Ethan looked back at the crew who had returned to their duties.

This had been a tough week on the Alma Soñada Ranch. With his father, Ansel Baldwin, getting sick with severe abdominal pains and being rushed to the hospital in the middle of a spring roundup, Ethan had continued the job. Ethan took control of the position with ease and full cooperation from the hired hands, that of whom some were over fifteen years his senior. The toughest part had been the time alone with his ex-fiancée, Paula. She had used his parents ' absence as an opportunity to rekindle a relationship that existed only in her mind.

"I gotta get back. We want to finish today," Ethan excused himself as he walked away.

"Wait," Paula called. "Can't you talk a minute? I've been so lonely all by myself."

Ethan ignored Paula's plea and made tracks back to the swarming dust and bellowing cows. He preferred their bellyaching over Paula's constant need for conversation and companionship.

Frowning as she stared at the back of Ethan's head, she wished she could throw something. Paula jumped off the fence where she had sat and headed to the house. She needed to finish making dinner for the crew. With no one else at home right now, it all rested on her shoulders.

Paula was like a daughter to Ethan's parents, Ansel and Vida Baldwin, long before she and their son became engaged. The Baldwins were her godparents, her mom and dad's best friends. The Baldwin family mourned the loss when Paula's folks were both killed in a tragic auto accident. After her parents' funeral less than a year ago, Paula came to live on the ranch.

It was hard on Paula to lose her family in an instant and even harder when it happened two months after Ethan had called off their wedding. Living as a brother and sister was not what Paula wanted. She was sure Ethan would come to his senses and she and he could be married according to the original plan. It was only a matter of time.

Paula lifted her chin with resolve and went back inside to plan a romantic interlude for tomorrow. It was her and Ethan's last night. If the men finished branding the calves today as Ethan prophesied, the hired cowboys would be gone after dinner and it would be her and Ethan alone in the house until the Baldwins came home on Sunday.

Ethan had none of the usual excuses to keep his distance from her. With the roundup done, the cattle resting up for the drive to the high country, and his father's return, there was nothing else to preoccupy Ethan's mind. Paula couldn't see Ethan having anything more important to think about than her.

Chapter 2

The same warm spring air that had blown the dust around the working cow hands at the Alma Soñada Ranch blew farther down the valley toward the city. Speeding up the highway, straight into the wind in her SUV was a young lady from back east. The same wind that had almost removed the cowboy's hat now aimed for car the driven by Miranda Dunn. With all the windows down, speeding along the country road, Miranda relished the tickle across her face as the wind forced renegade strands of thick black hair out of the clip secured on her head. This was her last travel day. Miranda would spend her last night of this trip in a motel.

Miranda had been traveling for two weeks from Connecticut to her new adventure in Montana where she hoped to expand her non-profit agency. She had seen many sights as she drove her Land Rover through the seven states that lay between her old life in Torrington and the life she expected to build in the small community called Rambletap Springs. This, she hoped was the beginning of keeping promises made.

Since becoming involved in horseback riding therapy when she was a teenager, Miranda dreamed of having a facility of her own. After years in the non-profit sector promoting and facilitating for others, she was still almost too afraid to branch out. Along with her continued work at her agency, she now dreamed of having an equine therapeutic program on an authentic working cattle ranch. For a young woman from the city, there was the possibility she was biting off more than she could chew. But she was determined to try her best to succeed.

The last leg of the journey took her across the Missouri River, west through Helena, and then northwest to Rambletap Springs. Miranda planned to reach the Alma Soñada Ranch shortly after noon tomorrow. She was meeting the owners and intended to make a good impression. The place of her dreams was on the line.

Through her non-profit agency, Miranda created a model program that connected and managed horse owners with therapy providers to offer their services for the physically and mentally challenged. The success of her organization was very satisfying, but she longed to expand. She dreamed of a facility where riding students and their families could all enjoy horses together.

Miranda envisioned an equine academy that could not only see to the needs of students at various levels of ability, but also get the children riding outside the arena. She proposed her dream of expanding to her attorney, Albert Bennett. Albert took Miranda's plan a step farther, suggesting she take it to a ranch setting. Albert Bennett set her up with his wife's cousin, Ansel Baldwin, who owned a place on the outskirts of Helena, Montana.

Miranda was communicating with the Baldwins after her attorney introduced them over a conference call. Miranda's plans appealed to them and her business proposal was well received. Her numbers added up favorably, and it thrilled her to get the green light. The Baldwins were amenable to the possibility, but also expressed some concerns.

The Alma Soñada Ranch was the last of the open spaces to be threatened by the big push from the suburbs of the state's capital city. The close-knit town of Rambletap Springs had been suffering growing pains. Urban sprawl from the greater Helena metropolitan area was relentless. The onus was on Miranda to assure the Baldwins there would be no negative impact on the land or their community.

Miranda eased on the breaks as she approached Rambletap Springs city limits. She entered a driveway, and steered the large SUV into an available parking spot outside a supermarket. She stepped out of the truck and stretched. She had enjoyed the last miles of the trip and was ready to eat.

The shopping center was filled with the Friday lunch crowd. There was a pizza place, cafe, and a deli. At the corner was a Burger King franchise that didn't fit the theme of the town. Better than the fast-food option, Miranda chose the delicatessen. The deli's clever name, Deli Up to the Table, was creatively inviting. As she walked from her car to the sandwich shop, Miranda noticed the other vehicles were trucks with tools and equipment in the beds. Construction workers, another sign of the growth in the area.

"Can I help you?" the woman behind the counter asked after giving Miranda time to study the menu.

"I'll have a turkey breast on dark rye with everything on it except mayonnaise and onions." Miranda had eaten a protein bar with her coffee that morning and now she was hungry. She paid for the sandwich, a flavored mineral water, a pint of potato salad and went outside to eat. From her table, looking in the direction she thought the Baldwin ranch to be, she could view the mountains.

Rambletap Springs, with its convenient proximity to the big city, seemed miles away from everything but many people discovered the small-town charm and began moving in. When they ran out of space to build new houses in the valley, they spread up the mountain. Miranda noticed the build sites making their move into the foothills of the granite topped mountains that jutted skyward. The Rambletap ridge was part of the Rocky Mountain range. The largest mountain system in North America, the Rocky Mountain range extended from Canada into the United States and south through the state of New Mexico.

They'll build on solid rock when they can make enough money at it, Miranda thought, looking up the slopes, as she finished her sandwich.

With a satisfied stomach, Miranda had the energy to walk around to further acclimate. Rarely had she ever been outside the big city and she was concerned being in the country might take some getting used to. She was already opening up to the relaxed feel and as she strolled along the sidewalks, she could picture bringing clients to the area for family fun.

She knew her plans were a win/win for everyone involved. Her ideas had gotten the attention of investors. Albert had made inquiries. Now, she just had to pick up some advocacy on the local level. After walking around, Miranda headed over to the hotel to check in.

The mountain cast a shadow over the valley as sunset came early to the little community of Rambletap Springs. Miranda carried an overnight bag into the room, one more night in a motel and tomorrow she'd be staying as a guest at the Alma Soñada Ranch.

Chapter 3

High noon at the Alma Soñada the next day looked the extreme opposite of how it had looked all week. To Paula's relief, the extra cowboys had gone home. Ethan gave the Crawley twins the day off, so there were no meals to prepare. It surprised Paula to have taken her all morning to get done the chores she needed to do before her godparents returned home from Helena.

It disappointed Paula that Ethan made himself scarce. Giving the twins the day off was a double-edged blade; she and Ethan were the only ones on the ranch which gave them privacy, but Ethan being the only one working at the ranch today meant he had triple the chores. It made her unhappy but, Paula knew she had to accept it. Paula hoped there would be some quality time with Ethan during the day as a prelude to what she was planning for the evening. She would have to condense her script into a smaller act.

"Who could that be?" Paula said to the black cat sitting on the chest of drawers. Paula peered through the upstairs bedroom window at what had caught her eye, a truck she didn't recognize turning off the highway. Based on the rooster tail of dust behind the vehicle, Paula knew it was coming fast.

Alone this afternoon in her room, Paula was putting on the finishing touches, setting the stage for her evening with Ethan. After searching the internet, Paula had read up on some romantic ideas. She set out candles, and softened the lighting with scarves hung over the lampshades. Set glasses on the nightstand for the champagne she had chilled in the refrigerator and she even got fresh strawberries. She questioned the romantic qualities of the berries, but read it brings out the flavor in the champagne.

Paula scattered rose petals on the bed, softly scolding her cat as the feline rolled and played with the scented pieces of flowers. It had surprised her when she noticed the oncoming car. By the time Paula got downstairs, the approaching vehicle was halfway up to the house.

Paula went outside the kitchen door and looked toward the barn to see if Ethan had seen the coming of an intruder, but there was no sign of him. Maybe he was in the barn cleaning the tack and getting ready to take the herd to the high country. Paula looked down the gravel road, but by that time the truck had gone past the arena and pulled to the front, out of sight from the corrals.

Feeling vulnerable, Paula cautiously followed the veranda that ran the perimeter of the home to the formal entrance on the side facing the road to town. The burgundy Sport Utility Vehicle had parked and climbing out was a woman Paula had never met. Her hair was black and in sharp contrast to her fair complexion. The woman wore a tailored, pale blue jacket with matching dress pants that accentuated her height and slender figure nicely. Paula wished that she was lost and could quickly be sent on her way. There was still lots of work to do to prepare for Ansel and Vida's home coming tomorrow. Paula needed the rest of today to carry out her enticing evening plans with Ethan. Paula didn't need any interruptions.

"Hello. My name is Miranda Dunn. I am here to see Ansel or Vida Baldwin," Miranda said politely to the young woman who appeared on the veranda at the corner of the residence.

"They aren't here." It disheartened Paula that this woman knew Ansel and Vida by name and might not be easily dismissed.

"When will they be home?" It puzzled Miranda, and she hoped she hadn't gotten the dates mixed up. "I had an appointment with them today."

"I don't believe the Baldwins are expecting anyone at all." Paula was adamant.

Miranda wondered how she made that mistake. She spoke by phone on two separate occasions about the best time for everyone to get together. Miranda spent weeks arranging her work schedule back home in Connecticut. Starting with the two week drive out to Montana and culminating in the meetup this weekend, Saturday to be exact. Mr. Baldwin had also been very specific about Miranda's stay at the ranch after the spring roundup when he and his wife were able to focus on what Miranda offered.

"There must be some mistake," Miranda started. "Mr. and Mrs. Baldwin…"

"Are not home, and I reckon you ought to be leaving." A man came from around the house, interrupting Miranda mid-sentence, as she was trying to explain things. The man was too young to be Ansel Baldwin. It left Miranda wondering.

The guy was quite tall, with a muscular frame, and the bluest eyes Miranda had ever seen. With hat pulled low over dark blond locks that were too long to be short, and too short to be long, he appeared to be covered from head to foot in a thick layer of grime and Miranda would have laughed if not for the intense look on his face.

"I'm Miranda Dunn. I was to meet…" Miranda began again, only to be cut off.

"You," the man's eyes narrowed, "better do as I say. We don't want to sell. I've had it with you real estate people. We won't let you tear up our land to develop it and sell it off in pieces. For the last time, leave us alone."

Ethan was constantly warding off pushy realtors in the past and had a cumulative anger toward them. This lady was especially irritating as it was her untimely arrival that not only interrupted his work but it was her accelerating tires as she rounded the curve into the gravel yard that was the reason, he was now spitting dust from his mouth and knocking bits of gravel from his ears.

The spray of rocks on the fence sent airborne when Miranda spun her tires had spooked Kit, the young horse Ethan was training in the round pen, causing the colt to buck. The horse's unexpected behavior surprised Ethan, and he lost his balance, which further confused the green horse. Ethan's efforts to ride it out were futile. The athletic horse unseated his rider, sending Ethan to the ground, rolling behind him in a cloud of earth.

"I'm not a realtor," Miranda attempted to clarify, certain now there was a misunderstanding, but her words stopped at her tongue when she saw red in the man's blue eyes.

Hoping for an ally, Miranda made eye contact with the woman who sidled over to stand beside the man. "There has to be an explanation. There's been a mistake."

"The only mistake made here is yours. You have no business being here, so if you will just excuse us and take your leave, there won't be any trouble."

Miranda didn't need to try anymore. The two people were not to be reasoned with. She was certain she wouldn't be able to set the record straight right here and now, so retreat was the only option. Miranda took her leave, as was so eloquently suggested.

Miranda was relieved when she turned the key that ignited the spark that brought the brawny twin-turbo V-8 engine to life with a comforting, powerful grumble. Gaining her composure, she put the automobile in gear and put a lot of gone between her and the scene on the Baldwin's front porch.

"What was that all about?" Paula asked, regarding the now retreating unexpected visitor. She looked at Ethan standing next to her, then laughed at the dirt that covered him from hat to boots. His face had a fine powdered application, and the dirt grains were stuck to his eyebrows. "What happened to you?" she exclaimed, surprised by his appearance.

Ethan didn't answer. He pulled off his hat, redistributing the dust that had settled upon it. In the fresh cloud, Ethan coughed, swiped his shirtsleeve across his brow, turned, and headed back to work. Paula didn't get an explanation. She had seen before what a thrown cowboy looks like. The colt Ethan was riding, Kit, was coming along nicely in his training but just suffered a setback. The horse would need extra care to build back his confidence. It irked Ethan to no end that this one negative experience could stay with the impressionable youngster for some time.

Paula watched the car disappearing as Ethan made his way across the gravel drive to the corrals whence he came. Paula wondered about the person who may have been invited by the Baldwins. It was certainly plausible. Without a second thought, Paula shrugged her shoulders and returned to the house.

Paula didn't pay attention to the business affairs of her surrogate parents. Paula simply didn't have time to think about it. She was glad Ethan ran the woman off. Paula wanted nothing to interfere with her plans for tonight. In the back of her mind, Paula assumed the female intruder's visit wasn't important, especially after the way she and Ethan treated the woman.

"Oh, well," Paula thought out loud, "It's not my problem now." She turned away and went inside. "And besides," Paula stated to her cat, who had followed her downstairs, then jumped on the windowsill, curiously watching the action. "We don't need anyone around to distract Ethan from me, now do we? Especially anyone who looks like that."

The cat's tail switched back and forth, and he continued looking out the window as if smugly watching the burgundy car disappear down the gravel road.

Miranda glanced in her rear-view mirror and saw the Alma Soñada homestead getting smaller. She began to process what had just happened. This was not how Miranda's first experience at the ranch was supposed to end. She had been looking forward to meeting the Baldwins in person.

The opportunity to not only see, but feel the majesty of the mountains and the power of the river as described to her by Vida had been the subject of her day dreams. Miranda wanted to breath in the musk of the meadows and the spiciness of the forests. Seeing is believing, but feeling is proof.

As she dealt with her dismay, Miranda became angry. She had a lot riding on this collaboration with the ranch owners, there was a lot at stake. This confusing encounter threatened to bring down her entire plan. Who were those two adverse adults she had just met? Where were Mr. and Mrs. Baldwin? Miranda needed answers.

"Hey, Siri," Miranda said. The Range Rover's Bluetooth responded when Miranda asked it to call her guardian, Albert Bennett.

Chapter 4

The rest of the afternoon was uneventful around the Alma Soñada farm. Ethan had plenty of work to do but enough time to finish and get things ready for an early start the next day. Driving the herd up to the summer pasture was the last event in what had been one of the most unusual spring roundups he had ever experienced. Tad and Noah, the twins Ethan grew up with, would be there in the morning to help. Ethan hoped to have the cows and calves moved and settled efficiently. He predicted the three cowboys and two border collie dogs could be off the mountain before nightfall.

Ethan began the evening routine, thinking how grateful he was to have the Crawleys on permanent hire. The twins worked for Ethan's father when their father sold his spread to developers. The boys had grown up in Rambletap Springs and had no interest in moving to Helena with their parents. They now lived in the bunkhouse and hired on at the Alma Soñada Ranch to do the only work they knew.

What with his recent health scare, this was a perfect time for Ansel to be resting on his better health. It was fortunate they had Noah and Tad to help. They were the best ranch hands around, not to mention Ethan's childhood friends. After tomorrow, with the cows and calves delivered to the high valley pasture, it would be a worry-free summer.

Moving into the barn for the rest of the chores, Ethan called to the dogs as he scooped from the bin in the feed room, then poured their kibbles into a big shallow pan on the ground. A couple of tabby cats, one orange and one tortoise shell, jumped down from their resting place high atop the stacked bales of feed to sniff at the dog food. The canines ignored the feline intrusion as they ate. The two cats lost interest and returned to polishing Ethan's ankles, anticipating their own meal, which was coming forthwith.

Ignoring the cats, Ethan bent over to pat the heads of the well-mannered border collies. "Good work today, you two. Get some supper. We have more to do in the morning." Ethan knew the importance of skilled working herd dogs, and his father raised the finest. Ansel believed a man on a decent horse with two excellent working dogs is all a rancher needs.

Ethan fed the cats while the dogs finished eating. Then Ethan tended to the horses they'd need for the morning drive.

Nobody wants to do this for a living anymore, Ethan thought, and it was true. The Crawley twins and Ansel and Ethan were like the last of a dying breed. All the other ranchers had retired and were living off the money they made by selling out. They bought places in the city and sent their kids to college and on to careers.

Ethan went to the university in Helena because his mother had always dreamed he should. But the work Ethan preferred doing for a living required no college degree. Ethan thought the education was a waste of money, but he found there was a lot to learn business wise about running a successful ranch. Upon graduation, Ethan brought home valuable ideas he had since applied.

Ethan walked over to the corral, climbed up to the top rung, and swung his legs around to watch the sunset. He thought about his mom and pop. How they were getting along in years, and now his father had been in hospital. This last week had been a real scare. Ethan wanted his dad to slow down. Trying to convince the old man the three younger cowboys could handle things was a challenge, and there was also his father's pride to consider.

Perched on the fence enjoying the evening's quiet, Ethan knew it would soon be dark, but he was in no hurry to go inside to a house full of nothing but Paula. Ethan tried to ignore the traffic noise rising from the once serene valley floor. The work force that commuted from the booming bedroom community of Rambletap Springs was equally active on the streets driving around on weekends. The border collies came out and sat down below Ethan. They knew he'd know when it was time to sleep. Until then, they remained ever ready.

~****~

From inside the main house on the Alma Soñada, Paula took note of the setting sun. Looking across the gravel court yard, she had seen the shadows grow longer. The now darkened structures built in a circle around the area saw a lot of the activity of ranch life, day and night.

From above, the area looked like a lollipop; the buildings formed the candy and the long driveway was the stick. The main house on the left and the guest house on the right were the anchors. The carports and equipment bays were between the main house and the bunkhouse.

Next stood the largest building, the barn. Stretching alongside and beyond the barn were the big arena and all the paddocks and corrals. In the center of the lollipop's candy circle stood a giant Sugar Maple tree, whose leaves were deep green now but would turn to a stunning mixture of yellow, orange and red when touched by Autumn's chill.

Paula had fixed dinner for Tad and Noah when they returned to the ranch after their day off. They had eaten voraciously from the left overs she heated up, and then they retired to the bunkhouse for the night. Paula, who had become quite the accomplished cook since coming to reside with the Baldwin's, had dinner ready for Ethan. Paula set the table for two with candles and cloth napkins. She planned for them to dine together and now sat waiting for Ethan to come in.

Vida did most of the cooking, but for the past week in her absence, Paula had been cooking to feed the hired crew lunches, and some of them stayed for dinner, plus meals for Ethan and the twins. But that was just her chores. Tonight, she had enjoyed making Veal Parmigiana. She had lovingly prepared the meal for her and Ethan's special night. The ruined meal still sat waiting in the oven.

Paula ran out of patience, annoyed by Ethan's tardiness. She switched off the overhead lights, fixing to watch TV in the other room. She knew Ethan eventually had to come in. He always entered through the back door. It would be more effective in conveying her mood to Ethan if the kitchen was dark and empty.

Ethan would flick the light, see the table Paula had prepared and know tonight was supposed to be romantic. Feeling guilty when he saw the spoils of the meal, Ethan might realize how hard Paula worked. Maybe he would feel compelled to make it up to her.

Paula blew out the half-burned candles and watched the smoky tendrils from the flameless wicks curl upward to the ceiling before disappearing into the air. Paula walked past the iron, pot-bellied stove with its low burning embers that were just enough to keep off the overnight chill of the brisk spring air. Following her into the other room, Paula's cat gave a hiss and cackled as he passed by the wood stove. In response, two orange paws stretched out from under, then drew back in.

Ogee, the tomcat, an orange tabby in his teens, held no animosity toward Paula's cat, but the newcomer with no credentials who came to reside in the house seemed quick to pick a fight. The big orange, who had earned his stripes as a working barn cat, had contributed his genetic signature to the many offspring who followed in his footsteps as a champion mousers.

Earning his retirement, the old cat was now afforded the luxury of lounging around for the life of leisure. Regarding the other cat, perhaps, the veteran feline decided it wasn't worth the effort to rise and make a fuss. The orange cat never even opened his eyes and the black cat retreated in a huff.

The cat jumped onto Paula's lap as she reclined in Ansel's chair and began making biscuits. Paula started the TV and searched for something to see. The news was on. She wasn't in the mood to watch anything and she stared blankly at the faces, zoned out the voices of the talking heads. Her fingers drummed unintentionally on the armrest. Nothing left to do but wait until Ethan came in.

~****~

Ethan sat where he was for a solid twenty minutes after the kitchen lights went out, then climbed down and slowly made his way in. The dogs followed at his heels and settled on their beds among the scatter of muck boots, cowboy boots, hiking boots, and rain boots that lay on the floor of the service porch.

Knowing his mother liked to keep a spotlessly clean house, Ethan stepped out of the outer layer of clothes that were still packed with the permeating dust, the results of the tumble to the ground after losing his seat in the saddle. In his tee shirt and boxer-briefs, Ethan proceeded into the dimly lit, empty kitchen.

Deep in thought and trying to make a clean, unnoticed line to the stairs, Ethan saw the light in the living room and heard the soft volume of the TV, but didn't look at the two place settings on the table. He also didn't notice the dinner that sat spoiled on the stovetop.

Showered, shaved, and dressed, Ethan came back down to the fridge to find something to eat. By the dim light of the open fridge, Ethan noticed the dishes weren't washed. Not only were the dishes unwashed, but the pots and pans on the stove still contained food.

“What the heck?” Ethan said under his breath. Dinner had been over hours ago. Where was Paula? And why hadn’t she cleaned up after dinner?

Ethan glanced from the stove top to the table set with two dinner plates, cloth napkins, and two blown out candles. As the meaning became clear, Ethan’s heart sank. Paula had other things on her mind for the evening.

“Oh, no,” Ethan groaned. He wanted a quick bite to eat before he could sleep. That would be impossible now. Ethan braced himself as he heard Paula’s footfalls coming from the front room. Paula doused the kitchen in light so Ethan could see the crestfallen look on her face. She said nothing and hoped her silence would inspire some desperately wanted attention.

Ethan was familiar with that look. He had seen it many times when they were dating and later engaged. What always followed was Ethan avoiding Paula until he could figure out what he had done to cause the hurt. He usually had to wait it out until Paula eventually explained her reasons. It was always something Ethan did or didn’t do, that left Paula disappointed. It was exhausting. Ethan felt obligated no more, nor had he the energy tonight, to appease Paula. She was no longer his girlfriend.

Paula was sticking to the old dramatic script, and began the silent treatment to wear Ethan down until he would come to her with an apology. Ever since the ending of their engagement, Paula’s scheming drama never got her anywhere, though still she tried.

“Paula,” Ethan said, “I am so sorry I was late for supper. I was focused on getting things prepared for the cattle drive tomorrow.”

Paula allowed Ethan to speak and said nothing as she turned on the burners to reheat Ethan’s meal.

“You don’t have to go to any trouble on my account,” Ethan replied. “I’ll just throw a plate full into the microwave and we can clean up the kitchen together.” He hoped Paula would defer and agree to the offer, but she stayed at the stove reheating the meal as she readied a plate.

“Can I help you with anything around here before Mom and Dad get home?” Ethan tried again to offer Paula some help.

Since the break-up with Ethan, Paula didn’t know what to do when Ethan disappointed her. While they were a couple, Paula ranted and raged, after which she became quiet. Ethan would usually spend the days bending over backward to appease her. Paula would let Ethan stew until she decided he had suffered enough, then she would reward him with sex.

“I’ve got everything under control.” Paula’s voice was slow and smooth as the river in September. She set Ethan’s steaming plate on the table.

“Great,” Ethan sighed, relieved by Paula’s unemotional response, “because I’m spent. If you are sure, you don’t need help, I will turn in after I eat.”

Maybe Paula wasn’t angry after all. Maybe she had seen that her dramatizations were childish. She finally wanted to move on and get past their failed relationship. Before Ethan could even take a bite, Paula pulled out a chair and sat down by her empty plate at the dinner table.

It surprised Ethan Paula wasn’t eating with him. Hadn’t that been her plan? Ethan braced himself for what might be next, but Paula remained silent as she stared out the window into the darkness. This was not a healthy sign. Ethan reluctantly took a few bites, unsure of how this was going to play out. It was as if Paula had reverted to the deep depression, she experienced following the death of her parents.

“Aren’t you going to eat?” He asked with trepidation.

“Do you like the veal?” Paula asked, then paused. “It’s your mother’s recipe.” Another pause. “I’m sure it tasted better when it came out of the oven hours ago.” Paula’s eyes remained fixed on the black glass. She wasn’t looking for feedback. Her question was moot.

“The dinner is fine. Delicious. Thank you,” Ethan pointed to the empty plate in front of her. “You already ate?”

“I lost my appetite while waiting for you.” Paula’s words dripped with implication. Her staring eyes suggested she was contemplative. “I’m still hungry, but not for food. Why don’t you sleep in my bed tonight?”

Ethan stopped chewing, taken aback by Paula’s forwardness. Thrown off balance, Ethan swallowed. He needed to respond without being confrontational. “Tonight I need to get some rest, Paula.”

“You will get some rest, remember? You always sleep better after. My mattress is better. Wouldn’t you rather sleep in a more comfortable bed?”

“My bed is fine. Paula, we don’t sleep together, we are not a couple.”

If the ruined dinner hadn’t pushed Paula over the edge, the rejection certainly would, but Paula’s behavior left Ethan with his back against a wall. Paula was making a full pass at him and he had no intention of obliging. This had happened once since Paula moved in with the Baldwins. One night Paula was distraught, and Ethan comforted her. He and Paula ended up sleeping together even though they were no longer engaged. Ethan vowed he would never again make that mistake.

Ethan still felt the guilt of that single act. Luckily, his parents hadn't found out. Ethan knew they would surely have disapproved of the behavior. Ansel and Vida were Paula's godparents and even though Paula had betrayed their son, they decided as a family to forgive her and take her in. Knowing it might be difficult for Ethan, they had all three talked about the situation making it clear he and Paula were to live as brother and sister.

Ethan assured them he had no other intentions. He was confident he could let go of the past like he had done with Noah. It turned out Ethan was better at letting go than Paula. If any of the Baldwins had known how Paula really felt, they would have come up with an alternate living arrangement.

"I could help you relax." Paula turned absently from the window to gaze at Ethan with exaggerated bedroom eyes.

Ethan concentrated on the plate in front of him, wondering how much he should eat. Maybe a few more bites would be enough to prevent insulting the cook. Then he could politely excuse himself.

Paula stood up, moved behind Ethan, and began massaging his shoulders. She lowered her head and kissed the nap of his neck. Ethan tensed and dropped his utensils. His mind raced to find a diplomatic way out of this situation.

"No, Paula." Ethan moved his chair back to stand, moving Paula out from between the chair and the wall.

Ethan's words did not discourage Paula. She moved to the front, pushed his dinner plate aside and stood with her back to the table to face Ethan. Caught now between the chair that was up against the wall and Paula who was backed up against the table, Ethan would have had to physically push Paula aside to get away. He raised his arms, hands up like he was being held at gunpoint. Paula took Ethan's arms and wrapped them around her waist with his hands resting above her buttock, then she ran her fingers up his chest and laced them behind his head. As soon as his hands were free, Ethan let his arms drop away from Paula, then he reached up to pull apart her hands. "No, Paula" he repeated.

"Why not? I love you and still want us to be together." Paula reached up again, hands gripping her opposite elbows over Ethan's shoulders as she jumped up and wrapped her legs around Ethan's torso.

"This is ridiculous. I am not a jungle gym," Ethan chuckled, feeling embarrassed by what it must look like. A man standing in a kitchen, arms at his sides, with a woman draped over him like a backpack on his front. Ethan was glad there was no one around to witness this nonsense.

"Why is this ridiculous? When two people love each other, this is how they show it. Ethan, when will you start paying attention to me again?"

"Get off," Ethan said firmly.

Ethan extricated himself from her clutches and set Paula gently down. He picked up his plate, dropped the remaining food into the garbage, rinsed the residue, and left them to be put into the dishwasher.

Paula stood behind Ethan as he was shutting off the running tap. "Let me show you what you've been missing out on and chase the stubborn little boy in you away. We have given this enough time to heal. You can forgive me. Show me how much you love me."

Paula pressed her breasts onto Ethan's back and slid her thumbs under the waistband on the front of his jeans as she hugged him from behind.

"Enough," Ethan reached for Paula's hands, "this is no time for a wrestling match. I am not playing a game." Ethan cuffed Paula's wrists, raised her hands up, ducked under and twisted until he was facing her. With his fingers still clasped around her wrists, her arms now crossed over each other. He put an end to Paula's advances.

"When will you stop this?" Ethan flung her arms away when the look on Paula's face reminded him of the expression she wore the day he had confronted her with the truth about her unfaithfulness. The force with which Ethan threw Paula's arms caused her to grimace.

"You are not innocent, you know." It frustrated Paula. "If you had only shown me the proper attention I deserve, I wouldn't have…" Paula's voice trailed off as she had never put to words what she had done.

"Wouldn't have what? If I had paid more attention to you then what, Paula?" Ethan scowled. "I couldn't always be at your beck and call. I have other responsibilities. You were never satisfied, no matter what. No man alive can give you the attention you need."

Paula paused, found her words, then said, "I am not asking for all your attention. Just a little. I am living in your house and you still won't treat me with respect."

Ethan retreated to the veranda just to get out. It was difficult to treat Paula respectfully when he was avoiding her advances. He longed to be comfortable with her, wanted to be friends like how they used to be in grade school. The two of them had been like peas in a pod. Paula was popular and Ethan was shy. Paula was Ethan's link to social connections with the other kids in school.

Ethan was like a brother protecting his sister from the other boys when she took her flirting too far. As time went by, Paula wanted more than a friend or brother. She was ready for a boyfriend. Paula's need for attention and Ethan's lack of attentiveness created a wedge between them. The ties that bound them stretched. The separation between them grew. It finally snapped irreparably the night before the wedding.

Into the darkness, Ethan walked haltingly across the driveway, not knowing where he was going. The dogs had followed Ethan out the swinging screen door and stood waiting for a command. When Ethan came to the corrals, he leaned against the fence. All he could think of was saddling up and riding into the night. The cattle needed to be moved, he and the dogs could get the job done now.

Ethan glanced back at the house and saw Paula taking care of the clean-up. When the downstairs lights went out, Ethan waited for but never saw the upstairs lights go on. Surely, he would soon see the square shaped light cast on the gravel drive below from the window of Paula's room that would show she had turned in for the night. Wanting to avoid finding her waiting in his room, and unable to be certain Paula had gone to bed, Ethan had no way of knowing if the coast was clear.

Abandoning the idea of running off alone with the herd, Ethan dragged his tired self out to the guest house that sat kitty-corner between the house and barn. Ethan crashed on the couch in the little living quarters, but sleep didn't come quickly to his tortured mind.

There were so many things that ran around in his head. How was he to handle this situation with his ex when she refused to accept reality? Could they come to an understanding that would bring peace? And on a different subject, what about his father's health? Both his folks were getting on in years and deserved to take it easy. Would Pops be willing to step away from some of the daily duties? Would the real estate brokers continue their assault, making offers to buy the ranch? And what if they sweetened the pot so much, his father stopped saying no?

Ethan willed his mind to clear, and finally found rest. He and the twins would head up the trail tomorrow, pushing cattle up the mountain and everything up there would make sense. It would all be better tomorrow.

Chapter 5

Miranda walked up the pathway to the motel office, out of breath from her morning run. Still processing the events of the previous day at the Alma Soñada Ranch, she was counting on burning off some frustration through sweat. It had upset her the more she thought about the hostile reception. When she spoke to Albert Bennett, he assured her there had to be a logical explanation. Albert promised he would investigate and encouraged Miranda to relax. Sometimes, the best plan moving forward is to let off steam. "Why don't you explore some more of the town," Albert had suggested.

Running through the streets of the sleepy Sunday town, Miranda had felt her tension melt away. She had run straight into the sunrise, letting the healing rays blind her as if to erase from her mind the images of the less than welcoming people she had encountered. Miranda visualized clearing up the misunderstanding. Miranda drew in a cleansing breath, opened the door to the office, welcoming the warm greeting by the proprietor, Betty Arthur. "Good morning, Ms. Dunn," said Betty. "Did you have a pleasant run?"

"Very nice, Mrs. Arthur, thank you. And please call me Miranda. I was hoping to add a few more days to my stay. Is my room available for an extension?"

Miranda needed to stay in town for a few extra nights. She wasn't certain how things would go and didn't want to get left out in the cold. She had hoped to be done with hotels, but the Dinmont Motel was a clean, well-run establishment which made her disappointment easier to process.

The room Miranda was staying in was comfortable. It had a respectable kitchenette, making it seem more like an apartment, and the price was reasonable. She could handle a few more nights in town.

"Of course we can extend your stay, Miranda. We are glad to have you." Mrs. Arthur ran through a file, flipped through a few papers, and told her it was all taken care of. It amused Miranda that the motel didn't have their reservations on a computer. They were still doing things old-school, paper and print.

Miranda left the office and as she walked to her room, she could feel the rising energy of the community waking up. A woman was walking a little dog, and on the other side of the street a man was washing his car. In the air, Miranda detected the smells of breakfast cooking and her stomach reminded her she hadn't eaten since grabbing a late lunch on her way from the Baldwins ' place the day before. She unlocked the door of her motel room and went to eat and get cleaned up. She planned to call the Baldwins later, and she wanted to be prepared.

~****~

Paula could hear the phone ringing as she ran inside with the eggs she had gathered. She had woken up at sunrise to an empty house, which was no surprise. The breakfast and lunch she packed for the boys and left in the fridge were no longer there. She also noticed she had been alone in the house all night when she found Ethan's bed still made up. On her way out to the chicken coop, Paula checked in the guest house.

There was no evidence Ethan stayed the night there. The dogs were not on the service porch or in the barn. Paula knew they had hit the trail early. They all probably made it to the slope's far end by now, and were starting up the switchbacks. Paula was completely alone in the home complex.

The answering machine picked up the impatient phone call before Paula got to it, and she heard Vida's voice clearly. "Paula? Are you there? We are waiting for Ansel's last doctor's visit. The hospital is short staffed on Sundays. I will call back just before we leave Helena." Then Paula heard a dial tone before the machine quit recording to rewind the outgoing message.

Paula headed upstairs to shower. She had stayed awake last night listening for the sound of Ethan going to his room, still hopeful she and he might spend time together, even if it was for old time's sake. In retrospect, she felt embarrassed. What was she thinking? She had shamelessly thrown herself at him and judging by his reaction, she couldn't have been farther from the mark. He laughed as if their broken relationship was amusing.

Paula wondered how much more energy she should put into reconciliation. It was tiresome, but she would not be the one to give up. It was stuck in her mind since childhood that they would be married, and she wasn't ready to stop trying. Paula refused to accept that her cheating was a clear sign they weren't right for each other. She had promised herself a successful reunion, but the prospects were daunting.

Still deep in thought, Paula was hung up on how she behaved last night, despite her shower that did little to raise her spirits. She thought about Ethan's negative reaction and what would be her next move. Then the phone rang.

"Hello?" She got there on the third ring.

"Hi. This is Vida. Is everything alright?"

"Yes, of course," Paula tried to sound casual and energetic. "I was out collecting eggs when you called earlier."

"Oh, I understand." Vida knew how hard the girl had been working, keeping the household running during her absence.

"How are you doing? Are you on the road home already?" Paula asked.

"Yes, dear. We got the all-clear after seeing the doctor. We will check out of the hotel shortly. Then we'll be heading home. We should be there around lunchtime. We'll be glad when we're back. Ansel would like to know how is it going with the roundup?"

"The guys left early this morning. It went well. Everything's going great. They expect they will settle the cattle in the valley early and hope to be down off the mountain before dark." Paula recited the information.

"That is good to hear. It will please Ansel to know." Vida detected a false energy in Paula's voice. "And how are things with you? I hope it hasn't been too difficult, with the extra work." Vida was well aware of the work it took feeding the hungry crew during roundups.

"I am fine. It is not easy, but I am happy to do it," Paula said flatly. It was important that her godparents understand she appreciated their hospitality. They were kind to her, had always made her feel a part of the family. The last thing she wanted was to appear ungrateful. She only wished things were better between her and their son.

"Thank you, dear. We love you and we'll see you soon."

Vida clicked the end button on her cell phone, then double checked that the call had indeed ended, before turning to her husband to relay the information. She wondered if something more than the added work was bothering their goddaughter.

Paula had had a tough time dealing with her parents 'death. Her whole life changed in one instant. After spiraling down following the break-up with Ethan, there was no chance she could look after her deceased folks 'affairs.

Alone, Paula could not afford the rent on the house they lived in. Moving her up to the ranch where she would have their support seemed like an option. The only caveat was Paula and Ethan's finished engagement. Vida believed the kids were working out the kinks in their new relationship as friends. She wanted them to be like brother and sister, as they were before. Instinct told her they weren't quite there yet.

~****~

"Slow up the pace, will ya? You're gonna kill the beasts." Tad noticed Ethan and the dogs were pushing the herd hard from the rear, but Ethan didn't respond. Tad looked across the backs of the cattle toward Noah, who was flanking on the left side and shrugged his shoulders. They had no choice but to continue.

Ethan felt he was rushing the herd. His own frustrations spurred him on. Things he had to address with Paula were now affecting his work. Her attempts at seduction were exhausting. He had been going easy on her, considering her loss. The humorous approach hadn't worked, and ignoring her changed nothing. He couldn't go on ignoring the ridiculousness of her behavior. Paula needed to face reality, deal with the truth and either recover or it drives her insane and they send her to an institute. It bothered Ethan to have such harsh thoughts.

It wasn't at all like him to be insensitive, but Paula's incessant pursuit drove him to it. He was taking it out on the innocent creatures. It was critical that the mamas and babies arrive at the summer pasture in good shape. At this rate, they would end up stressed and weakened. Ethan put his own problems out of mind and thought of the herd. Why should they suffer, too? Easing his horse down to a slow trot, he whistled to the brothers, who circled to ride three abreast.

"Let's slow up a bit. Anybody ready for lunch?" Ethan said, making it seem like the other cowboys had a say in the matter.

"We don't need to stop just yet, but can we let the herd walk a while?" Tad spoke over his brother, who was on the verge of saying yes to a lunch stop. "Let's get up to the valley. We can rest and eat when the job is done."

"Speak for yourself, Brother." Noah grumbled. He wanted lunch. It frustrated him that Tad was always running a buffer between him and Ethan. Noah knew they had some unfinished business. He suspected there would come a day. He would tell Ethan how he felt about everything. Ethan had mistreated Paula and Noah wanted to let Ethan know it was not okay at all.

Tad studied Noah to gauge his emotional state. He often could see the embers burning in his twin brother's eyes. He saw firsthand the dangerous territory that lay between the two former best friends and hoped he'd be around to run interference. Logistically, he recognized that was a pipe dream. He wouldn't always be there.

Tad reached into his pocket for his cylinder-shaped container of chewing tobacco, took out a pinch and inserted it between his gumline and his cheek. He admitted the health implications of his chewing habit, not to mention it was offensive to many people. Still, whenever Tad desired to calm his nerves, he found sucking on the ground tobacco leaves was calming.

To Ethan's relief, the twins each rode up to their positions on the flanks of the roving three hundred head of cattle, but he heard Noah's grumbling protest. Ethan felt a twinge of guilt for being so sullen and withdrawn. Usually they all enjoyed the drives, passing time teasing and joking and laughing, and before they knew it, the job was done.

Ethan and the Crawleys spent their childhoods wondering the many acres of their ranches that shared a boundary for acres and acres up the slopes of the range. Friends since early on, their parents called them the three musketeers back then.

Paula, who grew up in town, went to a different elementary school. She knew of the boys and eased into the group, hanging with them when they met later in middle school. They were together as a happy group when Paula took an interest in Ethan as more than a friend. She flirted real well and most of the guys in school were smitten with her. All except Ethan. He had other things on his mind. He had spent more time with horses and dogs and vocally expressed his dislike of the make-up and tight clothes Paula wore.

Ethan remembered Noah had fallen hard in puppy-love with Paula at first sight back then. Trying desperately to catch her eye, his love-sick antics had opened him up for a lot of teasing from the others. Noah's attentions went unnoticed by Paula, who only had eyes for Ethan. It was obvious; she loved the attention of all the boys, Noah's attempts got lost in the crowd. Paula was focused only on the one boy who paid her no mind.

Ethan wished they could go back to being kids, before the ways of adulthood could intrude. If he could, Ethan would have insisted Paula leave him alone, and encouraged Noah to go for her. How easy it was in hindsight? Life would be simpler if lived backward.

Chapter 6

The lupines on the slopes of the mountains seemed to radiate their purples and lavenders a little brighter, with Ansel and Vida Baldwin rolling up the road. With a sense of relief, they turned off the highway and passed under the wooden arch at the beginning of their gravel road that displayed the name of the ranch, the Alma Soñada. Their home. It was good to be back at the place from which they had never spent much time away. There was the honeymoon, two weeks on the French Riviera, and an occasional trip back east to visit relatives. Other than that, they preferred to be home. Running a cattle ranch was an all-consuming endeavor. This ranch meant everything to them.

The time away from the ranch reaffirmed their sentiments. To distract themselves from being homesick, the couple decided to be tourists. There was lots of downtime while they were in Helena, so in between tests and exams, rather than sitting around and worry, they enjoyed the sights the city offered.

They made simple plans and rested when Ansel seemed tired. The prescribed medications for severe abdominal pain were relieving the discomfort. All there was to do was wait for a diagnosis and prognosis. What better way to pass the time than to have a little fun?

First, they toured the Cathedral of Saint Helena. Completed in 1914, A. O. Von Herbulis designed the church to replicate the Votivkirche churches in Austria. With its gold-leafed crosses set atop 230-foot twin spires, the cathedral was visible from far away. The interior of the church is lit by 59 masterfully exquisite stain-glass windows that, during the day, cast a spectrum of light. The intricately designed windows created by artist are the originals that came by ship from Munich, Germany.

The Baldwins also visited the Montana Historical Society and found the gallery containing paintings and sculptures by their favorite artist, C. M. Russel. While at the museum, Ansel and Vida took a special tour called, 'The

Last Chance', a train ride through Helena that stopped at many places of historical interest.

The train took tourists to the Old Pioneer Cabin, which turned out to be the original home of one settler with whom Ansel's grandfather had traveled shortly after immigrating from Europe. It pleased them to take in the accurately depicted, well-preserved artifacts. Spending their time touring the city was a great way to keep their mind off Ansel's health.

During the week, the doctors ran tests which revealed the cause of Ansel's discomfort. He had a mild case of diverticulitis. Though this would mean some changes in eating habits, there were no other signs of which to be concerned. Upon hearing the news, the Baldwins arranged a celebratory evening. They went to a movie and unabashedly displayed their affections for each other, necking like newlyweds in the darkened theater.

The next day, they informed the family of the medical findings in brief, promising to explain it all when they knew more. After being gone for a week, they were going home healthy and it felt wonderful. From cross the seat, Vida studied her husband's profile as he drove. She saw the young man she fell in love with some thirty-four years ago.

The lines etched in his face told the story of an honest, hardworking man who endured his share of sorrow. One such sorrow was their struggle to have a baby. That struggle turned into their greatest accomplishment of all, the birth of their only child, Ethan.

The couple tried for seven years to have a baby. They enlisted doctors and fertility experts, but nothing helped them. Finally, Vida's OB/GYN spoke to them candidly, advising they stop trying, stop with the medical intervention and stop thinking about it. It did not surprise the seasoned physician to get the call six months later. When Vida went in for an exam, she and Ansel had conceived.

Ansel felt his wife's lingering stare, turned to her, and smiled. He was glad Vida wasn't still worried about his health; the doctors assured them he was doing fine and with management, they could prevent future diverticulitis attacks. But Vida was a worrier. If she wasn't obsessed about one thing, she'd find something else. During their week away, Vida also worried about Paula and her fragile psyche.

The Baldwins had welcomed Paula into their home, and handled her with care regarding her grief. Had the pressure of added responsibility been too much for Paula? True, Paula had suffered life-changing events, one of the most tragic. But coddling the girl did her no good, either. Ansel firmly believed, regarding Paula, Vida needed to stop fretting.

Pulling around the back side past the house, Ansel parked his wife's sedan in the carport next to his Chevy Suburban. Paula's Toyota Camry was parked in its spot next to the carport. Eager to get inside, the Baldwins grabbed their bags from the trunk and headed toward the house.

Upon entering the kitchen, they found everything in order and neat as a pin. Vida's kitchen was in spotless condition, Paula had obviously done a fine job holding down the fort, and the stocked shelves in the pantry showed Paula had done the shopping as well. Everything was as it should be. It was as if Vida hadn't been away.

Ansel took a quick glance at the living room, expecting to find Paula.

"She might be upstairs," Vida read her husband's thoughts. "Let her come down. In the meantime, I'll make us tea."

"I'm gonna have a quick look around," Ansel started for the door, but Vida blocked his progress. Doctor's orders were for Ansel to slow down and Vida intended to see that her husband did.

Ansel caught his wife's subtle drift and cleared his throat. "Ut-chum. I'd love a spot of tea," Ansel said. "On the veranda would be nice."

"Um-hum," came the response from Vida. She was pleased that Ansel gave in before she had to actually remind him to take it easy.

Together, the couple made tea and gathered the accumulated mail and newspapers for the week. They sat at the table on the morning side of the house and chatted. Ansel and Vida thoroughly enjoyed each other's company the way they always did. They left the stack of envelops unopened, the periodicals folded, and instead took in the pleasure of their piece of heaven on earth.

So, in tuned to each other on the quiet veranda were they, the couple didn't hear Paula come from the house. Paula held back and from the corner, watched jealously her godparents 'interactions. She realized her guardians had in their relationship what was missing in her relationship with Ethan, intimacy.

"Hi, you two," Paula finally interrupted, and kneeling down between them, put an arm over each shoulder in a side-squeeze. "I missed you. I'm so glad you are back." She gave them each a kiss on the cheek.

"Hey, girl. It's good to be missed," Ansel teased his goddaughter. "Come join us."

"Hi, Paula dear," Vida stood up to give Paula a full hug. "You have a seat. I'll get you some tea and start the oven. We brought a take-and-bake pizza for lunch."

On the way through town, Ansel and Vida picked up lunch. The pizza chain, though an obvious sign of the modernization their son despised, was one convenience the rest of the family enjoyed.

Paula sat down, gratefully accepting relief from the kitchen duties. Paula relayed all the events, big and small, that had happened over the last few days. Her voice was firm, her expressions, animated. Ansel detected no signs of stress on the girl.

"Some real estate lady was here yesterday," Paula finished with the most recent event. "A pretty woman in a sharp-looking suit diving a burgundy SUV." There was a hint of envy in Paula's voice as she described the visitor.

"Oh?" Ansel's interest piqued. "Another real estate agent, you say? Hope Ethan didn't catch them here."

Remembering how rude she and Ethan had been, Paula stayed away from too much detail. "She gave us her name, Miranda Dunn, and then left."

"Miranda Dunn? She isn't a realtor. She is a potential business partner." Ansel recognized the name. "We had an appointment to meet with her. Vida, didn't you call Randi from the hospital and tell her we needed to postpone?"

"I did," Vida confirmed. "I left a message on her answering machine. She mustn't have gotten it."

Paula's ears rang when she realized the woman they effectively threw off the ranch appeared to be someone more important than she imagined. This woman was someone with whom the Baldwins were doing business. They had been expecting her. It made Paula wonder why Ethan didn't recognize the woman's name? Surely Ethan would know about someone as important as a likely business partner.

"Well, it's leaves in the wind, now," Ansel said. "Nothing we can do. I'm sure Randi will get back in touch to arrange another meeting. We will get it sorted out."

Chapter 7

"Hey, do you guys feel like going out tonight?" Tad said as the three cowboys rode back down the mountain. "We can go down to Wolf Creek and check out the party scene."

With the herd safely delivered to the summer valley, the men had set their sights on their return trip. Settling in nicely, the cows helped themselves to a long drink of cool, fresh water from the river that flowed along the valley floor. Once their thirst was sated, they began peacefully grazing. On familiar grounds, once again, the cows were at home in the valley. Since they were young heifers, they summered in the high country. Now they came with youngsters of their own. Thanks to the record-breaking pace and the ease with which the cattle settled in their new surroundings, the cowboys headed home even earlier than predicted.

"Yeah, that sounds perfect. Let's all go out," Noah agreed with his twin's suggestion. "It's been a while since we tied one on, and we deserve a break. We should find out what's happening at the Bronze Spittoon."

When Ethan didn't respond to Tad's blanket invitation for a night on the town, Noah chatted about their favorite night spot, and all the fun they had had there in the past. Tad wished Noah would stop talking about the local bar. He knew Ethan did not like hanging out at the Spittoon since the night of his bachelor party. It made Tad think about the history between his brother and his best friend.

The three boys had been inseparable, spending most of their time together at school or on their ranches. As children, they grew up more like brothers than mere neighbors. Tad thought nothing would ever come between them until it did.

From the days when they were all in junior high, Noah talked about Paula, the new student who came from an elementary school on the other side of town. Tad encouraged his twin to make his move, but Noah was afraid. By the time Noah worked up the courage, Paula showed her interest in Ethan.

Tad believed Paula would learn that Ethan wasn't interested and stop her relentless pursuit, but she did not. Noah could have made his feelings known, but Tad discouraged him. "There are more girls out there," Tad had said. "You should find one that actually notices you, too." Noah took his brother's advice and tried to forget about Paula. In high school, Ethan stopped ignoring Paula, and they began officially dating.

For a while, Noah accepted that Ethan and Paula were an item and they all went out together, a big friendly group again. It wasn't long, though, before it became obvious, Paula was way more into the relationship than was Ethan. As they continued dating through college, Paula kept up the pressure and before graduating college, she and Ethan became engaged.

Noah's reaction to the engagement brought to the surface all the feelings he had been ignoring. He told Tad he was going to tell Paula how he really felt. "Ethan doesn't love her," Noah had said. "Maybe if she knew how I feel, she'd forget about Ethan."

But Tad warned Noah to stay out of it. "No good will come of it," Tad warned. "You will lose friendship with both of them."

Tad recalled nights out with the entire gang. When Ethan and Paula argued, usually about something Paula wanted, Ethan did not. Noah would rage inside about Ethan's disrespectfulness. To Noah, it wasn't about the torch he still carried; it was seeing Paula constantly in distress.

With the wedding approaching, Tad saw the intensity of the triangle grow. Paula was pushing for the marriage; Ethan was digging in his heels. Noah began comforting Paula on such nights, and Paula was starving for the attention she didn't get from her man. Paula believed Noah's attention would bring out some jealousy in Ethan, and Tad hated to watch his twin being used.

Tad assumed the wedding would put the triangle to rest. Ethan expected marrying Paula would give her what she needed. Paula hoped Ethan would finally pay her the consideration she deserved. And Noah wished Paula would forget Ethan and run away with him instead. Everyone was holding their breath waiting for time to bring a change.

Tad shook his head to clear the negative memories. Noah was still chattering on about the great times they had had at the local watering hole.

Ethan rode on in silence, trying not to listen to Noah or Tad and their evening plans. He also wanted to stop thinking about his father's health or Paula's obsessions. It was time to clear his crowded mind. A rancher had to think ahead. A herdsman had to understand the market and sell at the most opportune moment. Evaluating their stock in terms of dollars they fetch at market, Ethan learned in college how to compare the value of selling off the younger cow versus keeping her for the value she may produce with a few more years as breeding stock.

If all that weren't enough to be thinking about, the Crawley's caterwauling about heading to the Spittoon threw Ethan into the past and reminiscing. Ethan loved remembering the old days. He and his two best friends had many fantastic stories to tell of their childhood adventures. Today's subject, however, was dangerously close to the memory Ethan didn't want to share. It was the night Ethan caught his best friend stepping out with his fiancée. Ethan didn't see that the betrayal had actually saved him from making a huge mistake. The fact is, what Noah did was the worst disloyalty a man could do to another.

After catching Noah with Paula that night, Ethan went through some changes. He spent most of his time working with very little social interactions. He stayed away for days up in the log cabin near the summit, claiming he was tending to the cattle, mending fences, securing the water sources.

Noah came up to the cabin after Ansel demanded the men to stop this foolish quarrel, bury the hatchet, and return to being friends. Noah had dutifully apologized, yet Ethan doubted the sincerity. Paraphrasing Tad's vulgar words, 'bros before hoes', Noah said to Ethan, "men should put their friendships in higher regard when it came to dating women." Ethan got the message. He wouldn't forgive but, for the sake of harmony, offered to forget.

Once again, the musketeers were together. Ethan abandoned his self-inflicted exile, and they started hitting the bars and clubs as far away as Helena. The Bronze Spittoon, the quaint place in their hometown, had fallen out of favor.

Wolf Creek, an unincorporated area along the highway between Rambletap Springs and Helena, had a nightclub that was a happening place. Folks came from miles around to dance to the new, young country music that was popular across the nation. There was never a shortage of pretty city girls looking for a good ol'boy to show her how to party country style.

It had amazed Ethan that he could do no wrong in the eyes of these ladies. No matter how bad the joke, the women laughed. The taller the tale, the more they believed it and hung on every word. At first, it was cool to be so popular, but after a while, Ethan grew weary of the fake adoration. He realized these young women didn't care a thing about him; they were in love with the image, and when he invited a willing lady out for a drive to an orchard or a hayfield to neck, it was to fulfill her fantasy, and nothing more.

Ethan soon left behind the singles scene when he had seen one too many girls using too much make-up and wearing tight jeans. It embarrassed him for the guys who had never been near a horse but dressed like dime-store cowboys, hoping to fool a girl into spending the night with them. It all seemed so ridiculous. Everyone pretending to be someone they are not to get something that didn't mean a thing.

After a few months of hard partying, Ethan began staying home. It was about that time Paula's parents were involved in the fatal accident. Though things between Noah and Ethan had settled into a working relationship, Paula's moving to the Baldwin ranch threatened to resurrect the feud.

With Paula's return to the scene, everyone with eyes saw the tension escalating. Sometimes the boys locked horns over the silliest of matters. Ansel once saw Ethan and Noah circling an issue over whose turn it was to clean one of the water troughs. They resembled two angry bulls, heads lowered and kicking up dust, about to throw down. There was always someone handy to settle the dust, but the dynamic was exhausting for all.

The Crawleys had finished with the details of their impending evening out when Ethan pulled himself from his thoughts and realized he was staring at Noah. Luckily, neither Tad nor Noah noticed Ethan's glare as they focused on navigating their horses through the more difficult terrain of the downhill trail they were now on.

"So Ethan, are you in?" Tad asked directly.

Ethan quickly came up with a better plan. "I'm not going, but you guys should go. Take Paula. She hasn't been out in a while."

Noah did not receive Ethan's suggestion well. "And, whose fault is that? You ain't been out either." he scoffed.

"Noah is right, Ethan," Tad tried to find the neutral position. "All of us should go."

"Like old times, huh, Ethan?" Noah took another jab.

“It’ll just be you three. That’s how Noah wants it, right Noah?” Ethan countered the attack, then softened the intention. “I want to stay home with my folks.”

“Are you serious, Ethan? It’s your idea to take Paula out, but it’s too much trouble to come along? She’s your girl, Ethan.” Noah came out swinging.

“Knock it off, Noah,” Tad continued to place himself between the angry men as the horses became unsettled by the tension between their riders.

“Oh, so you think Paula is my girl? So what? Since when do you recognize boundaries?”

“Both of you, cut it out. Y’all need to grow up.” Tad closed the conversation.

A kerfuffle between the two men usually could be written off as teasing, but this had escalated to a more serious level. Ethan would normally take the high ground and not react to the harsh and inappropriate comments, but because they were all tired after a long work week, or Noah’s passive-aggressive attacks were less passive. For whatever reason, Ethan wasn’t backing down. Digging his heels way too hard into the sides of the horse he was riding; Ethan bolted ahead and rode the rest of the way home in peace.

“You dummy,” Tad unloaded on his brother. “You never know when to quit.”

“Sorry, man,” Noah tried an excuse. “Ethan is too sensitive to take a joke.”

“No, Noah. The problem is you pretend to be joking, but you are not being funny. You are inciting discord.” His brother’s behavior annoyed Tad. That kind of stirring of the pot solved no problems, it only made it worse.

“I’m not inciting… or whatever you said. I’m just going by what Paula says,” Noah defended his actions, not really sure what his brother meant. “Paula told me they are practically together again.”

Too tired to talk anymore about it, Tad swore at his brother under his breath, “Feckin’ Eejit!” Using his father’s Irish slang expression, Tad felt the swear words of frustration helped.

Was Noah falling into the old trap? Was Noah putting himself in the third corner of the triangle again? Tad considered letting the chips fall where they may. Keeping two bulls from locking horns was an effort in futility. Everyone knows that when bulls are fighting over the same cow, you gotta step aside and let them settle it themselves.

Chapter 8

The sun reached its highest point in the sky and shone directly down on the shadowless pass of the very mountains that had been home to the Shoshone Indians before the settlers came. The land that supported a nomadic way of life became too populated with white men for the natives to continue their ways and it forced them into change.

Miranda yawned and stretched and set down the book she was reading. *How interesting*, she thought. Here it is, one hundred and fifty years after they chased away the Indians, the area is once again being cleared out. The inhabitants that had pushed away the indigenous people were themselves being forced to make a change.

Miranda had walked to town for some breakfast after her run and stopped at the bookstore. She had some time to kill before she made the call to the Alma Soñada Ranch and, depending on when her hosts could see her, might have some time thereafter. While perusing the shelves, Miranda found books on local history and decided she needed to educate herself.

The region she hoped to call home was rich in lore, from the Lewis and Clark Expedition, to the first steamboat to travel the Missouri River; from the Indians who'd occupied the land since the beginning to the brave young men and women who chose the 'Wild West' to be their new home. So many fascinating stories, Miranda devoured the books, becoming entranced with the intrigue, the families who set out for adventure, the tragedy when trouble struck. The pioneers stuck to their dreams. Many survived and built a rich history through generations. It left Miranda feeling nostalgic for something she didn't have: family history.

To say Miranda knew very little about her own family was an understatement. She knew nothing. She went to live at an orphanage when, as a baby, she became a ward of the state. There was no back-story beyond the firehouse where the authorities were called in to pick her up. One could surmise her parents abandoned her, literally dropped Miranda off at a safe place, with nothing but a first name. Miranda didn't even have a birthdate.

Miranda was unlucky with foster homes and bounced around until she reached school age. From Kindergarten through 2nd grade, Miranda lived with one family. There were seven children in the household and though her environment was stable, the years she spent moving from one foster home to another made her shy and reserved. Miranda required very little attention from her foster parents, so it was a good fit for them, but the agency removed her when a counselor labeled her as "failing to thrive."

The counselor took an interest in Miranda's case and through a network of personal connections, a man, Mr. Gordon Howarth-Dunn, adopted Miranda. At age sixty-one, Mr. Gordon Howarth-Dunn decided he didn't want to die alone. He was an only son of a wealthy family who made a fortune in the booming auto industry of the twenties and thirties. Upon inheriting the family business when his father passed, Howarth-Dunn devoted his time and energy into expanding and diversifying until he became even more wealthy.

But the choices that made him very rich came at a price. He was an old man with no family and figured it was too late to find a wife and have children of his own, so he sought to adopt a child he could raise and provide the finer things money could buy. He longed for a son to carry on his legacy, but as a favor, agreed to meet with a little girl, Miranda.

Captivated by her, he fell in love with the child and promised to care for her and spoil her until his dying day. Unfortunately, that day came sooner rather than later. Gordon Howarth-Dunn had a massive heart attack and died five months after the adoption papers were inked and dried. Before she was eight, Miranda became an orphan once again.

Fortunately, she did not return to the orphanage. Her late father's will was read and, according to the terms, Miranda was heiress to a vast fortune. Carrying out the instructions of the will, Miranda stayed on at the mansion she hadn't even gotten used to, and was cared for by servants she never grew to know. Though she could have anything she wanted, the things she needed, money can't buy. A family, someone who loved her, a home, brothers and sisters. Those were the things Miranda dreamed of having.

Miranda finally received some satisfaction and a sense of belonging at school. She had friends to play with and teachers who cared, but she still hadn't anyone to love her. At the end of the day, the other boys and girls had mothers and fathers, sisters and brothers. Miranda came home to an empty mansion with a butler and a maid.

By thirteen, Miranda was eligible for the 9th grade and could go to boarding school. It was then she negotiated with her late father's attorney, Albert Bennett, a kind and generous man who was in charge of Miranda's interests. Albert agreed Miranda should go to the school the late Howarth-Dunn attended in his youth, the Camelot Academy in New Haven, Connecticut.

While at the academy, Miranda connected with a classmate, Amanda Ferris, who lived in New Haven. With Albert's permission, Miranda spent vacations with Amanda and her family. It was then Miranda experienced her first taste of family life. The Ferris' treated Miranda as if she was their own. Amanda had two older brothers who looked out for their kid sister and her new friend. They nicknamed their sister Mandi, and when Miranda joined the family, they dubbed her Randi. The boys considered Miranda their sister and labeled the girls 'unjoined' Siamese twins. The girls were fine with the nicknames and being referred to as twins validated externally their inner connection. They were inseparable.

Miranda and Amanda stayed close throughout high school and college. They attended the university together and shared everything, as best friends often do. Upon graduation, Amanda stayed in New Haven and found work in her field of interest, publishing. Not wanting to be too far from her surrogate family, Miranda opened her non-profit and began her quest for an equine therapy program.

Leaving Amanda to come to Montana was the only hard decision Miranda faced when she left. Her passion for the riding program and her desire to expand it to include family members pushed her forward. The Ferris's were her strongest supporters and encouraged Miranda to follow her dreams.

Miranda fell out of her reverie and glanced at her watch. Yes, she left her stable home in New Haven to take a risk. Now she was going to see if there was a future for her here in Montana. It was time to make the call to the Baldwins.

~****~

“Thank you for the iPod. That is such a thoughtful gift. I’ve been wanting one for a while,” Paula inspected the gadget she had received from her godparents.

“You’re welcome, dear. It is a little something to show you how much we appreciate you.” It pleased Vida to see Paula smiling.

“We are glad you like it. It’s the least we could do. It means a lot to have you here this past week.” Ansel found it easy to express to Paula how he felt.

“You are right. It’s exactly what I want. Now I can listen to my music without bothering anybody.” Paula kissed Ansel on the cheek and gave Vida a hug. “Thank you both. Can I use the computer to download some music?”

“Of course, dear,” Vida said as she collected the leftover lunch. “I better get started on dinner for the boys. I’m sure they’ll be a mite hungry ’bout now. Anyone want more pizza before I put it away?”

“No more for me, thanks. I’m full. Pizza is the one food I could eat and eat, but then I’d be big as a house,” Paula joked as she rounded the corner heading to Ansel’s, and more often lately, Ethan’s office.

Ansel waited for Paula to get completely through the office door before he turned to Vida. “Well, she seems fine. It seems you are worried about Paula for nothing.”

“I’m trying to stay aware. She sounds okay, and looks rested, but her eyes have a sadness to them I haven’t seen for a while.”

“Really, Love. You worry too much. Of course, she can look somber now and again. She has been through a lot already in her young life. Grief is an emotion like all the others. She needs to experience it, to work through it, and clear the way for the other, more pleasant emotions to come.”

“Such words of wisdom,” Vida teased. “You should have been a preacher.”

“If I had been, maybe you’d be more inclined to listen.” Ansel stood from the table, gave his wife a hug, and held on just a little longer for effect. He looked down at her upturned face, and she lifted to stand on tippy-toes to kiss his lips.

Vida was a foot and a half shorter, and four years younger than her husband. She was a pretty woman, though not delicately. She had a healthy figure because she worked at it. Vida used the exercise machine, a joke gift from her friends on her fiftieth birthday that she took seriously, and rarely missed a workout. Vida let her husband hold her and then skittered off to begin preparations for a special dinner on this evening when her family would be together.

Ansel watched his wife for a moment. Admiring her strength and stubbornness, while appreciating her soft and vulnerable side, was his lifelong endeavor. He took pride in his ability to read Vida's moods in order to complement her multi-faceted personality. Ansel grabbed the unopened mail and headed to the office where Paula was sure to be buried deep inputting music on her new device.

Ethan taught them all about computers when he was studying at university, and Ansel wondered how they had ever functioned without it. The computer allowed them to keep better track of the stock for better management. This year, by replacing the older cows with heifers not yet bred, they had seventy-nine calves more than the last season.

By selling off the breeding cows at a younger age, they brought a higher price at market. The risk was using the younger heifers not proven as breeders, but the change in practice already resulted in more calves, not less. It turned out to have been a valuable risk.

Ansel set the mail on the desk when the phone rang. "I got it!" he shouted, but Vida had already picked up on the line in the kitchen. Paula looked away from the screen briefly when she heard Ansel shouting. She already had on her ear buds and was listening as she downloaded her tunes.

"Ansel, it's Randi," Vida announced.

Ansel went into the front room and picked up the phone by his recliner chair. "Hi, Randi. I'm so relieved you called. Are you still in Rambletap Springs?"

"Yes, I am. I'm at the Dinmont Motel. There seems to have been a slight mix-up," Miranda's voice came through the line. "I must have gotten the days confused."

"No, you didn't," Vida was still on the phone. "We had an appointment yesterday. There was a missed message, I think."

"We are so sorry," Ansel joined in the conversation. "We had an emergency. Vida left a message at your work a week ago."

"Well, that explains a lot," Miranda laughed as the facts became clear. "I've been gone for over two weeks. I arranged it so I could take my time driving out. On my way to Montana, I have been sight-seeing as I traveled across the country. The only way to reach me is my cell phone. Remind me to give you that number."

"Oh, my goodness. So, that's how it happened!" Vida exclaimed.

"Well, now that we have that straightened out, let's get back on track," said Ansel. "What is the soonest we can meet? We are looking forward to meeting you in person, and there's no time like the present."

"We'd love to see you today. And if you have no plans, will you stay for dinner?" Vida extended Ansel's invitation. "We will all be here, and you'll meet the lot of us at once."

"So, what do you say? Can you make it?" Ansel urged.

It only took Miranda a split second to respond affirmatively to the invitation. She had left behind all other obligations and her calendar was open. She was tired of eating alone. It would be a welcomed, and possibly overwhelming, experience. Miranda suspected she may also see the two she already met informally on the front porch. As was her way, diving in head first and hoping for the best, Miranda would make sure her second impression was much better.

Chapter 9

"I'm gonna get the mail." Paula announced to no one in particular. She came down from her room with her sneakers, a hat and her new music device, freshly loaded with songs she loved. With her ear buds securely in place, she could hear nothing but her tunes.

"What?" Ansel yelled from the office where he was catching up with paperwork. He had heard someone shouting.

"Did you say something?" Vida came from the pantry.

"I think Paula was talking," Ansel answered, meeting his wife at the window facing the courtyard, where they both saw Paula walking down the driveway, her black cat following like a dog.

"I want to tell her we're having company for dinner. I'll catch her on the way back," said Vida.

While Ansel evaluated the outdoors, Vida returned to the preparations for tonight. On the menu for this special meal, she was pulling out the stops. Coq Au Vin, roasted string beans, buttered bowtie pasta sprinkled with Asiago cheese, Caesar's salad, and, for dessert, Chocolate Mousse. Vida was a self-taught chef who loved to be creative and deviate from the customary comfort foods one would expect to eat when dining on a ranch.

Beef stew or fried chicken, mashed potatoes, baked beans, biscuits and gravy, cornbread were all often on the menu. But Vida liked to experiment and hoped it broadened the minds and palates of her family. For different occasions, especially when they had guests, she relished the opportunity to show off her skills.

"Do you need any help here, Love?" Ansel offered. He appreciated seeing Vida taking care of her household, but he was not a chauvinist. He would gladly help in the kitchen, just as he knew she would be more than willing to work with the cows and horses if necessary.

“I would have to say no, thank you. The house is spotless, thanks to Paula.” Thinking for a moment, she added. “On second thought, you could set the table. We’ll eat in the formal dining room and use the China, and you could check the silverware. It may need polishing.”

The wheels continued to turn as Vida thought about the evening meal. She was looking forward to welcoming Randi in style, but felt no pressure to perform. They had nothing to prove and only wanted to show hospitality. Vida’s motivation came from a place of generosity. She simply delighted in providing a decent time for all to appreciate.

After getting the stacks of China ware down, and checking the silverware, Ansel moseyed out into the breezy afternoon, the signature of weather at Springtime in the Rockies. The valley floors warmed as the rays of sun grew in intensity. The warm air rose and the cooler air rolled down the mountain slopes to take its place. It was all so deliciously pleasing to his senses. Ansel loved everything about this land. This is where he was born and the only earthly home, he hoped he’d ever know.

Stepping carefully through the gate to the garden he and Vida cultivated, Ansel inspected the daffodils still blooming long after their normal season had passed. As he picked through the flowers to choose the blossoms that were at their best, he remembered teaching Ethan about gardening.

Ansel felt it was important for a young man to have respect for all living things, including the flora. By encouraging Ethan to garden, he was demonstrating to the boy self-sufficiency. Ansel taught the basics of Farm to Table long before it was a bourgeois thing to do. Ansel wasn’t sure his offspring would ever cotton to gardening. That apple may have fallen far from the tree, but Ethan was handy with the tools and had a green thumb, just the same.

Having shuffled through the daffodils with skill, Ansel had secured enough decent blooms to make quite the bouquet. He stood up with the flowers in hand and came face to face with Magic, his stallion Ethan rode.

“Sorry, Magic. These are not for you.” Ansel patted the friendly and curious stallion and looked up to see a goofy grin on the rider’s face.

“Hey, Pops,” Ethan couldn’t contain his emotions. “So wonderful to have you home.” He swung from aboard and reached over the waist high garden fence to embrace his father. “I can tell you must feel better, but what did they do? Turn you into a girl?” Ethan’s eyes twinkled as he teased his papa for standing there holding a bouquet. "Is Mom taking you to the spring Dance with that bouquet?"

"Why, yes, kind sir? Yes, she is," Ansel raised his voice to a falsetto and attempted to flutter his lashes, which brought both men to laughter, then with his normal voice, "I am grateful to be home. I should take the switch to your behind to tease your old man that way."

Ansel slipped through the garden gate to stand next to his horse, who nuzzled his master in search of a treat. "Thanks for getting ol'Magic out. How'd he do?"

"He did fine, Dad." Ethan had ridden his father's prized stallion on the drive. The horse had been standing idle during the roundup. "He'll do fine for me, but he never does as well as he'll do for you."

Magic stood, head up, ears pricked forward, locked in a stare with Ansel. The connection between the two was obvious.

After pausing, Ethan said, "I hate to break up this love fest, Dad, but you better go take those posies into the house before anyone sees you. You'll get a lot more teasing from them. Come to the barn and I'll catch you up on the roundup."

Ethan waited for Ansel to come from inside and then they walked across the driveway with matching, even strides. Father and son were the same height, built structurally long and lean, though Ansel was slightly more slender than his son. Their facial features were the same, too, and other than a five o'clock shadow, they both liked to keep clean shaven.

Ethan wore his hair longer than Ansel's, though not as a fashion statement. Ethan was too busy to go for a haircut. And Vida swooned over her son's curls. When left to grow out, the curls framed his brow and formed ringlets down Ethan's neck.

Before the two men could make it to the barn door, the border collies ran out and jumped, and danced all around Ansel. "Did ya 'miss me? Huh, guys? Did you miss your daddy?" He patted and scratched as the dogs fell over each other, trying to be closer to their master. Ethan led Magic inside, where the twins had already untacked their horses and were putting away equipment.

"Hi, boys," Ansel greeted the men more like sons than as employees.

"Hey, Ansel," Tad hung up the bridle he had been using every day for the better part of a week. "You're home."

"How are you feeling? Are you okay?" Noah expressed concern.

“I’m going to be fine, boys. I have what’s called diverticulitis. The lining of my stomach becomes irritated and inflamed with infections when particles of undigested foods are trapped in the tiny pores.”

“What that means, guys,” Ethan explained, “is Dad can’t eat strawberries, blackberries, or sesame seed buns, or anything with small seeds.”

Upon hearing the diagnosis from Vida, Ethan did the research. He had found many online sites on how to manage the disease through diet and homeopathic teas and tinctures. Ethan planned to be helpful by supporting the dietary changes and needed to be informed. He planned to do everything he could do to keep his dad healthy.

“Let’s turn your horses out, guys,” Ethan finished removing the tack from Magic’s back as the stallion stood patiently.

Tad and Noah continued caring for their mounts, taking extra time with the curry brush to remove any signs of sweat from their necks and chests. The cowboys chatted as they worked.

“How did Kit do today?” Ethan asked Tad.

“He went as solid as a veteran, Ethan.” As per Ethan’s advice, Tad had ridden the green broke colt for evaluation. He seemed no worse for the wear after bucking off Ethan the day before. Ethan had put some quality hours on the youngster and was proud to know he had proven himself today as Tad put him through the paces with nary a flinch.

“Do we still have those three horses from McGuire’s coming in for training?” Noah asked.

Ethan filled Ansel in on the training appointment they booked during his absence. “You remember McGuire’s boy, Nathan? He is a dentist now. Went to college off the money they got selling their place. Anyway, he bought these three fillies, and he’s bringing ’em out here tomorrow.”

Ansel digested the information. “That’s fine. We will handle the work. I bumped into ol’McGuire at the Spittoon a few months ago. He told me about his son and two of his son’s friends and how they were fixin’ to ride and learn to rope. Nathan was a good handler. It was in his blood. The other two apparently knew nothing about riding or roping. As usual, city slickers with money who think if they buy a couple horses, spend more money on training, they will be a cowboy overnight.”

“Yeah,” Noah added, disdainfully. “They take these fine horses that we’ve poured in our time and sweat to make them solid mounts. With their lack of skill, they ride them hard for a while, ruin their mouths, desensitize them by overusing their spurs, then bring them here for us to fix."

"It's a vicious cycle, and I hate we make money at the expense of a lot of excellent horses," Tad agreed with his brother.

"It's always about the money, with them. But if we don't do it, someone else will. At least when they get here, they are treated well. It's a vacation for them," Ansel said, then walked over to Magic as Ethan began to untack the stallion. "Hey, boy," Ansel softened his voice.

The horse nuzzled Ansel's side pocket and his human produced a small, crunchy treat. It amazed Ethan that his old man, who hadn't been home, hadn't been around the animals for days, still had a treat handy.

The twins led their horses outside to the gate, turned them loose in the pasture, then leaned on the fence to watch them mill about. The horses dropped their heads and walked slowly with their noses to the ground, sniffing for the perfect dusty spot so they could roll and scratch and rid themselves of the feel of riding equipment.

Once their itch was scratched, the horses rose and shook and puffed up their coats to allow the dust to settle deeper between the hair shafts, then they joyfully loped off with renewed energy to join the group of horses grazing at the far end of the ten acres they stayed on.

"I'm getting cleaned up," Tad said to Ansel, who had joined the twins in watching the stock horses revert to nature. "We got some major partying to do."

"You boys heading into town tonight?" Ansel asked.

"Yeah," Noah answered. "We're all going to the Bronze Spittoon, taking Paula out for some fun. Well, all, except Ethan."

Ansel picked up on a slight sneer in Noah's voice and said, "That is just as well. We have company coming for dinner. You guys can head out, but Ethan needs to be here."

"Company? Tonight?" Ethan overheard his father talking.

"Yes, tonight. I know you're tired. It's been a long week for us all, but we want to proceed with our plans. Randi is generous enough to come out today." Ansel noticed Ethan seemed mildly agitated whenever they spoke about Randi and their plans to diversify.

"Oh," Ethan groaned. "Not this again." Ethan tried to avoid talking with his parents about their ideas for the future.

"Your mom and I have tried to include you. If you would allow us to show you, you'd understand Randi's ideas and you wouldn't have to rely on whatever cockamamy nightmares you have imagined we're proposing."

"Mumpf," Ethan snorted.

"And don't go thinking of running off to the cabin like you usually do when you are uncomfortable. You'll be there for dinner tonight."

On that note, Ansel walked away. The dogs, who had been sitting by the fence, followed Ansel, then stopped and looked at Ethan. They hesitated, as if contemplating which way to go, then bounded off to follow Ansel.

"Fickle as a woman," Ethan tossed the words at the retreating tails of the canines. Ethan admitted jumping on a horse and heading up to the high country to Carmen's Camp for a few days was a marvelous suggestion. It was what Ethan did rather than stay around and deal with unpleasantness.

Ethan recalled how long he had stayed on the range for other occasions. One could survive nicely up there. The cabin was well stocked with provisions, augmented by any game he could hunt. There was no electricity. No telephone, no internet, no TV. Only beautiful sunrises and sunsets, and cattle peacefully grazing among the lush grass and flowers. Regarding this Randy guy Ethan's parents insisted on dealing with, who wouldn't rather be up there than here?

The interaction he had witnessed puzzled Tad. The Baldwin men at odds on an issue? They almost never disagreed. Tad had never seen Ansel end a conversation by walking away. "What plans? Who is Randy? What's going on, Ethan?" Tad demanded.

What Tad also didn't know is the Baldwin men had butted heads on this issue so hard that Vida had had to step in and mediate the peace.

"You remember last year," Ethan explained to the brothers when Noah came to listen, too. "Dad was worried about finances, more so than usual, that is. We had lost too many calves after that severe, late spring storm that rolled through right after we had moved them up to the summer valley. We discussed ways to lower costs and ways to add to our income streams to get past the setback."

"With some ways to help immediately, we were fortunate the market was good, but selling off stock only works short term. Luckily, we muddled through, our finances recovered. I understood we were done with it, but Mom and Dad were not. They had started with this guy. I think he's a consultant or something. He has these plans to save the day and apparently, they are still thinking about using his ideas."

Geez, that doesn't sound so bad. Tad thought it might be interesting to know what the consultant had to say. If it had been his father, Tad would have been supportive of ideas that may have kept their business profitable enough they wouldn't have had to sell.

"Is the Alma Soñada still in trouble financially?" Noah asked.

"No, man. That's the frustrating part." Ethan grabbed his saddle from the rail and stomped into the tack room where he slammed the saddle down on the rack and pushed it back so hard it rumbled the wall.

Ethan felt apologetic when he heard Magic spinning in his stall from the ruckus. "Even last year, when we were barely making ends meet, it was never as bad as that. A consultant? Some guy from the city who probably doesn't know the first thing about ranching, and he's gonna tell us how to run our business?"

"Sorry, man," Tad conceded. "I see what you mean."

The three men went out to witness the stock horses go through their ritual as the newly turned-out horses become part of the herd again. As they nipped and kicked playfully, reestablishing a pecking order, the dust rose.

"What are you guys doing?" Paula came up behind the men. "Why do you always watch the horses when you turn them out? It's like spying on rocks. What is so interesting about a bunch of horses grazing in an enormous field?"

"Hi, Paula," Tad and Noah said in unison.

Ethan remained focused on the horses. It was fascinating to watch the herd dynamic as the group co-mingled. Studies showed that horses 'heart rates syncopate within the herd. Ethan believed this regulation of heart rate explained how, when startled, the group reacted in unison. If one horse detected a predatory threat, the entire herd would respond. It wasn't as if one spooked, then the others did, in a chain reaction.

Ethan struggled to introduce Paula to the mysteries of the world of the equine communication, but she didn't understand. Paula hadn't the ability or the desire to consider things from a different perspective.

"Hey, Paula. We're going out dancing to celebrate a successful spring roundup. Wanna come?"

"All of us?" Paula cast a hopeful glance toward Ethan and didn't see the scowl on Noah's face.

"No, not all of us." Noah answered Paula's question with less enthusiasm.

"I have to stay here and try to put an end to this 'rescue operation'." Ethan almost wished he were going with the group. He couldn't decide which option was worse. He never dreamed his folks would carry this notion so far.

"Who's being rescued?" Paula inquired. "What does that mean?"

"Let Noah explain it to you," Ethan said sharply, then turned and walked away. "I'm too tired right now."

Ethan was tired. Tired of Paula and Noah, whose only aim it seemed was to torment him. And he was tired of his parents and this scamming consultant. He was fed up and longing for relief. Despite his father's warning, Ethan wanted to saddle up and ride away.

Chapter 10

Miranda stood at the little closet in her motel suite with a towel wrapped about her wet head and studied the meager wardrobe from which she had to choose something to wear to dinner. Should she wear a suit, or something dressy? Or maybe she should go more casual? A shirt, boots and jeans? After all, she was dining at a ranch. No, she laughed derisively." Don't be ridiculous." She told herself. They were having dinner, not hitting the trail.

If she were at home, she would have a lot more of a selection. Though she was an incognito heiress most of the time, she had quite a full closet for the occasions that demand she look the part. Tonight, Miranda wasn't sure which part to play. Business attire would show the Baldwins she took her job seriously. But if she opted to dress up, it was a symbol of her financial capabilities and might appear too boastful.

Miranda reached into the closet and pulled out her favorite dress, a sleeveless, scoop-necked, flared floral print in shades of royal and white, with a high-low hem line and a sash tied at the waist. "This will need some ironing," she said. She was going to be herself tonight, simple and humble. She hung the dress on the hook on the bathroom door and started putting on make-up while she waited for the iron to warm up.

Miranda learned from Amanda's mom how to wear make-up to accent the best features and conceal the flaws. The result was a natural beauty that never appeared painted on. Miranda was blessed with a blemish free, lily-white completion, and excellent color in her cheeks. The only make-up she applied tonight was to her eyes. She used bluish-gray eyeshadow on her lids, then applied black mascara on her already thick eyelashes.

Next, Miranda pulled the damp towel off and her hair came down in a wet clump. It was thick and straight and so black it shone blue in the sunlight. She could curl it and wear it up with small streamers to frame her face, or just let it hang loosely. She decided on something in between; curled but hanging down with the hair on the side pulled into a ponytail hanging down over the rest. With it drawn back, it accented her prominent forehead and brought out her features even more.

"There," Miranda said to her reflection with satisfaction. Mrs. Ferris had taught her well.

Last, Miranda applied to her lips a glossy, red lip balm in keeping with the more dramatic print design of her dress, make-up and hairdo. Not knowing what was in store for the evening, she was confident she could handle the pressure. There were many people counting on her to carry out their plans. Albert had gone out on a limb, promoting her idea to investors. A summer camp/therapeutic equestrian program that includes all family members had never been done.

Miranda had invested her hopes and dreams in this endeavor. In its elusive form, she never worried about failing. Now that there was the opportunity to make the dream a reality, failure was a possibility. To pretend it didn't scare the wits out of her would have been a complete lie.

Miranda glanced at the digital clock by the bedside and banished the self-defeating thoughts from her mind. Grabbing her light blue sweater, she stepped out into the late afternoon air. The chill told her the sweater was a sensible choice. She glanced at her cell phone and saw she had enough time to drive out before sunset. It was a twenty-minute drive to the Alma Soñada Ranch.

Miranda drove through the opened gate under the archway with the name of the establishment, 'Alma Soñada', written across the top. "Soul's Dream," she whispered. As she drove on, the residence and outbuildings came into view in the distance. Sitting higher than the lowland she had climbed out of; it was a sight to behold. She concentrated on the driving and tried not to think about what had happened the first time she visited. She pulled her vehicle to the left to park. It was then she saw a man and a woman coming down the stairs to greet her.

The man, a tall, physically fit specimen, bounded down the steps and opened her door before Miranda could set the E brake and shut off the engine. He was the spitting image of the guy she had met yesterday, but upon closer inspection, the differences became clear. This man was thinner and his hair was short. His eyes were intensely blue, like the guy Miranda had encountered previously, but the biggest difference was in attitude.

The fellow held out his hand and Miranda reached out as she swung her legs and gracefully stepped out.

"Hi, Randi," Ansel greeted their guest. "I'm Ansel, and this is Vida."

"It is so nice to meet you both." Miranda shook each of their hands warmly.

"My, but you are tall, and slender, and pretty," Vida complimented the girl unabashedly.

"You're making the poor child uncomfortable, Vida," Ansel stated.

"Come inside, dear. Can we get you a glass of wine? We also have fresh lemonade."

As they walked in, Miranda noted there was another person who had come out. It was the man who had unceremoniously asked her to take a hike, and he was now leaning against the opened door frame with his arms folded across his chest. He looked different without the layers of dirt he had been wearing before, but the stern expression was still on his face. There was also a trace of confusion in his expression.

"Why's she here? Is this some sort of trick?" Ethan recognized Miranda Dunn, the realtor.

"Ethan!" Vida gasped. "Where are your manners?"

Miranda ignored the anger but noted Ethan's confused expression. "Miranda Howarth-Dunn," she held out her hand. "We met yesterday."

Instead of shaking the outstretched hand she offered, Ethan looked at his parents.

"What's gotten into you, son? Is that any way to treat a visitor?" Ansel glared at the boy. Although they were the same height, Ansel seemed to tower over Ethan at the moment.

"This way, dear," Vida said to Miranda, shooting a warning glance at her son. Ethan slid out of the doorway to let Miranda pass through.

"Will you please pour us some drinks?" Vida sternly instructed Ethan. Her words were swift. With no choice but to act immediately, Ethan obeyed. It made him feel like a child being chastised.

It surprised Ethan that the lady he and Paula had run off the property the day before was not a realtor. He was even more shocked to find out Randi was not a dude, but a dudette, a beautiful woman he had been rude to twice in two days.

Ethan suddenly realized his own appearance, his jeans, shirt and work boots were clean enough, but they were the clothes he wore every day. He had showered and shaved after the long day, but had been too tired to pay much attention to how he looked. Ethan contemplated his choices, pulling idly at a ringlet, and remembered he had been putting off getting a haircut for weeks.

"Damn," Ethan pressed with both hands on the top of his head as if to push the growing strands back in. "I mean, shoot." he corrected himself out loud in an empty room.

He willed himself to get it together, and poured some wine and lemonade. When Ethan regained his composure, he carried in the glasses on a tray.

Ethan approached their guest first to offer her a glass and stated, "I must apologize for my behavior. I wasn't expecting you. What I mean is, I wasn't expecting you to be Randi." He felt like he was cleaning a stall, and the faster he shoveled, the more it filled with manure.

Miranda accepted the lemonade as Ethan stuttered but only offered a 'thank you'.

When nobody else spoke either, Ethan tried again. "Let me start from the beginning," Ethan passed the beverage tray by his folks, then continued. "When Randi showed up the other day, Paula and I thought she was a real estate lady. I'm not saying that is an excuse for my being so rude, but maybe it's at least a reason."

The three other people remained quiet, so Ethan kept talking. "I have assumed since the beginning that Randy was a man. When Miranda came to the house and introduced herself, it never dawned on me she also goes by Randi. I am really very sorry for the mix-up."

Ethan declared his regrets. He had done his duty.

"I understand," Miranda spoke next, accepting the explanation. "It was an honest mistake, and I accept your apology. Let's begin again." She humbly extended her hand. "I am Miranda Howarth-Dunn from Connecticut."

"It's a pleasure meeting you, Ms. Dunn." This time, Ethan shook her hand politely. He had forgotten that male or female, Miranda is still the threatening consultant, and was not a welcomed presence in his opinion.

Everybody relaxed and fell into casual conversation. Ethan studied this tall, black-haired girl with dark eyes as she explained the origin of the childhood nickname that had created such confusion. Ethan thought she had an exotic look about her, Asian or Pacific Islander. So, unlike the girls he hung out with at the Spittoon. Her looks were rich in contrast; ebony hair and alabaster skin, dramatic features that softened expressively when she talked, masculine height and feminine and very appealing figure.

"If you'll excuse us," said Vida. "I have some finishing touches to do for our meal this evening. In about ten minutes, dinner will be served. Ethan come with me."

When Vida and Ethan exited, Miranda asked Ansel, "So can you please tell me the history? How long has this place been in the family?" She sat and listened to Ansel tell the legend of the settlers. While Ansel spoke, Miranda observed Vida and Ethan coming in and out of the kitchen, bringing the meal out. Ethan reminded her of how helpful Amanda's brothers had been to their mom, and she found it endearing. When Vida officially presented the dining table set in all its glory, Ansel paused the historical narration so they could all sit down and say grace.

"Everything looks and smells delicious, Vida. You shouldn't have gone to so much trouble." Miranda was overdue for a home cooked meal and was intrigued by the menu. It whetted her appetite.

"It was no trouble at all. Everyone, dig in," Vida said with pride.

When everyone had food on their plate, Ansel went on with the history, resuming where he had left off; his father and uncle at odds, and nearly jeopardized the future of the ranch with their fighting.

"When my grandfather, the only son of Elias, the original settler, died, my dad, Nicolas Baldwin, and Uncle Fred were each given an equal share. They assumed the estate would continue in both their care, but it didn't quite go as planned. My dad married first and started a family. They built the guest house for my uncle, who was still a bachelor."

"When Uncle Fred took a wife, he needed a larger house for his growing family, but my dad always found some excuse. The two brothers battled over this and many subsequent issues. Though the guest quarters are only two-hundred feet away, it may as well have been across the continental divide."

"From that time on, they pulled farther and farther apart until, because of their unchecked anger and inflated egos, they divided everything in half. The cattle and the acreage, the buildings. It all became separate ranches. We worked our side; Uncle Fred worked the other. It was almost comical. Some silly plot in a sitcom where the main characters put tape across their apartment when they break up. My mother and I kept the lines of communication open. My cousins and I could play, but our fathers never spoke."

"When I was fifteen," Ansel continued. "Uncle Fred broke his leg in a nasty fall during roundup, so I volunteered to help. This enraged my father. He refused to help and my mom, having gotten fed up with the feud between brothers, threatened to go. My father's merciless behavior pushed Uncle Fred to the breaking point. He sold off his portion of the livestock, refusing to let his brother buy him out. He hired an attorney to split the deed, and he sold his half of the ranch. It turned out, unbeknownst to us, Uncle Fred had left the deed in trust to be given to me when I turned eighteen."

"The brothers remained estranged, and the feud left my pop a bitter man. My mother couldn't stand it any longer and made good on her threats to leave. I was eighteen, so I stayed on with the old man while Mom and Sister moved to the city. I stayed in touch with them, but my mother remarried a military man and they all moved to Germany."

"This last insult pushed my father deeper into his anger and he shut himself off from the outside in. Those were dark days for me until I met, fell in love with, and married my wife." Ansel stopped talking and, for emphasis, gazed lovingly at Vida.

"That's a story for another day," Vida peeked adoringly at her husband.

"In conclusion, when Vida and I married, we came here and Vida's energy brought back the joy into the household. On my eighteenth birthday, as directed by his trust, the deed to my uncle's land went to me. My late uncle's gesture humbled my old man, and he prayed for forgiveness. He lived with regret for the days lost, but drew some comfort knowing that the divided homestead would once again be whole. A few years later, my dad passed. I was the sole owner of the entire place."

"What an incredible tale," Miranda almost clapped at the end, "dripping with tragedy, trumpeting with triumph."

"Baldwin Brothers Feud: the motion picture. Coming soon to a theater near you," Ethan's sarcastic comment flopped out on the table, gasping for a connection, but got no response. Ethan wondered why his father was sharing such personal information with this person they had only just met.

Ansel continued, "When I took back the area that had lain unkept for years, I felt obliged to give my cousins some restitution, so I tracked them down. Both his girls were hitched. They had no ill feelings toward me and wanted me to have the homestead according to their father's wishes. Of course, my sister technically inherited half of our father's half when our father passed. She has a life in Germany now and has no interest."

"And," Ethan took advantage of the pause, "that is the end of the story. Our family has been here for over one hundred years. I believe that was Ms. Dunn's original question, wasn't it?"

"Yes, that was the question." Miranda met Ethan's eyes. She was not a fan of his condescension. She could tell Ethan felt a passion for his homestead. He also must have a strong sense of privacy. Miranda would try to calm his defensiveness. She changed the subject, "So, your cousin is married to Albert Bennett, right?"

"That's right," said Ansel. "My cousin Barbara. Her husband is Albert Bennett."

"I met Barbara after my father's passing. During the weeks Albert spent settling his affairs, Barbara was a key factor in making sure I wasn't overlooked. Barbara made sure everyone treated me with dignity, and not as another line entry of instructions to an attorney." Miranda saw Ethan tense up at the mention of attorneys. Perhaps he would soften with a fragment of sympathy for an orphaned child without parents and whose guardian was a lawyer.

"And that's how we found you, Randi," Vida chimed in. "Ansel's cousin, Barbara, was instrumental in getting us connected. She is still looking out for you."

"Hmph." Ethan caught his reaction under his breath and stopped himself from making another inappropriate remark. Knowing there was a familial connection didn't ease his concerns.

The conversation went on and soon after everyone had finished a satisfying meal, Ansel asked, "Shall we move this party into the other room? The seating is much more comfortable."

"I'll brew up a pot of tea, ginger and chamomile. Unless you prefer coffee?" Vida turned to Miranda with the question.

"A cup of tea would be lovely."

Everyone rose to their feet as Vida made her way to the kitchen. Ethan did not follow his mother, but bowed slightly and swept his arm, exaggeratingly inviting Miranda to walk past him in the other direction. "Right this way, Ms. Dunn."

"Please, call me Miranda." As she stepped in front of Ethan, Miranda's shoulder brushed ever so closely, and though she felt there was no physical contact, the energy between them gave her a lingering electric sensation on her skin.

Miranda moved toward the sofa and caught sight of the painting hanging on the wall behind it. "Is that a C. M. Russell painting?" She stared at the art piece with admiration. "I just read about him, his history, his fame. Fascinating character."

"That piece is an original," Ansel boasted.

"Sounds like there's a story behind that painting." Miranda sat on the sofa facing the recliner Ansel was settling into. "Please tell."

Ansel admitted he had stumbled into an antique store and scored an original piece of artwork worth thousands of dollars for twenty bucks. Painted by the famous Charles Marion Russell, one of the most recognized American Old West artists.

A true adventurer, the painter who lived a portion of his life as a cowpuncher riding the plains and mountains of Montana, was inspired to paint what he saw. From its place of prominence, depicting a live-action scene that one expected to encounter on a cattle ranch, it was fate that brought the museum quality art piece to live with the Baldwins.

Ethan was standing in the archway that separated the two rooms. An odd sensation had rendered him temporarily immobile. Ethan contemplated the residual heat from the passing brush of Miranda's shoulder. Vida slipped by him, carrying the tray of cups and a teapot full of the warm, soothing beverage.

"Okay, Vida's here. Let's talk a little about business while the tea steeps." Ansel leaped up and gently eased the loaded tray from his wife's hands and with gracefulness one wouldn't expect to see from an old cowboy, Ansel set the tray down gently.

Vida sat on a petite, beautifully upholstered rocking armchair, then noticed her son hovering in the doorway. "Have a seat, Ethan."

Ethan glanced around and based on the current arrangement; his only option was to sit with Miranda on the sofa. Instead, Ethan grabbed a dining chair and swung it briskly into the living room.

"First, we want to show you the complex of buildings, corrals, and pastures." Ansel had waited patiently until everyone was settled, then resumed. "We can head out early, ride up to the peak where you'll get an aerial over view. Next, we'll ride to the lower valley with the meadow and the river running through it. I know you will find it to be as beautiful as we described."

"That sounds perfect. I have done some legwork as far as plans for the valley. In what condition is the old barn down there? I have a contractor with expert experience renovating old buildings. He brings them up to code while preserving the rustic look." Miranda was so excited she hardly paused for breath, "How close is the stand of aspens to the river?"

Distracted no more by the physical effects this woman had on him, Ethan zeroed in on the discussion. *Miranda needed an overview? Of what?* he thought. And what about the meadow? That part of the land was full of historic significance. The aspen stand has some of the oldest trees to be found, which date back to the early sixteen hundreds. And what use did she have for his Uncle Fred's broken-down old barn? Ethan intended to raise the structure. What were his parents thinking?

"We can also check out the slopes around the valley for suitability," Ansel suggested, between sips of herbal brew.

Ethan had missed some of the conversation leaving him even more confused. Suitability? Suitable for what? Ethan couldn't understand.

"I'd like to know if the trails are interconnected. It'd be nice to have several options for small loops or bigger loops, depending on the ability of my clients," Miranda explained.

Her words ricocheted inside Ethan's head and lay scattered about incomprehensibly. It was sounding to him as if they wanted to turn their place into a dude ranch! Had his parents lost their minds? Surely, they were not serious about this. He pictured a bunch of greenhorns running around pretending this was the wild west, abusing his stock horses and destroying the barns and corrals. And what about accommodations? How many guests was this proposed dude ranch supposed to entertain? Were they going to build campsites, or cabins? or worse? What if Miranda proposed they build a lodge?

"Well," Ansel's voice broke through Ethan's thoughts, "I think we are off to a suitable start. Do you agree?"

"Wonderful, yes," Miranda said.

Ethan wished to interject, but couldn't find his voice. *Wait*, Ethan thought. He wanted to say 'stop, I do not agree' but he couldn't move the words from his head to his tongue.

There was some more casual conversation after the business was settled for the evening, and when Miranda's tea cup was empty, she announced she should be going. She noticed Ethan seemed to be brooding and Miranda had no intention of wearing out her welcome with him a second time.

"Thank you for a lovely evening and for making me feel so at home." Miranda enjoyed another hug from Vida. Ansel held the open front door.

"Then I'll see you all in the morning," Miranda stepped outside.

Ansel and Vida followed Miranda onto the veranda. "Until tomorrow," Vida said.

Miranda climbed into her Land Rover, fired up the engine, waved to her hosts, and it was then she noticed Ethan hadn't joined in the sendoff. She contemplated his absence and decided not to dwell on the few negative vibes she had picked up. Ethan hadn't contributed to the conversation. He was quiet during the meeting, but for what reason? Miranda speculated.

He may be tired after finishing a week's worth of work. Miranda thought the encounter had been a success overall. She had made a proper impression on the senior Baldwins, and her first impression of them was sparkling with promise.

As she guided the car onto the main road, she continued thinking of Ethan. She remembered the heat she felt when her sleeveless shoulder skimmed past his chest. She tried to focus on the road, illuminated by the broad beam of the car's headlamps. Her thoughts kept meandering onto a different path when Miranda wondered if the skin on Ethan's chest was as bronzed as that on his muscular arms.

Chapter 11

Paula's abdominal muscles contracted, her breath caught, when she abruptly fled from the warm, stuffy air inside the club to the cold exterior. The blast of cold air, typical for a springtime night in the valley, hit her as she swung out the double doors passing by Noah who followed her out the main entrance of the Bronze Spittoon.

"I've got to catch my breath." The words knocked around in her mouth as Paula tried to quiet her chattering teeth.

"It sure is getting cold," said Noah. "Here, take my coat." Noah set his jacket around Paula's bare shoulders and his hands brushed up and down her arms to suggest friction would warm her from the outside in.

Paula had started out the evening planning to make Ethan jealous by flirting and dancing with as many guys as she wanted. She was wearing her short leather skirt, and a ruffled, off the shoulder peasant blouse. The skirt drew attention to her curves and brought out the roundness of her booty. The ruffles on the blouse added to the action of her bouncy breasts as she shimmied and grooved to the music.

It was a good plan until Ethan didn't join them. It did not easily discourage Paula. She created a Plan B, the same plan only she would rely on the gossip machines to relay her activities to Ethan. Paula expected someone to tell Ethan about her behavior and he would have to take notice.

But Noah had derailed the plan. He had been dogging Paula all night, and so far, though there were plenty of gentlemen to choose from, Paula had only danced with Noah. The place was teaming with suitable men that would make it easy to carry out her plot. Frustrated, Paula lashed out, "Noah, you don't have to come out here with me. I just need to cool off for a minute. I need some space."

"Okay?" Noah said. "But your teeth are chattering, Paula. Come back in."

Paula turned with a huff. Why was Noah being so attentive? "Did Ethan put you up to this? Did he tell you to keep an eye on me?" Paula hoped he had. It would mean Ethan still cared.

It felt like grit in his boots every time Paula said Ethan's name and he went from concern for Paula to annoyance. "Oh, that is rich, Paula. Me watching over you? That would be like putting the cat in charge of the mice."

"That is not funny, Noah. Because of our actions, I lost everything. I lost it all, and you lost nothing. You and Ethan were back to being friends long before Ethan would even talk to me. He forgave you, and I'm still out in the cold."

Noah was sorry for his poor attempt at humor. He knew it had been his unrequited love for her that drove him to extremes the evening of her impending nuptials, but he maintained he would do it again. If only Paula would realize the significance of what she said. Noah had been there for her then and he was trying to be there now. Regarding his and Ethan's friendship, there was no forgiving. There was only a fragile truce. For Noah, being around Ethan was like walking on broken glass.

"Paula, don't you think that if Ethan loved you, he would have forgiven you by now?"

It was a legitimate assessment, but as soon as he spoke, Noah regretted it, and based on Paula's reaction, his regret was warranted.

"You don't know a thing about me and Ethan. You will never understand our love. Don't talk about something you know nothing about!" Paula spun her compact frame and lunged forward toward Noah. With fists clenched, arms swinging, Paula laid into Noah, letting out a considerable amount of pent-up frustrations and he silently absorbed it.

Noah felt like he deserved the lashing punishment for the part he played. His heart ached in sympathy for her pain. Paula's energy, once spent, left her leaning on Noah, her shoulders heaving in silent lament.

Reaching around her in an embrace, Noah flexed and straitened his fingers in a gentle caress on her back. "I am so sorry I made you cry."

Paula buried her face in Noah's comforting chest. Noah was so kind, so thoughtful. So different from Ethan, Paula mused. Comparing the two men seemed ludicrous, there were few similarities. Paula wished Ethan was more like Noah. Maybe she wished she could forget about Ethan altogether and go for a guy like Noah instead.

Obviously, she needed so much more from a man than Ethan gave her. How much time should she expect to waste waiting for Ethan to come around? She realized he probably never would. "It's my fault, Noah. Not yours. I wish that night had never happened. You're not responsible for these tears, Noah. Its Ethan."

"Ethan! Ethan, it's always Ethan!" Noah lifted his chin as if howling at a moonless sky. Though unintentionally, Paula's words stung like a scorpion. She wanted to forget a night that was emblazoned in his soul. Noah couldn't forget that night. The passion she could not have faked. He could taste the sweetness of her lips and hear the soft, satisfied sounds of her pleasure. "Don't forget that night, Paula, don't forget about me," Noah pleaded.

Paula raised her head and stared at Noah.

"Do you ever think of me?" Noah implored. "I love you, Paula, always have, but all you see is Ethan. What happened between you and me, the love we made, is more real than anything you've ever had with Ethan. When will you see that?"

"You're hurting me." Paula looked at Noah's hands on her arms. He noticed his death grip, then back at Paula's face.

Noah pushed himself away and let go abruptly, backing away in fear. His anger at the situation had allowed him to squeeze Paula to the point of pain. Noah spun away and started walking. He did not look back, wanting only to disappear into the darkness where the club's exterior lights could not reach.

"Noah, where are you going? Come back," Paula started after him.

Paula's pleading voice caused Noah to walk faster until he broke into a run. What he had to say needed to be said. It was a long time coming. Now, it was in the open. There was no going back. Noah ran for the town's edge, then slowed to a fast walk. Without his jacket that was still draped over his lover's shoulders, the midnight air blew through the cotton threads of his dress shirt, but it was invigorating, inspiring. With every step, Noah became lighter. The weight of too many years longing for what he couldn't have lifted when he finally spoke the truth.

As Noah turned down the main street, which was also the highway on the north end and south end of town, he saw a big rig grinding his jake brake coming around the corner. Noah popped out his thumb, and the truck driver brought the simi to a stop. Noah delivered a brief greeting as he climbed into the cab, then glanced at his watch. It was eleven thirty. He would be home before midnight. He was glad the operator of the rig wasn't much of a talker. With each gear the driver grabbed, he let more of the diesel engine's power loose and Noah felt his own self unwind with it. Soon they had reached highway speed and were purring away from the night lights of Rambletap Springs.

Chapter 12

Ethan woke to the smell of bacon tweaking his nose. As he rubbed the sleep from his eyes, he caught a whiff of the freshly brewed coffee and got up to get dressed. He had tried to talk to his folks after Miranda left, but they were tired. Well, it was morning now. Ethan didn't want to waste another second. He would speak to his parents right away.

His suspicious nature had him convinced Miranda must be up to no good, and he was determined to uncover her hidden agenda. As Ethan dressed, he planned to approach his parents with honesty and compassion. There was no need to insult them, or criticize their enthusiasm. There was no need to question their business sense, but somehow, he had to convey his concerns and make them see things clearly.

Ethan tucked his shirt in, slid his belt through the loops of his Wranglers, and stepped out of his room with socked feet. Tip-toeing in an effort not to awaken Paula, to his surprise, her door was ajar, and the room was empty. Ethan continued to the bathroom, took care of business, then made a hasty descent to the kitchen.

"Good morning, Hon." Vida held out a mug of the eye-opening liquid.

"Thanks," Ethan accepted the beverage, then went out to the service porch to put on his boots.

"Where you headed, son?" Ansel asked from his seat at the table.

Ethan stopped with one boot on and looked at his father. "Feeding chores, of course." It was what Ethan did every morning.

"The animals were hungry and couldn't wait for you to wake up," Ansel teased, knowing lazy was not in Ethan's character. "Noah and Tad were up early. They are out feeding the stock. They should be in for breakfast shortly."

"Where's Paula?" Ethan pulled up a chair.

"Paula stayed in town last night," Ansel answered. Tad told us she ran into Suzanne Mitchell, whom she hadn't seen for a while and apparently, they had a lot of catching up to do.

"A sleepover? At their age?"

"It surprised us, too," Vida said. "Tad acted casual when relaying the information, but I wonder if anything else happened."

"It's just Paula being her free spirited self. Maybe her friend needed a shoulder to cry on." Ansel provided the voice of reason.

"Suzanne is getting married. What could she have to be crying about? Maybe it was Paula who needed support?" Ansel's reasoning did not stifle Vida's suspicions.

Ethan couldn't help but wonder if his rejection of Paula's advances was bothering her more than she let on. He wondered if his parents should know about what had transpired. They were her guardians and her best interest might be at stake. But they were also his parents, and the incident was too embarrassing to share, especially with his mother.

Before Ethan could think twice about it, they could hear the twins tromping up the steps, then clamoring into the mudroom to remove their boots. Their laughter soon filled the place.

"Si'down, boys. Let's eat," said Ansel.

Tad grabbed two mugs and poured the coffee. He then handed the other to Noah as they both sat down. Ansel and the twins engaged in idle chatter as Ethan sat listening, but he did not join in.

Vida sat back and watched for signs and clues. The energy between the boys was different. Of course, there was the wedge between Noah and Ethan. Vida knew that had never gone away. When they talked, the boys often would exchange sharp comments, and the teasing was, in her opinion, mean spirited.

Normally, it was Noah on the attack while Ethan turned the other cheek. Today, Ethan was unusually perturbed by Noah's energy. When had that started? Did Paula's absence have any connection with the extra-chilly space between the boys? Vida saw how damaging had been the repercussions of the love triangle and only halfway believed they had all buried the hatchet.

With her ears tuned in and her intuition in gear, Vida listened as the men discussed what was on the agenda for the day. Vida decided Tad and Noah were fine. They both asked about meeting Randi and got a laugh when they were told the story of mistaken identity and confused gender. Out of the group of them, Vida noticed the only man who looked sullen and displeased was her own son, and she deduced it was nothing to do with the twins. Ethan must be sulking about their plans to expand the services by providing the venue for Randi's therapy program. It saddened her that Ethan was against it. He wasn't allowing himself to enjoy the next chapter in the history of the Alma Soñada Ranch.

~****~

The alarm on Miranda's cell phone, which was linked to her music library, went off playing an old Garth Brooks song as it gently roused her from a dreamless sleep. Miranda climbed out of bed and ambled to the kitchenette where the automated coffee maker had sprung into action only ten minutes ago. Miranda silently blessed modern technology as she poured herself a cup of brew that held the power to clear away the fog of slumber.

Grabbing a container of cubed watermelon from the tiny refrigerator under the short little countertop, Miranda sat down on the chair by the desk that also served as a table in her temporary accommodations. There was no time for a run this morning, but Miranda expected she'd have enough exercise touring the homestead on horseback. Miranda was around horses while operating the therapy riding program, but she rarely had time to ride. She had years of lessons as a child and hoped riding a horse was like riding a bike. She might start out a little rusty, but felt confident her experience would return along with her skills.

Miranda remembered her boots were still in the trunk full of horse tack and equipment she had stored in the expansive interior compartment of her Range Rover. She slipped into her Wranglers, a lightweight, long-sleeved blouse and her running shoes. She would change into her boots before they hit the trail.

It had been tough packing most of the belongings for this epic trip into her car, and living with a suitcase was getting old. Miranda looked forward to moving in to some more permanent accommodations soon.

Other than the shoes, Miranda's outfit was complete, and she inspected herself in the mirror to be sure. She liked how the jeans fit. Dungarees were not a regular component in an heiress's wardrobe, but it pleased her to pull off the cowgirl look brilliantly. She gathered her hair in a ponytail and pulled it through the back of her ball cap that sported an acronym, CETO. On the front, her attire suited the activities of the day.

Last, Miranda snatched her denim jacket off the bed where it lay, and was ready to leave. It was five minutes to eight, and she would arrive at the Alma Soñada on schedule.

~****~

Ethan stepped through the pasture gate to pick the horses they would need to take Miranda on a tour. All the equines gathered around him, wanting attention, and it made him smile.

"No, Kit. You get to sit this one out." The young horse nuzzled up to Ethan, at ease and familiar with the human. Ethan had worked Kit hard every day during the roundup and though he was a colt, Kit had earned his stripes. Ethan considered the horse to be a veteran now.

Pushing through the crowd of horses toward the human, amid nipping and tail switching, was Rowdy, the top dog of the pasture. He made it clear that when he was near, none of the others could nuzzle with the two-leggers. The ruckus he created stirred up the dust, and would seem a dangerous place for anyone to be with the squealing and kicking up of hooves.

Ethan never concerned himself with the risk of any misdirected aggression. Ethan recognized every horse intimately, and they knew him the same. Regarding Ethan, even Rowdy was second in command.

"Okay, okay, guys," Ethan soothed, and the herd quieted as he slipped the rope halter on Rowdy's head. "We'll let Rowdy take care of the guest. She'll need a babysitter." Ethan heard chuckling from behind him and turned to see Tad standing at the gate.

"Sounds like you are having a pretty pleasant conversation. I'm glad you are talking to someone." Tad brought up the subject of Ethan's quiet moodiness at breakfast without actually mentioning it.

"Eaves dropping is not a virtue, and I am choosey with whom I carry on conversations." Being with the animals had brought Ethan far enough out of his funk to tease Tad in return.

"Okay, Wilbur," Tad made his voice unnaturally shaky to imitate the equine actor from the vintage TV show, 'Mister Ed'. "Let me know if Mr. Ed has something to say, will ya?"

Tad collected two more halters from the fence post and let Ethan pass through before taking Style and Sonnet, the three-year-old fillies from Ansel's stallion, Magic. Rowdy followed behind them, halter on, lead rope swung over his back. Once the halter was on his face, Rowdy knew the drill and could probably do the ranch work without a rider at all.

"You watch too much re-runs on streaming TV," Ethan laughed at Tad's wacky attempt to impersonate the sitcom character of a talking horse voiced by the great Western actor, Allen Lane.

"Your father wants you to log some more hours on Winston." Tad informed Ethan as he entered the pasture to collect the last remaining horse needed and brought him out. They were all set for mounts. Noah joined his brother and Ethan as they busied themselves getting the horses ready.

With their mounts securely tied to the hitching posts, the three men started chatting like they used to do as young boys when grooming and tacking horses. Happy to be in their element, it was as if everything else slipped to the sides. They could reboot to the better days, the innocent times before the troubles of an adult world that threatened to rip their joy to shreds.

Noah had woke up still feeling the lightness he felt the night before after he unloaded on Paula with the truth, took back his heart, and vowed to never let a woman have a hold on it again.

"So?" Tad asked. "This Randi dude turned out to be a dudette, and Vida says she's a knock-out. Is she, Ethan?"

Tad knew Ethan had met the Baldwins 'new partner, and hoped to find out more, but Ethan reverted to silence, his mood toggled back to sullen.

"Yeah, I wonder how good-looking she really is," Noah spoke, because Ethan wasn't answering the question. "Pretty or not, I bet she's just another city girl looking for a wild ride on an authentic cowboy. You should go for it, Tad. You've had a bit of a dry spell. Hasn't it been a while since you've roped a filly from the herds of women that hang out at the clubs?"

"If all she wants is to ride a cowboy, she is going through more trouble than she needs to," said Tad with a smirk.

Ethan was about to respond, hoping to clean up the conversation that, in his opinion, was denigrating toward women, but Tad continued.

"There is a surefire way to win a buckaroo," Tad said. "She should spend some time at the Bronze Spittoon, wait for a local boy to become plastered, then jump on. If he doesn't buck her off, she's got herself a cowboy."

Noah's laughter in response to Tad's joke sounded mocking and disrespectful. He felt no reason to stand up for Miranda, a woman they didn't even know, but Ethan decided Noah's words were insulting to women.

As Noah put the saddle on Sonnet, Ethan warned, "Mind how you set and cinch that saddle, or you'll be in for a wild ride with a filly yourself. And, if memory serves me, the last time you rode Sonnet, wasn't it you who got bucked off?"

It was true, Noah had ridden Sonnet, his saddle slipped, the hypersensitive youngster felt it, and panicked. With a little pop of her hips and a twist of her powerful haunches, Sonnet sent Noah spiraling in the air and crashing to the ground with a thud.

Noah glared at Ethan for bringing up a sore subject. His ego had suffered the biggest bruise, and his emotions were too exposed to brush it off. The question was, what could Noah do about it? He resentfully took Ethan's advice and gave the saddle extra attention. He didn't want to repeat the trick. Noah calmed his anger.

Tad sensed the animosity between his best friend and his brother was brewing and came to the rescue. "Hey, Ethan. Wasn't it you who came off Kit the other day?"

"Ahhhh, see? It can happen to anyone." Noah took hold of the white flag his brother waved.

"Shoot," Ethan exclaimed. "Yeah, he spooked and moved out from under me. Left me rolling in a cloud of dust," Ethan laughed in recollection, accepting the opportunity to keep the peace, gratefully recognizing Tad's effort. The laughing and joking began again. Tad had successfully deflated the tension.

Soon, the horses were tacked up and left to stand for a while as the three cowboys set about the daily chores. They moved the brood mares with new foals out of the barn and into paddocks, then cleaned the extra-large stalls. The routine was so engrained, they didn't have to think. They moved in harmony like a well-oiled machine and just as they were finishing up; they heard the crunching of gravel from an oncoming car.

"She's here." Noah and Tad burst forth like toddlers at Christmas. Ethan stayed behind and finished saddling Magic for his dad to ride.

Chapter 13

The courtyard in the center of the complex of buildings that formed the heart of the Alma Soñada appeared deserted as Miranda drove over the rise. As she continued her approach and began to circle counter clockwise the giant Silver Maple in the middle, she caught sight of two figures emerging from the barn to her right. She parked beyond the main house facing the way out. From the driver side Miranda looked over the top of her Range Rover as she stepped out of the vehicle.

"Good morning," Miranda spotted Ansel on the veranda and beside him stood two men she hadn't met. It amazed her their resemblance. They were like a carbon copy, and she knew instantly she was looking at the Crawley twins she had heard about.

Ansel began the introductions. "Randi, this here's Tad, and that's Noah. Boys, allow me to introduce Ms. Miranda Dunn." Each man took Miranda's hand as she stared from one face to the other.

"Pleased to meet you," Miranda said to each man. They were both nice looking, with amiable smiles that showed very white teeth under twin mustaches. As they removed their hats respectfully, Miranda noticed Noah's hair was a tiny shade lighter, and he placed his hat back down slightly tilted to the left side. She couldn't help wonder how many other differences she'll discover if she got the chance to know them better.

"We can barely tell them apart either," Ansel laughed, accurately reading Miranda's expression. He knew exactly what she was thinking. "Come on in and we'll talk a minute before we hit the trail."

As the group filed in to the kitchen, Miranda noticed there was one person missing. She thought better than to ask, instead she said, "I think I'd like to freshen up. If you'll excuse me?"

"There's a facility on the right before you exit the vestibule, dear. Help yourself," Vida instructed as she was finishing the clean-up from their breakfast.

As soon as Miranda exited, Tad fairly jumped for joy. "Does anybody believe in love at first sight? Because y'all are about to witness it."

"Calm down, boy. She'll hear you," Noah gave a warning, along with a wide grin.

"She's not just pretty, Vida. She's gorgeous." Tad was beside himself. "You won't ever see any woman the likes of her down at the Spittoon."

"Pipe down, boys. You don't want to embarrass her, do you?" Ansel put a stop to the gushing chatter and began explaining the day's plans. They were to take a series of single-track trails that ran up the canyon, a faster route to the summit than the wide trail for moving the cattle. Ansel finished talking as Miranda returned. She was adjusting her pony tail that had become loose under her cap. Tad leaped to her side, holding out a chair for her at the table.

Miranda smiled at the gesture, "Thank you… Tad?" she asked. "Did I get the name right?"

"Yes, m'am," Tad answered proudly. "CETO? What does that stand for?" Tad asked, referring to the letters on Miranda's ball cap.

"I noticed your hat, too. Is it the acronym for your therapy program?" Vida asked.

"Yes, Vida," Miranda began, "It stands for the Connecticut Equine Therapy Organization, part of my non-profit organization." Tad and Noah both sat down to listen, so Miranda continued to explain. "It's the part of my business about which I am very passionate. CETO is a resource group comprised of horse owners and stable facilities that work collectively with the professionals to provide horseback riding therapy for physically, developmentally, and differently abled children."

"We do all the work on the business end so the doctors and therapists can access the programs effortlessly. The easy access to the program allows the service providers to focus on their work; building confidence in their clients' abilities and give them the opportunity to live a fuller, enriched life."

"The kids come to us with varying degrees of abilities and mental conditions and we introduce them to horses. It's amazing to watch the transformations as the children interact with the equines. We chose horses that are most inclined to be quiet communicators, condition them to support and care for their riders, and for the children, having that support turns the world into a much more inviting place to be."

"And that's where we take part," Ansel continued the explanation. "We feel it would be rewarding to donate a portion of the ranch to Randi for her riding program, only we wish to help her expand the concept, get the kids out of an arena and into the real world, our world."

Miranda hung on Ansel's words, admiring his and Vida's generosity. She was grateful they not only would help her, but understood her dream with a passion of their own.

"Wow, that is so great," Tad spouted, unable to wipe the rapturous grin from his face as he listened to Miranda talk.

"I'm impressed, and what a noble cause. So, do you already have the children for this program here in Rambletap Springs?" Noah diverted the attention away from his twin.

"Most of the clients will come from back east at first. The sessions are going to be a week at a time. It'll be like a family vacation for them," Miranda answered.

"Family vacation?" Noah wondered. Maybe Ethan was right. Randi intended to turn Rambletap Springs into a tourist destination. The Baldwins were going to open a vacation resort right there on the ranch. "Won't that bring more people to Rambletap Springs?"

Randi answered, "Each week-long session will have a small number of students along with a few family members."

Ansel cut in, "The therapy is available to kids from all over. They will travel a distance and we will set them up with a place to stay. We thought it would be great to incorporate the therapy time for the kids with family time, invite the mothers and fathers, sisters and brothers to join in and enjoy the fun, together, as a family."

"So, where would they all stay?" Noah demanded to know.

"That is a question for another day, Noah, let's talk about this later. Today, let's focus on the tour. We'll start out going up to the bluff on the Wash-out trail. It'll be an easy climb up. We'll get there in time to have lunch at Carmen's Camp, and then we shall go up the Peak trail to the ridge. It's a fifteen-minute climb straight to the sky, and the view will knock your socks off." The last sentence he directed at Miranda, sweeping his arm in a horizontal arch as if laying the view in front of her.

"After the horses have caught their breath," Tad chimed in, puffing a little as if he had just now finished the climb to the peak himself, "we will take you down the back side of the peak a ways and catch the Old Wagon Trail."

"Ah-hum," Ansel cleared his throat to interrupt Tad's contribution before continuing. "After we have lunch in Carmen's Camp, there'll be a perfect opportunity for you boys to check fences. We have had no one ride those lines since fall, and we all know the importance of a sturdy, well-maintained fence line."

"What is Carmen's Camp?" Miranda asked.

"Carmen's Camp is a cabin below the ridge built by a settler in the late 1800s. The settler, a lonely fur trapper, was a curiosity among the tribe of natives, particularly to one young maiden. The white man fell in love with the maiden, a Black Foot squaw, but they had to keep it a secret from her people and his."

"They kept it on the down-low," Tad interrupted with a silly comment that evoked a loud guffaw and a smack across the shoulder from his brother.

"Dude, you don't have the street cred to pull off that slang. Get it together, man," Noah said under his breath as Tad shoved his brother, nearly knocking him over on the chair.

The boisterousness made Miranda flinch. She had little experience with this kind of rowdiness, but it was endearing and made her chuckle, too.

"Why don't you boys settle down, hmmm?" Ansel was not pleased. "I'm sorry, Randi," Ansel apologized and resumed the story.

"The settler and the Indian maiden continued hiding their affair and met whenever they could. One night they were discovered and when the information got to the town's leaders, they put the settler in jail. The girl followed the men to town and the Chief announced that the white man stole her from them. By locking up the settler, the townsfolk hoped for a way to show the native people they respected the native sovereignty. The Indian squaw returned to her tribe by day, but at night, she would steal away and go to the window of the jail cell. She wanted to be near her lover, for in her womb she carried his child."

"The people of the town, when they could no longer legally hold him, released the settler and he fled to the mountains. Shunned from her tribe when her body showed the infant growing inside, the maiden had been on her own when the baby came. She was frightened. The settler, having just been freed, ran deep into the back country where he knew the maiden's tribe would be, but all that was left of the village were the smoldering ashes in the fire pits that had warmed their tents."

"Fearing his lover and the child she carried had fallen to the worst fate imaginable, the young trapper decided he would go after them, but he stopped short when he heard the weakened cry of an infant a little distance away. He found the baby in a bundle, but the Indian maiden was nowhere to be found. The settler stayed with the newborn at the abandoned Indian village and waited."

"It is said that they forbid the maiden to rejoin the tribe even though she had left the baby behind. She didn't belong in the white man's world either and it is believed in final desperation, she took her life. Not knowing her fate and still filled with hope his maiden would return, the young settler brought the infant to town to save her life and he found kindness at the church. The pastor and his wife agreed to help, no questions asked, and the trapper went alone to the abandoned native village in the mountains to wait."

"Time passed, the young mother didn't return to the camp, and the trapper returned to town. The infant girl grew, but the townspeople were not kind or welcoming. They merely tolerated the single father and his half-breed child. When the girl was old enough, the trapper took his daughter to raise her in the cabin he had built at the site of the deserted Indian camp. The settler created a comfortable homestead for him and his daughter and they both waited for the Indian squaw that never returned."

"When Carmen, the little girl, grew up, she stayed in the cabin and lived on her own. Her father left, they say, in search of his lost love. Carmen, who had a way with all the woodland creatures, stayed in the high country alone with only her animals to keep her company. The few people in town that knew about her left her alone, checking on her welfare only a few times a year."

"Such a lonesome soul," Miranda felt deeply the pain of that kind of lost and disconnectedness.

"The rumors circulated through the generations. Some said Carmen was a witch and told their children tales of how she could talk to the animals and order them to do her bidding. The people grew to be afraid of the Carmen in the stories, and the folklore that developed said she cast enchantment spells on the forest that caused travelers to become lost, but my great-grandfather Elias, the original Baldwin who knew the truth, let Carmen live in peace in the cabin that became his when he bought the land upon which it was built."

"My grandmother Katherine, used to visit and bring Carmen gifts and supplies in her old age. One spring after a harsh, long winter, Katherine went to Carmen's cabin and found it had been empty for some time. Legend has it Carmen went to find her mother and father and now the three of them together in spirit roam the forests and meadows around Rambletap Springs in eternal peace."

"That is so beautiful." The story had captivated Miranda's imagination and pulled at her heart. "Beautifully tragic, and heartbreakingly romantic."

"When I came to live with Ansel, his father told me about the legend of Running Fawn." It was Vida's turn to add to the story. "Running Fawn was Carmen's mother, the native squaw. Like it did to you, the tragedy deeply moved me. I wanted to memorialize the spirits of those souls whose only crime was their love for each other. Punished by societal constructs for being honest with themselves and compassionate with each other, I couldn't ignore the past, so we erected a small monument at the cabin site. We keep the cabin in good order and stocked with supplies. The weather in the high country can change in a flash, and it's a good idea to have a refuge. The cabin is always ready for the next occupants, be they spiritual or of this realm."

"Speaking of always ready, are you folks ever coming out?"

Miranda turned to see Ethan standing in the doorway between the vestibule and wondered how long he had been there.

Chapter 14

Miranda marveled at Ethan's ability to appear out of nowhere, undetected, like a cat stalking their prey. The polite thing would be to at least make his presence known with a friendly gesture if he preferred not to interrupt. Ansel and Vida were finishing up the story of Running Fawn, and Miranda was still deep in thought when Ethan's words interrupted. "The horses are ready to go."

As she acknowledged Ethan, Miranda's heart beat slightly faster. Was it from being startled, or was it from her annoyance? She reasoned it was because of the elevation difference for which she had not yet become acclimated. At home in Connecticut, the elevation was only five hundred forty feet above sea level. Rambletap Springs was almost a whopping ten times more at forty-eight hundred, and the ranch was a slight climb above town.

"I'm ready," Miranda followed the others out into the morning sun.

Ethan studied Miranda as she walked down the stairs ahead of him, surprised how normal-looking the big city girl from back east was in her jeans and blouse. The women that came from the cities around here to the Bronze Spittoon and other clubs always took their idea of western wear to the extreme until it appeared cartoonish.

Ethan's positive evaluation came to an abrupt halt when his eyes got to her feet. To be exact, Miranda's running shoes. *There it is*, he thought, *wanting to find fault*. In his mind, the absence of proper footwear added to his suspicions that this woman was up to something.

Ansel had described Miranda as an experienced horsewoman, but her footwear said otherwise. She wanted something from the ranch, and was reaching to great lengths to gain their trust, but Ethan saw right through it. Miranda's footwear choice was a dead giveaway. Ethan was collecting data to present to his parents. By the end of the day, he would have more than enough information to convince them to abandon their ideas.

Aware that she was being sized up, Miranda opened the storage trunk she carried inside the back of her SUV, "Let me get my boots," Miranda spoke directly to Ethan and couldn't help looking smug as she pulled on her well-worn boots, a pair of practical Justin brand Ropers.

"You have only that little jacket?" Vida questioned from the top of the stairs. "Come back in here and pick out a parka. You can tie it to the saddle. You might need it at the summit."

Now, it was Ethan's turn to wear a smug expression as Miranda stepped past him to get a heavier coat. A comfortably worn pair of boots wasn't enough to prove to him Miranda wasn't a greenhorn. She still had a lot to learn about the natural forces of nature.

Miranda walked into the tiny mudroom just inside the kitchen and searched around. Stacked on the shelves was a pile of folded rain slickers. Above her hung a plethora of coats in varying lengths and sizes on hangers on an open rung suspended from the ceiling. It was like stepping into a Land's End or Eddie Bauer clothing and apparel catalog. Miranda grabbed a parka that would fit well and do the job, threw it over her arm, and sped out to catch up with the others who were making their way to the barn.

Ethan studied the coat Miranda chose, glad to see she had the sense to choose one that is waterproof and had a hood. There was no predicting the weather despite all the meteorology tools there were to employ. Mountain weather could shift on a dime. Clouds can gather from out of thin air, and temperatures would drop ten degrees in ten minutes. There was no way to outrun a storm and no place to run to, anyway.

This was shaping up to be an interesting day, Ethan thought, deciding to find entertainment in watching this newcomer handle the ins and outs of cattle ranching beginning with horses. He was certain Miranda was about to dig herself into a hole. Why not up the ante? With a last-minute change in the lineup, Ethan let her ride Winston.

When everyone had mounted up, the first twenty minutes of the ride found each horseman with their hands full. Their mounts were feeling playful and energetic. Ansel's horse, Magic, had sat idle in his stall during most of the past week, while Ansel was out of commission. Sonnet, with Noah aboard, was acting like a bronc. Not at all unusual for her as she was still green broke and needed time to settle.

Style was catching Sonnet's energy and was playful as Tad did his best to keep her moving forward, though not in a straight line. Ethan, who was riding Rowdy, the oldest and most experienced horse on the ranch, looked to be the only one enjoying the ride. As for Miranda, she found that riding a horse was exactly like riding a bicycle if you hadn't done it for a while; you might be a touch rusty, but you never forget how.

Though originally Ethan had picked Rowdy out to babysit the city slicker, he changed his mind and, as part of the testing process, gave Miranda Winston to ride. Winston, a four-year-old chestnut gelding, hadn't been started with the rest of the colts last year because of an injury to his shoulder. They started riding Winston earlier that spring, but he showed good progress and the cowboys had even worked him on cattle.

Miranda easily adapted to Winston's shortness of stride compared to the thoroughbreds and warm bloods she grew up riding, but she was finding it harder to adjust to his quick reaction to any rider movement. Trying to stay as still in the saddle as possible, she stayed with the little horse, but every time Winston moved a bit this way or that in navigating his hoof placements on the ground, Miranda felt awkward.

Miranda tried to move with the horse, but her over compensation caused a shift in weight that sent Winston back in the other direction. Next, Miranda tried raising herself off her seat. This only sped Winston up. Miranda lifted her legs off Winston's sides, hoping that might slow him down.

"Try to loosen your spine. Don't be so stiff. He can feel that." Ethan rode up alongside Miranda. "And don't lift your legs. When you pick up your legs, your buttock clenches, Winston can feel that, too. Put a little more weight on your tailbone, that will lift the weight of your legs off his sides. Then let the reins out a bit."

Miranda shifted her weight back as per Ethan's instructions, but she was not comfortable loosening her grip on the reins. It seemed to her like Winston was ready to bolt and letting go of the contact didn't seem wise.

"Trust me, Miranda." Ethan sensed Miranda was second guessing his instructions. "I gentled that horse myself. I promise Winston won't take off."

Ethan's soothing voice and calming presence made her relax, and to Miranda's relief, Winston slowed and stopped jigging and sidestepping. Miranda lightened the contact and Winston fell out of his trot and into a fast walk, matching pace with Ethan's mount, Rowdy. They rode together for a while, Miranda focusing on staying light, Ethan, with his presence alone, providing silent confidence to Winston and his rider.

After a time, Miranda eased her focus and glanced at her surroundings. They were no longer in the meadow and had been slowly ascending the trail into the forest. She also noticed they were alone. "Where are the others?"

"You left them behind, but not by far. If you can stop that runaway horse, we can wait for them to catch up." Ethan winked.

Miranda leaned farther back, and Winston came to a stop. To her, it was a foreign concept to stop a horse without using the reins, but she was getting the hang of it. "When in Rome…" she muttered.

"There, you see? You communicated clearly. Winston, read your intentions. It's not magic." Ethan was proud of Winston and a little condescending. He observed Miranda had skills but wasn't ready to give her credit.

"I know how to communicate. It starts with an open mind." Miranda prided herself upon her communication skills, and she didn't like Ethan's tone. "A scant more information would have gone a long way, too. You could have given me instructions before throwing me and Winston together to figure it out on our own. That is just dangerous."

"There is nothing dangerous about Winston. I trained him myself. I know what I'm talking about. He deserves simple messages from his rider. It's misunderstandings that are dangerous."

"You are the expert in misunderstandings. Simple messages, however, don't seem to be your strong suit." Miranda was indignant. She thought about their first encounter on the veranda. If Ethan had asked a logical question that day, Miranda would have explained, but he attacked. "One cannot receive information without an open mind."

"You're calling me closed minded?" Ethan's response was larger than expected. "You don't even know me."

Ethan's outburst was a shock and Miranda tensed up. Maybe Winston sensed the physical tension, absorbing it from the air. It could have been the other riders approaching from behind that startled Winston, who was a less experienced horse. Most likely, it was the perfect storm of circumstances.

The results of it all spooked the little horse and when he lunged forward, Miranda lost balance backward. Her legs shot forward and when she pulled them back to regain balance, her feet lost the stirrups. She instinctively grabbed a handful of mane to hang on and away they went.

Miranda willed herself to calm down. First, she needed to regain her stirrups. Winston flying, his hooves pounding. They had left the designated trail and were tearing through the trees. Miranda knew Winston would eventually stop, and the safest thing for her to do was to stay with him. She tucked herself in over his neck to avoid the low branches. She didn't interfere with Winston as he navigated past tree trunks, shifting left, right, then left again.

The first ten seconds of the run, Winston went out of control. Between the thirty and forty-second marks, they found their rhythm. Winston slowed a bit. Just as Miranda was wondering if she should try to sit back and ask the horse for a stop, they came upon a creek. With no time to debate whether to cross, they were still moving too fast.

Miranda dug her heels into Winston's sensitive barrel and together they sailed over the stream like it was a Grand Prix water obstacle, landing heavily on the far side. The other riders had been racing up behind them and saw the whole thing.

"Wow, that was outstanding." Noah was the first to arrive on the scene, holding his hat in his hand and spinning his mount in a circle. He appeared to be jazzed by the show. Sonnet spun to a shining stop. "Awesome," Noah whooped. "That was some mighty fine riding."

"Randi! Are you okay?" Tad's horse, Style, sprinted past Noah and Sonnet, splashing through the water. Before Style stopped, Tad was dismounting and rushed to Miranda's side. He helped her off her mount and caught her on unsteady limbs.

Miranda turned to her mount to inspect him. She checked him for cuts or scuffs he might have sustained on his mad dash through the undergrowth and rocky terrain. To her relief, Winston was unscathed. Miranda turned the frightened gelding around to walk back across the creek. He was huffing and blowing, his sides were heaving as he regained his breath, but he followed through the water. "Poor little guy." When they were back on the other side, Miranda stopped to comfort Winston.

"Are you are alright?" Ethan moved up to where Miranda had crossed the creek and dismounted.

"I'm fine," said Miranda. She wanted to say, 'no thanks to you', but it wasn't worth it. Using her instincts, Miranda had been pushed into finding a communicative pathway with Winston. As difficult a task as it suggested to be, she was going to figure out a better way to communicate with Ethan, too. "I just need a minute."

Tad was by Miranda's side the instant he saw her teetering, and maneuvered her to a downed tree, encouraging her to sit before she might faint and fall. Though Ethan was responsible for the calamity and thus obliged to help, he saw Tad had things under control.

"At least she's got good instincts," Ethan muttered as he dismounted. "We should switch horses."

Miranda regained her equilibrium in response to Ethan's double-sided comment. He may have thought she hadn't heard. It insulted her he now requested to put her on the veteran horse? Who did he think he was? He had no business evaluating her skills, testing her abilities. She stood up beside Winston.

"Winston and I are fine, thank you. We took care of each other. At least Winston is looking out for me."

Ethan heard Miranda's comment to the colt and felt even more guilty for his decision to let her ride Winston. He put someone in a less than optimal position, even if it was someone he didn't like or trust, that was not how he was raised. Ethan glanced at his father and, from his narrowing eyes, knew instantly Ansel hadn't missed a thing. He and the other two cowboys had most likely heard the shouting as they approached just before Winston took off. Ethan knew there would be a discussion about it later.

Ansel moved Magic forward to stand by Winston as Miranda readied herself to mount up. "Honey, are you certain you're okay? You look a little pale." Ansel's voice was soft, his words were kind. The tenderness of how he looked at her made her long for the father she never had.

"I am certain." Miranda spoke quietly to the man on the beautiful black stallion. "My skin is always this color. I'm the definition of paleface."

Her voice still quivered, but her sense of humor assured the men she was indeed okay. Tad and Noah laughed at the joke and mounted their horses. They seemed relieved. The ordeal was over, and all's well that ends well.

Ethan, however, was not convinced. He had heard the tremble in Miranda's voice, saw the waver in her balance, and knew it was his fault. It was an odd feeling, but all he wished to do was protect her, make amends, and make sure Miranda was never in danger again.

"I think we need to change plans, Dad," Ethan said and moved toward Miranda to help her mount up. "There will always be another day to go to the summit."

"I'm fine. Really." Miranda put her left foot to the stirrup, but it surprised her how weak her leg muscles were. Ethan effortlessly and with one hand under her left armpit, lifted Miranda up while leaning his shoulder against her left thigh as she swung her right leg over Winston's back. "See?" Miranda said as she gathered up the reins.

Ethan and Ansel exchanged a glance, and Ethan shook his head 'no 'at the unasked question in his father's eyes.

"Ethan's right," Ansel took control. "Besides, it looks like the weather is taking a turn after all."

"Noah, you and Tad take Randi back down on the cattle road. It will be an easy descent. Ethan and I will keep going up and check those fences. If the storm gets bad before we are through, we can hole up at the cabin."

Miranda peered skyward, trying to catch what Ansel saw as a change in the weather. In the canopy of branches above, she saw no sign of clouds. There was nothing but patches of blue.

"Okay, I hate to break up this party, but let's go." Ansel moved his horse forward through the forest, where they would catch the trail farther up. "We'll see y'all at the house."

Ethan hesitated, looking up at Miranda as if he were going to say something, opened his mouth, then closed it again. Ethan gave Winston a pat on the shoulder. "Take care of her," he whispered softly to Winston and glanced at Miranda before jumping on his horse to take off after his father.

Miranda shivered. Maybe it was the weather change, or shock following her dangerous ride. It could have been the tenderness in which Ethan expressed concern for her care through talking to her horse. No matter the reason, Miranda felt chilled, so she reached back to gather the parka, which was still securely tied to the saddle with the latigo strings.

Feeling the warmth of the parka, and the security of two able-bodied cowboys riding with her, Miranda felt safe to head down the mountain. The summit would be there for her to explore another day.

Chapter 15

Vida looked out the window as she finished the breakfast dishes, her eyes focused on the sky. It was a rancher's inherent duty to keep tabs on the weather. She would look up again many times throughout the day without planning to. It was second nature. Before she turned her focus on her duties in the kitchen, a bit of movement caught her eye. A car she didn't recognize was coming over the rise. She dried her hands and stepped out the back door to wait for what turned out to be Suzanne Mitchell driving up with Paula.

After bringing the car to a halt, Paula got out of the passenger side and immediately explained, "Suzanne brought me up here to pick up my car. I'll be staying in town with the Mitchells for a while. I came to grab some things."

Suzanne leaned out of the driver's side window to exchange a greeting. "Good morning, Mrs. Baldwin."

"Good morning, dear. And please, no need for formalities. Call me Vida." Vida appreciated the respectful address. "I understand congratulations are in order."

"Thank you Mrs.... I mean, Vida," Suzanne smiled shyly. "Well, I better get back. I'll see you at my house, Paula," Suzanne said. She circled around the courtyard and was gone.

Vida returned to the kitchen, and studying Paula's expression, looked for but saw no signs of distress. All Vida saw was a girl coming to pack an overnight bag for some time away. If there was something for Vida to be concerned about, Paula was getting good at hiding it.

"Paula, if you have a second, I'd like to sit and chat before you go."

"Sure, Vida. I always have time for our chats."

"You go on up and pack and I'll finish my work here. Then I'll put the kettle on."

Vida wasn't British, but she was well versed about tea, an essential part of any conversation. Social convention suggested a hot beverage was to be offered for many reasons; to soothe a breaking heart, calm an angry mind, or to console the grief-stricken soul. The tea in Vida's kitchen could do all those jobs and more. Vida had an elixir to heal that what ails the body, physically and mentally.

"Paula, I was wondering," Vida got right to the point when her goddaughter came back down with her suitcase in tow. "why did you stay in town last night? What made you decide to stay for a while with Suzanne?"

"Like I told Tad, I met up with Suzanne at the Spittoon. It's been a while since we've seen each other. We needed to catch up."

"Why are you going to stay with them for a while? How much catching up do you need to do?" Vida grilled the girl.

"Well, Suzanne is planning a wedding. I offered to help," Paula wiggled uncomfortably in her chair.

"Is that the only reason?" Vida zeroed in bluntly.

Paula looked away. They were acceptable reasons; they made perfect sense and were more plausible than the truth, so how did Vida recognize it wasn't the whole truth?

Vida stood up, giving Paula a moment to consider her next words. The kettle of water would soon boil. "Can you tell me what's going on? I have more questions."

"Did Noah make it home?" Paula redirected, seeking to avoid a game of twenty questions with her godmother.

"Yes, he did," Vida answered. "Were you concerned he might not? Why did Noah leave the bar without you and Tad?"

"Noah was upset with me."

Now they were getting somewhere, Vida thought. *Do you know what upset him?*

Paula knew she was eventually going to tell Vida everything in pieces, question by question. It had happened before, and Vida was relentless. Paula decided to get it over with, so she took a deep breath and began, "When Ethan couldn't go out with us, it made me mad. I wanted to dance with all the guys I could. I just needed to have fun. But Noah wouldn't let anyone else dance with me. I accused Noah of trying to be my bodyguard."

Paula paused and tried to remember what happened next. Vida took advantage. "Paula, why were you mad at Ethan for not going? You are no longer engaged, and it isn't Ethan's duty to see you get to go out and dance. In your own words, you admit there were plenty of guys with whom to dance."

"I know, I know," Paula dropped her head. "I can't seem to let go of Ethan. It has been such a habit for as long as I can remember, me and Ethan. In my heart I get it. We are not a couple. It's my brain that isn't cooperating. Noah told me to stop chasing Ethan, and I got mad at him. He told me he loves me, Vida. Noah said he's tired of me hurting him," Paula's words caught in her throat. "And then he ran away." Paula sobbed, "I didn't know I was hurting him, Vida."

It was upsetting to talk about, and Paula hoped she'd satisfied her guardian's concerns. She was too embarrassed to elaborate or go too deep into details of how she had shamelessly thrown herself at and been rejected by Ethan.

When Vida and Ansel invited Paula to come live with them, they had all sat down to discuss the subject, hash it out, and get everything in the open so they could set clear boundaries. Paula hadn't intended to lie when she told Ansel and Vida she was over the break-up. When she said she understood she wasn't to be married to Ethan, she said she was ready to be his friend. She thought she meant it.

Paula stopped her tears and continued, "When Tad found out his brother had left the club, he tried to call, but Noah didn't answer his cell phone. We waited, but Noah never come back. I left with Suzanne. Tad said he was gonna head home."

"What do you think about Noah now? Does his confession of love for you change how you feel?" Vida pressed.

"I don't… I mean…" Paula stuttered. "I never even thought of Noah…"

The tea kettle began to whimper and Vida extinguished the flame under it, releasing it from the intensity of the heat that would bring it to a scream.

Vida heard enough to put the situation into perspective. Looking back on their decision to move Paula in when there was so much baggage in this three-way love triangle might not have been the best plan, but under the circumstances, they did the best they could.

Vida had only one more question for Paula. "You were with Noah the night before your wedding to Ethan, but you never considered what that meant?"

As the tea leaves steeped in the boiling water poured over them, Vida realized there was still just as much chance for the kids to all figure things out as there was potential for the wedges between them to drive them completely apart forever.

"Paula, you now know there is no chance of you and Ethan reconciling to become husband and wife."

"Yes, I do, Vida, I honestly do. I think I was holding on to the idea of marrying Ethan because it meant not everything was changing. I have been foolishly trying to stay in the past, maybe to better hang on to the memory of my parents. If I lose Ethan, too, I will have lost everything."

Vida set a cup of tea in front of Paula and the girl stared into it, looking past the steam and through the tinged liquid to the ceramic surface on the bottom. "I just don't want to lose him."

"If you can find Ethan as your brother, then you will have him forever."

Paula felt lucky to have someone to talk to. It helped her see things more clearly. Of course, Vida was right. Paula trusted Vida to know what was in her own son's heart, and now Paula just had to figure out how being Ethan's sister was to work.

And now there was Noah. He had confessed his feelings. He said he loved her, and she turned that love around and stabbed him with it. How did she feel about Noah? Did she love him, too? Had she the right to tell him, after the way she treated him? It was too much to think about all at once.

Vida saw the wheels in Paula's mind spinning and swooped in with cream and honey for the tea. "You should take a pause for reflection. Time for yourself. You take a break from everything and figure out what's next for you. The time away with your girlfriend will give you some space in which to do that."

Paula was the daughter Vida would never have. Vida had let go of the dream of having many children. Nature had other plans. She had been blessed to have the twins move in, and then out of the tragedy of Paula's parents came the gift of Paula. Vida's dream home with a big family was within grasp. Vida wasn't going to let it go.

Right now, Paula was the key. Paula could ease up on Ethan and bring peace to the household in that regard. By reconciling her feelings for Noah, she could give Noah and Ethan a chance to honestly mend the broken bonds of their friendship. Vida was tilling the soil, and planting the seeds in hopes of growing a family. Her intentions were pure, her actions came from love.

Paula sighed and gently mixed the honey and cream into her beverage. Vida was right, and Paula felt confident that it was going to be alright. She needed time to let the dust settle. She felt better already. Vida's miracle elixir was soothing to the heart, mind, body, and soul.

Chapter 16

It seemed like an eternity since Ansel and Ethan had split off from the other half of the group. Riding in silence made it worse. The trees in the forest offered no comfort as they darkened the mood. The riders continued to climb as the thickness of the trees decreased until the forest opened up at the timberline. They veered their horses to the right and brought them together to walk abreast through the velvety green grass at their feet. The two cowboys found the line of fencing they needed to inspect and got to work, but it was difficult for Ethan to focus on the task. He kept going over the events of the morning, all that had gone wrong and how much worse it all could have been.

Why had he put Miranda up on Winston? Why hadn't he let her ride Rowdy like his dad suggested? At the very least, he should have taken Miranda and Winston to the arena for a few minutes. Miranda was obviously an accomplished rider and a fast learner. Would it have been too much trouble to give the horse and rider a chance to get a feel for each other in the safety of a riding ring?

"Shoot," Ethan exclaimed, which turned his father's head.

"Nothing," Ethan answered before Ansel had even asked a question.

"Randi sure did a fine job handling Winston." Ansel had a suspicion he knew exactly what was bothering his son.

"If something would have happened to her, Dad… or Winston. It could have been a disaster."

"Well, nothing happened. We got lucky. We all learned a lesson, I hope?" Ansel was being tactful on the subject, not bringing up whose decisions were responsible, knowing his son was already punishing himself enough.

Ethan was tentatively relieved that his father might not lay into him about how Miranda ended up on a green broke horse when there were other solidly trained horses among the stock from which to choose. The conversation stalled and silence prevailed.

Ansel considered Ethan and what the boy had been through recently. It was understandable for Ethan to be a little head shy around women after the heartbreak and betrayal that came with finding his best friend and his fiancée had been having an affair. Following the break-up, Ethan had gone with the twins to the clubs and saloons, but nothing became of the time spent. Ethan wasn't dating, and Ansel feared his son had no intention of getting back out there.

Then, to complicate things, he and Vida invited Paula to live with them only a few months after the drama at the altar. Based on the information supplied to them, Ansel and Vida believed Paula and Ethan had worked things out and moved past their differences. Had they known the truth, they wouldn't have brought Paula into their home only to pour salt in their son's wounds.

It was a tangled web in which these kids had become ensnared. Ansel hoped he and Vida hadn't made it more complicated. He hoped they could work it out. There was no taking anything back, straight ahead was the only choice. It's not about what anyone did wrong, it is about what to do next that can make it right.

"Do you still love Paula, Ethan?"

Ethan wasn't expecting the question and answered without thinking. "Of course, I do. I care about Paula. I just can't think of a way to make her happy. At least, making her happy without making myself miserable."

"There are many kinds of love, son. Remember that. You and Paula both love each other, you are great together. I remember you used to get on so well, laughing, playing, enjoying silly conversations. There is a genuine connection. I suppose that is why you two keep showing up in each other's lives. But that doesn't mean you two are right for marriage. If you had the right love for Paula, making her happy would make you happy and if Paula had the right love for you, she wouldn't have gone to Noah looking for something else."

Ansel's truthful statement was simple and accurate. Ethan wondered why he hadn't seen it that way all along. Paula wouldn't have been driven into the arms of another had she been right for him. He and Paula were an energetic match, but they were not a match that could complement each other in marriage. It was making sense now, and Ethan hoped he could talk to Paula soon. Once Ethan spoke to Paula, he felt certain they would get to a healthy point relationally.

Interrupting Ethan's thoughts, Ansel pointed. "Look, up ahead." There was a spot along the fence they had been skirting, with a few poles pulled sideways by tight wires.

"Looks like something may have come down on the barbed wires farther down the line," Ethan theorized.

"I'll ride ahead and find out," Ansel announced. "You stay here, stabilize those poles and reconnect the lines." Ansel turned Magic toward the downside of the fence. "See you in a while." With a wave of his hand, the old man and his horse disappeared as the wind that was bringing the weather picked up.

Ethan dismounted and stood at Rowdy's flank, unpacking the tools he always carried in his saddlebags. He cut the wires that held the tension. The listing poles bounced back. The rewiring was a breeze. In about ten minutes, Ethan's job was done. With his tools safely secured in his bags, he and Rowdy rode off to find Ansel and Magic.

"Hah, get up there!" Ansel yelled at his horse, urging Magic forward. He had tied a rope to a downed, diseased tree, the culprit that took out the fence and pulled the strands that bent the poles up the line. Ansel had the other end of the rope wrapped around Magic's saddle horn.

The horse heaved and grunted, straining to pull the remaining root ball of the tree free from the ground. When the dirt finally gave, it sent Magic stumbling forward. The magnificent stallion caught his balance without upsetting a hair on his rider's head, then dragged the ten feet of tree far enough away for fence repair work.

Ethan came along just in time to see the action. His heart filled with pride for the horse and love for his father. Ethan thought about the love he felt for his family, then felt a deeper twang of sympathy for Paula, who lost her family so suddenly, tragically and without warning. It made sense now, Paula's need for attention, her need to hang on to anything she held dear to her heart.

Ethan wished he could help Paula feel security again, make Paula understand they were her family now, he and Ansel and Vida, unconditionally. Hopefully, that would help Paula be happy. That was what would make him happy.

"Let's get these poles reinforced and reattach the wires, then let's catch the quicker trail home. I think we are gonna get wet." Energized by his horse's performance, Ansel sprang from the saddle and grabbed his tools.

This life's work he had been born into was so satisfying, he thought, as he and Ethan worked side by side. A rancher's job, to the unenlightened eye, seemed never-ending, and many who tried quit for that reason. To Ansel, and probably most successful ranchers, every day was a series of minor tasks that, when completed without looking for results, eventually added up to visible fruition. Ranching was a long-term, lifetime commitment.

Working together, Ethan and Ansel made quick work with the repairs, doing the best they could do by hand. They knew it would hold and made note to come up with the four-wheel-drive truck and more powerful tools to do a more permanent fix.

Raindrops fell as they were putting away their tools. The temps had only dropped a few degrees. Their slickers would come in handy now.

Ansel glanced at his watch. "No wonder I'm hungry. It's eleven thirty and our lunch is heading down the mountain, getting farther away on Winston's back."

Referring to the saddle bags tied to Winston's saddle, Vida had stowed everyone's lunch there. With the wind whipping the raindrops sideways, it wasn't like they would stop now to eat, anyway. Getting back home quickly was the only goal. Ethan was eager to get back, not because he wanted to avoid getting wet. He actually loved the storms on the ridge with the many dynamics they brought to the land. Ethan was anxious about how the other three riders had fared. He was worried about Miranda. Forgetting she was still the enemy; Ethan's only concern right now was her safety.

Ethan allowed Rowdy to settle into a ground consuming jog, the seasoned horse new there was a dry stall waiting for him at the end of the ride. Ansel followed behind, and the dogs followed him. Looking at the group from afar, one could imagine them as the subject of a painting by C. M. Russell.

Chapter 17

Miranda ran from the barn to the house to dodge drops, but she didn't need to. The rain had already soaked her jeans. Still, running to avoid getting wetter made sense. In reality, the intelligent thing would be to have brought a change of clothes. Miranda had not.

"My goodness, Vida exclaimed when she saw Miranda come into the vestibule dripping like a wet dog. I wasn't expecting you to be home so soon, and when I watched the storm breaking over the ridges, I figured y'all might hold up at Carmen's Camp and wait for it to pass."

Miranda hung the sopping wet parka on a hanger and squeezed her boots off her feet. Her ankles were the only parts still dry.

"You must get out of those wet jeans. Let me find something of Paula's for you to wear while I put your Wranglers in the dryer." Vida scurried across the kitchen and disappeared up the stairs.

Alone in the room, Miranda felt a shiver and looked for a source of heat. She heard the wood-burning stove softly crackling, then spotted the orange cat who occupied a shelf on the wall behind. The old orange cat she had noticed before sleeping under the stove had taken a safer spot where he wouldn't be scorched by the stove, that now burned hot. Using his well-earned wisdom, the cat knew he could get the benefit of the rising warmth.

Miranda was standing by the pot-bellied stove, warming her hands and petting the old tomcat when Vida returned, carrying a pair of sweatpants. "You can borrow these. They'll be a scant short. Paula is not as tall as you. Take off the wet socks, too. I have some slippers for you to wear."

Miranda stepped into the little bathroom she had used that morning, and obediently did everything she had been told. When she finished, Miranda gladly accepted a cup of tea from Vida.

"Now, let this warm you up and tell me how was your ride?"

"We had to change plans after I had a near accident with Winston, but he's fine," Miranda answered.

"An accident? With Winston? Are you okay? What happened?" Vida knew how unpredictable horses could be. Miranda explained to Vida an abridged version of what had happened.

"I'm fine now, too, though it shook me up. When we saw the weather was changing, we decided Tad and Noah would ride back with me and Ansel and Ethan continued up the trail to check fences."

"I'm surprised you were riding Winston."

Miranda then filled in the details, starting with getting used to riding Winston, jumping the creek, resulting in the decision to abort the mission. She described the ride back and getting within ten minutes of home when the clouds let go.

"Well, I am glad no one was hurt. It sounds like you handled it well, but it must have been frightening."

"Actually, I hadn't the time to be afraid, at least not until it was over." Miranda was honest. "Oh, I forgot the saddlebags on the service porch. They were dripping wet, but I think the lunch stayed dry. I'll go get it."

When Miranda came back to the kitchen with the contents of the saddlebags, Vida was talking to the young lady Miranda had encountered day she came out to the ranch. The day she was kicked off the ranch.

"Miranda," Vida motioned with her hand, "come meet Paula. Miranda this is Paula Mariano, Paula this is Miranda Dunn."

"Nice to officially meet you, Ms. Dunn." Paula reached out. She hoped Miranda wouldn't mention her and Ethan' rude behavior the first time they had met.

"Nice to meet you, too. Please, call me Miranda. And thanks for loaning me some pants." It relieved Miranda to see no sign of the animosity she had felt from Paula that first day.

"Of course. We couldn't let you freeze in your wet clothes." Paula's smile was genuine. "I better get going, Vida. I need to make it to town in case this storm gets worse. Good bye."

"Good bye," Miranda called after the departing girl. "Hope to see you soon." The door had already closed.

Vida had followed Paula out the door, leaving Miranda on her own again, this time with wet bags of food in her grips and questions on her mind. *Very interesting*, she thought, sensing the young woman she had met twice now was an important person to Vida. Miranda knew Vida hadn't a daughter. Vida hadn't mentioned a daughter during any of their chats, but this young lady lived here. She could be Ethan's cousin, perhaps? That would explain a different last name, but it seemed Vida would have included that information in the introductions.

Vida came back in after seeing Paula off, and began inspecting the condition of the food as she pulled it from the soggy saddlebags, item by item. "The food is fine. It seems to have survived your cross-country run and the cascading rains. We can eat as soon as Tad and Noah finish in the barn. Ansel and Ethan will be back much later."

Miranda helped Vida empty the contents of the saddlebags. The lunch they were supposed to eat on her tour of the summit was sandwiches they now unwrapped to put on plates. Miranda's mouth was watering with appetite and she thought about the two men still out riding in the rain. They must be hungry, too.

In Miranda's mind, she pictured Ethan in the saddle, sitting straight backed and relaxed at the same time. Miranda remembered Ethan riding beside her, explaining Winston's personality as a mount, giving her suggestions in a very non-critical manner. Miranda couldn't help admiring his soft mannerisms of communicating the way he thought she should ride the horse. His gentle touch with his own horse made Miranda wonder why he couldn't seem to have the same touch when communicating with her. Was he so stand-offish with all people?

Miranda became more pensive as her thoughts wandered. She was still reflecting about Ethan, but she had now gone in another direction, speculating about how to better communicate with him. Miranda wasn't sure why, but it always seemed like they were not speaking the same language. There was definitely something under the surface between them. She had noticed it since day one on the front porch, a tension she couldn't quite identify.

Miranda would not deny there was a basic natural attraction. Ethan was a very good-looking man, athletically inclined, obviously physically fit. His physique, though trim and toned, was not the same as the frame of a bodybuilder who works out in a gym. Ethan's body was much better proportioned. Miranda shivered a little, thinking about it.

"Are you cold, Randi?" Vida detected the tremor. "Go into the mudroom and grab a sweater. The small sizes are to the left on the shelf."

Miranda immediately complied, embarrassed by her own thoughts. She was grateful for an excuse to turn away lest her hostess might see through her eyes and read her mind. Miranda would have to work harder to keep focused on business when interacting with Ethan. She needed to discover the reason there was a barrier and get beyond it. Staying on track and not letting physical attraction become a distraction was the key. But, oh boy, what a delightful distraction Ethan had the potential to be.

"I'm starving." Tad lumbered into the house and pulled out a chair from under the table.

"We will serve lunch soon," Vida said. Then she noted the obvious bulge in Tad's cheek and she ordered him back outside. "Chewing tobacco again? You know how I feel about that awful stuff, Tad. Get rid of it." Tad's chewing tobacco habit was vexing. "I thought you were quitting."

Tad did as he was told without hesitation. "Sorry Vida."

"I will get the drinks, lemonade?" Miranda asked Tad when he returned from throwing out the wad of chaw he had been sucking. She handed him a glass.

"Thanks," Tad grinned widely.

Miranda fought to keep her nose from wrinkling in disgust when the odorous evidence of Tad's habit lingered on his breath escaping from his mouth when he spoke.

Having warmed up to her after spending the afternoon in her presence, Tad boldly asked, "So, Randi. This morning you were talking about your riding program. Can you tell us more? What will you be doing here, with the ranch?"

Miranda leaped on the opportunity to talk about the work she loved. "I'd like to start small, invite some of my established clients to come to Rambletap Springs after I get a few certified therapists lined up. Then the kids can come and ride. There are also many other things to do in and around Rambletap Springs and Helena. There is an abundance of history. I think it could be a good tourist attraction."

"You want to bring tourists to here? I don't know if the folks in town would cotton to that." Noah had joined them and spoke the truth. He shared an element of concern with Ethan.

“It wouldn’t be floods of people. The riding program is small. I wish to focus on quality, not quantity. The program is expensive to run, and adding travel would make it cost prohibitive for most people. Through my non-profit, we can reduce the cost, and give the kids and families a time of their lives, plus, on a small scale, bring some positive cash flow to the locally owned businesses here.”

“Sounds quite involved.” Tad was listening intently.

“It promises to be a great deal of work, and a lot of reward.” Vida stopped the conversation. “Everybody sit. Let’s have lunch.”

Chapter 18

It had been raining for nearly an hour by the time Ansel and Ethan emerged from the forest and headed across the meadow toward the ranch buildings. They passed the livestock pasture where the horses in the field barely lifted their head to the riders approaching. The herd stood in a perfect row, side by side, butts to the wind. They had weathered many a storm before, worse than this one, and instinct always pointed them in the best direction to wait it out.

"Pretty cold for a spring storm," Ethan stated the obvious, watching his breath vaporize and disappear as he spoke. He looked longingly toward the house, was eager to finish in the barn and get inside, but both he and his father would take the extra care needed to look after the hot, wet horses. "We should get Tad and Noah out here to help."

"What's the hurry, son? Always take care of your horse yourself. That way, you know it gets done right." Not that Ansel had no confidence in his hired hands, but it was good practice for a rider to see to the needs of his horse. A cowboy wasn't worth a dime without a healthy horse and horses coming in from working in the rain needed special handling.

Ethan knew what his dad meant, knew the importance of proper care, and usually always put the animal's well-being above his own. When the cowboys brought their mounts into the barn, they noticed Tad and Noah had taken care of Winston, Sonnet and Style who were standing in their own stalls, draped in a cooling cloth designed to wick away moisture but provide warmth to ward off a chill. Munching on their favorite oat hay, the horses were content. It was time to cool down and dry off the last two mounts so they, too, could start munching on some comforting oat hay.

Ansel was first to lead Magic into the wash rack after he had removed the saddle and bridle. Washing an already wet horse seemed counterproductive, but it was important to rinse away the sweat or the coats would dry with the hairs all clumped with dander. A coat of clumpy hair provided no warmth.

Ethan took the saddle from Rowdy's back and released a wave of trapped heat that turned to rising steam.

Once Ethan had rinsed the residue from Rowdy's body, he began rubbing the horse down to remove the excess water. As he rubbed, he thought of lunch and being warm and dry inside. Ethan thought of Miranda. The thought of Tad acting like a schoolboy around Miranda made Ethan wish he was in there right now. He should be in there to run interference.

Ethan was certain a girl like her hadn't the patience to deal with Tad's childish behavior. When Ethan recognized his feelings as jealousy, he scattered his train of thought, reminding himself why Miranda was there at the ranch, and remembering it was his duty to prevent his parents from making a mistake.

Fueled by thoughts of Miranda, Ethan finished with Rowdy's rub-down before his father finished with Magic. He went to the tack room and grabbed two blankets from the rug rack. He hung one over the door of Magic's stall and threw the second one over Rowdy's back. The blanket came down hard and the horse jumped forward with surprise, nearly running out of the stall.

"Take it easy, son," Ansel said, hearing the commotion in the stall next door. "Haven't these horses been through enough today?"

This was the second time he had spooked a horse with brutish behavior. Ethan commanded himself to get a grip. He was allowing his emotions to take over his actions, and it was causing friction. So badly had he wished to make his way to the residence, he was willing to take a shortcut at the expense of the stock. His emotions were causing him to act in ways that put others in danger.

"Easy, boy," Ethan soothed. "That'll do." Calming the veteran horse with his hand and his tone. Rowdy relaxed and Ethan gently straitened the blanket on the horse's back, reached under to secure the belly strap while Rowdy went back to enjoying his oats.

Ethan spent extra time combing Rowdy's mane and tail. It was as much soothing for him as it was for the equine, and now it was Ansel's turn to be impatient.

"C'mon, boy. Aren't you done yet? I'm cold and hungry. Let's go inside." The old man had been standing at the open stall door with his arms crossed.

"What's the hurry, Dad? The horses come first," Ethan echoed his father's phrase.

Ethan closed the stall door and Ansel playfully punched his son's arm. The two men fell into a boxing stance for a mock fight that lasted all the way across the driveway and onto the back steps. As they dodged and ducked and danced their way in, the dogs joined in the fun, barking and jumping at their feet.

"You go on in, Dad. I'll dry the border collies," Ethan appeared the opposite of anxious, but was finding it difficult when he could hear the conversation coming from inside. Tad was telling Miranda how he and Noah had needed jobs and ended up at the Alma Soñada Ranch.

Ethan tempered his inclination to hurry, reached into the cabinet under the shelves of slickers and sweatshirts for some towels. First, he dried Quinn, for in his mind the pregnant dog deserved special consideration, then he dried Troy, the father of Quinn's pups. When he saw to it the dogs were dry and comfortable in their beds, he went in the house to find Tad, Noah and Vida chatting with Miranda like they were all old friends just hanging out.

Everyone was becoming enchanted by Miranda. She had them all eating out of her palm as she wiggled her way in. Her plan to exploit the good nature of his folks was working. She was pretty good at it, but Ethan could still get ahead of the deal and head her off. He just needed more information.

"I'm going to get dried off." was all Ethan said to the group as he strode hastily past the table. Why was Miranda still there? The tour was over. Was there any reason she should still be there, in his house, casually conversing with his friends and family like she'd known them all her life?

"I've got soup and sandwiches for you and your father when you come back down." Vida's words followed Ethan up the stairs.

Ethan retreated to his room to wait for his father to finish up in the bathroom, cursing that they only had the one. He and Ansel had been contemplating a remodel of the old farmhouse. It needed updating on many levels. Adding a second bathroom was long overdue. But renovation was not as easy on these legacy buildings and preserving the history was more important. There was a lot to be lost when making changes, and as was his nature, Ethan felt a deep sense of obligation to his ancestors to keep things the way they were.

"Bathroom's clear." He heard Ansel say, and the wheels in Ethan's head continued to spin. He would speak to his family about Miranda at the next available opportunity. For the sake of his ancestral home, he simply had to change his parents 'minds.

While showering, Ethan usually did his best thinking. First on his agenda was talking to his parents, but he also needed to speak to Miranda. Ethan would tell her, unlike his folks, he wasn't on board with her plans to turn their place into a dude ranch.

He intended to let her know it's nothing personal; he is just doing his duty as steward of the land, as an advocate for his late relatives who can no longer speak their own minds, and that she would have to go through him to have what she wanted. Ethan was going to throw down the gauntlet.

Once out of the shower, Ethan stretched his long legs into a dry pair of jeans and zipped up, leaving the top unfastened so he could tuck his shirt in. He opened the bathroom door and came face in face with Miranda.

"I was…" Miranda stepped to the left. Ethan's naked torso was there, "looking for…" she slid to the right, only to run into Ethan again, "Paula's room."

Miranda now had the answer to her question about Ethan's bronze-colored arms. His light amber colored chest was right in front of her. Holding up Paula's folded sweat pants like a shield, Miranda tried to clarify her purpose.

Miranda averted her eyes, but she could feel the radiating heat off of Ethan's skin that only minutes ago was wet from the shower. Her nose told her he used scented soap, but it was not a floral smell. Nor was it the pine scent type that never really captured the smell of the forest after a rain. It was natural and pleasing and begged her to move closer for a better whiff.

"Paula's room is that one," Ethan pointed, trying to be angry at this woman, this intruder who had now not only comfortably entered the house, but had penetrated the very sanctity of his privacy; the upstairs. Instead of anger, Ethan found Miranda's reaction to his half-dressed state amusing.

Miranda realized she had been staring at Ethan for far too long, and judging by his smug expression, Ethan noticed it too.

"I'll just leave these here. Paula can put them away when she comes home." Miranda set the pants on the bed.

Miranda wanted to go back downstairs, but Ethan, still half-dressed, was now standing in the doorway, blocking her exit, and to make matters worse, he appeared to be chuckling at her.

She was trapped, but instead of rolling over in defeat, Miranda came out swinging with the classic distract and redirect. "Tad was just telling me about the swimming hole in the meadow you all swim in during the heat of the summer."

Ethan stopped smiling, his amusement evaporated. He remembered this woman had an agenda. "I want to give you fair warning. You are wasting your time here. I don't know what you think you are doing, but I will not let you proceed without a fight. You swill not screw up this ranch."

Ethan moved with intent, from the doorway into the room where Miranda stood, and without digesting his words, Miranda reflexively squirted by and now she was in the hall looking in.

"I guess we can talk about it later, after you've dressed."

With the ball once again in her court, Miranda turned and was heading down the stairs without looking back. Once past the landing, she slowed down to give herself time to organize the assortment of feelings she had just experienced.

Even when Ethan seemed angry, it excited her. She didn't feel she was in danger. Miranda recognized Ethan's emotions. She had seen the same thing with riding students when they were afraid. Some kids displayed anger rather than confess their fears. As far as emotions go, anger and fear often went hand in hand. Fear was difficult to acknowledge. It came from within. It was easier to express anger than it was to face fears. If fear motivated Ethan's behavior, it was imperative to Miranda's success she figures out why. What did Ethan think she was doing? What was Ethan afraid of?

Chapter 19

Through the rain cleaned atmosphere, the sun glimmered in the early morning sky, and the air was mountain fresh. The bathing showers that had fallen from the sky like manna for the Earth had settled the dust and gave everything a look of newness. It was unusual for a storm this late in the season to last so long, or hold that much moisture, but after a day and a half of precipitation, the clouds finally passed, leaving the community ready for the sunshine.

As Miranda jogged through the neighborhood in Rambletap Springs, she felt more and more at home. The people recognized her and she them as they saw each other regularly since the first day she went running. At the park, she waved to the fellow she always saw walking his Rottweiler dog.

Today, Miranda was going back to the ranch to bring the Baldwins up to speed on the progress she had made. She had met with the director at the community center and was pleased to learn she could draw a lot of useful connections from them. She secured an office space above the Great Western Bank in town and had already made the calls to have equipment delivered.

Albert mailed her some more documents to get insurance for the donated portion of the Alma Soñada Ranch under the non-profit status. Now she needed the Baldwins 'signatures. It excited Miranda to share with her soon to be partners the advancements she had carried out while waiting for the rainstorm to pass.

Throughout the stormy day, Miranda had also thought about her encounters with Ethan and analyzed how full of contradictions he was. One minute he seemed to enjoy her company, the next he acted like he could throw her down a well. He moved quickly from friendly teasing to avoiding eye contact completely and for no apparent reason. Her initial approach was to stick to business and offer to include him with no pressure or expectation, but she had changed her mind. She recognized the withdrawing behavior as a sign of fear. But why would he be afraid of her?

With her students who were afraid when they began equine therapy, it served no benefit to force the issue, but, if you ignored it, nothing would change, either. Gaining the confidence of the child in an area they are comfortable, for example, letting them groom the horse, showed the student they could trust her. From there, she would gently introduce them to the peripheral items; the saddle, the bridle, etc. and slowly the fearful children's curiosity grew. Eventually, Miranda would tell them how it feels when she rides.

Biting off the unknown into small parts made it easier to absorb. Miranda had yet to fail at getting her kids aboard. By applying the same principle, Miranda decided it was time to inform Ethan of his parents 'and her plans in bits and pieces. She would not leave any room for misunderstanding. Miranda was certain, with gentle diplomacy, she would bring Ethan onboard, too.

~****~

Ansel and Ethan leaned against the rails as they watched a truck towing a trailer leave the highway. As the vehicle approached, they could see it was a dual wheeled Dodge Cummins diesel pulling a goose-neck stock trailer.

"Right on schedule." Ansel looked at his watch, then at Ethan, wanting to catch the look of anticipation on his son's face. Inside the container coming up the driveway was the three-year-olds Ethan was to train for the McGuires.

"Yep," Ethan quipped.

Ethan was always eager to train, but these horses, with their impeccable bloodlines, brought greater enthusiasm. Their sire was a direct descendant of Doc Bar, one of the more famous and prolific quarter horses of all time. It is said that Doc Bar and his progeny revolutionized the cutting horse industry. With horses Ethan considered royalty, his emotions flew off the chart. He had worked with Doc Bar bred horses before and was familiar with the common characteristics the stallion passed on.

Doc Bar was a first-generation descendant of the stallion, Three Bars, a horse from race track lineage who lacked the stamina to finish a race strong but held the record in the first quarter mile. When Three Bars was put out to stud, they discovered the strongest characteristic he passed on was his quick speed. Among the other qualities, a much harder one to track, was personality.

Ethan found some predictability with Three Bars and subsequently, Doc Bar bred foals, but when it came down to brass tacks, Ethan knew each horse, regardless of bloodlines, had a personality all their own. Some horses would suspiciously watch every move a man made, while others were compliant and trusting. One horse would take off bucking when they felt the tightening of the saddle while another might stand there, appearing to be confused, perhaps wondering, "Can I breathe with this vice-like ring around my lungs?"

"Let's put them in the paddocks by the corral." Ethan wasted no time and went past his father to intercept the approaching rig. The dogs barked enthusiastically, greeting the oncoming visitors. Ansel motioned for the driver to turn the rig around in the graveled circular area between the ranch buildings before stopping to unload.

"Howdy," said the cowboy, who climbed out of the cab with his hand extended. "I'm Jim. I'm delivering these horses from the McGuires?"

"Yes. We've been expecting you. I'm Ansel Baldwin. This is my son, Ethan." Ansel reached out to shake Jim's hand.

"I'll unload the stock," Jim said, but Ethan was already at the back of the trailer. He had no time to socialize. Ethan unlatched the back gate and lowered the ramp. He was ready to start the training immediately.

Ethan started teaching the instant he handled a horse. Every interaction between man and horse was a lesson, and each lesson built the groundwork for the following interactions. The opening encounter was the foundation upon which Ethan would build the entire relationship.

Ethan stepped into the trailer and approached the filly closest to the rear. She strained her head against the tie that kept her from facing the man she could only see with one eye, the man she hadn't seen or smelled before. She was curious and turned the other way in hopes the rope might allow her to see Ethan more clearly with the other eye. The young horse showed no fear. Ethan reached out his hand and placed it on the filly's shoulder. The energy that passed from human to equine said, "I am not a predator."

Before the little horse could think further, Ethan had removed the nylon halter from the filly's head and left it dangling, still attached to the trailer by a quick-release tie. In the same motion, he slipped over the horse's head and tied the latigo halter he preferred to use, then together they both moved toward the rear ramp. In what appeared to be one motion, the liberated horse stepped lightly from the trailer, head held high as she surveyed her new surroundings, then followed Ethan to the paddock on a loose lead.

The others still inside became anxious as their herd mate disappeared. Herd instinct was important for survival, but when Ethan followed the same procedure with the next two horses, their nervousness eased and the unloading was a breeze. The successful first lesson was in the books. In the brief time of exposure for evaluation, Ethan already knew these were excellent horses. This was going to be fun.

~****~

Miranda's energy inside matched the output from the engine in the Range Rover as it rolled smoothly down the highway. She was stoked to begin the day. As she approached the ranch gate, she spotted a truck and trailer driving away from the house and barn complex, and they were only halfway down the driveway. Knowing the road wasn't wide enough for them to pass each other without one of them leaving the graveled surface, Miranda waited at the entrance, until the other vehicle left. The two drivers exchanged a nod and a wave, then proceeded in opposite directions.

Miranda saw nobody coming out of the house as she brought her car to a stop by the gate to the garden. She had noticed three figures sitting by the corrals, so she strode over to check it out. When Miranda was close enough, she saw a fourth person standing just inside a paddock, grooming a beautiful little bay horse.

"Good morning," Miranda said when she was in earshot.

"Mornin'," came a response in stereo from Ansel and Vida.

"Good morning, Miss Randi," Tad dropped off the fence where he had been sitting and spooked the young horse with his exuberance.

"Whoa. Easy, girl." Ethan stood still as the filly circled about a few times, then settled.

"We're just checking out the newcomers. These three are here for training." Tad stated the obvious, making himself sound important by including the 'we'."We are getting them used to contact."

Ethan shot a crooked eye toward Tad as the circling horse came to a stop. Then he began briskly petting and rubbing with bare hands over the horse's back and down her legs.

"No brushes?" Miranda peered through the fence rails to observe the training.

"They have handled these horses, but Ethan likes to go back to the beginning with them as if they hadn't been," Vida answered. "He uses his hands rather than brushes for the energy exchange. It makes the communication more direct, more intimate."

"More direct." Miranda repeated. *A gentle desensitizing procedure through touch*, she thought.

"Yeah, I don't get it either," Tad said, "but it sure seems like the horses do. If it were me, I'd throw on the saddle and see what these youngsters know."

"Hmm," Miranda thought about it. Tad's idea seemed harsh and abrupt, in contrast with what Ethan was doing.

In her therapy programs, touch was the most basic component. For kids who suffered with shyness, human contact was painful, even eye contact. When the horses looked at the children, there was nothing threatening about it. The kids could touch the horses, and with no hidden consequences. Kids who were in the programs for emotional trauma, who had been abused, physically or verbally, had adverse responses to being touched.

When therapists gave a child a treat to hold in their hand, as the horse gathered it up with its lips, the children were soon smiling, giggling, and laughing. The softness of the muzzle on their hands and the tickle of their whiskers allowed the children to feel the pleasant sensations without fear of pain. The way Ethan interacted with horses was touch therapy. Ethan was using therapy on the horses. "Fascinating," she said.

Tad gave an unimaginative, "Pfufff" and shook his head. "Hardly."

The process with the filly continued. Ethan stood alongside the equine, diligently rubbing her withers above the highest point on the shoulder blade with his fingertips in a circular motion. The horse was responding by stretching her neck out and wiggling her upper lip. Miranda giggled at the comic display. As Ethan continued the shoulder massage, the horse bent her neck over, continuing the wiggle of her lip, and began nuzzling Ethan's shoulder.

"Bet you thought she was gonna bite him, right, Randi?" Tad grinned.

That thought hadn't even crossed Miranda's mind.

"They are rubbing each other's backs. It's a bonding exercise," Vida said to Miranda, ignoring Tad.

“That’s enough for today.” Ethan spoke to the horse, then noticed Miranda had joined the audience. He normally didn’t take to strangers watching him work, but he was glad she was there to witness him starting the fillies. Based on observation, Miranda’s handling of the incident with Winston gave Ethan the impression she understood more about horses than some folks.

Miranda had watched intently while the cowboy worked. She continued to stare as Ethan approached the paddock fence. Ethan held her gaze, climbed through the rails, and stood up on the other side, very near Miranda, and still she held eye contact.

“Mornin’, Miranda,” Ethan said.

“Randi… Randi?”

A voice that seemed from far off broke Miranda’s focus on Ethan. She turned her head toward the frantic calls. “What is it, Tad?” Miranda asked.

Tad sighed with relief when Miranda turned away from Ethan to listen to him. “Ansel was talking to you. He’s ready to get down to business.”

“Ah… oh,” Miranda stammered. “Yes, of course.”

“Thanks, Tad. I’ve got it from here,” Ansel practically dismissed Tad, making it clear he was not a part of the work they were conducting.

Miranda glanced at Ethan, expecting to catch a mood change, the kind that always appeared with any mention of business, but there was none. Instead, Ethan walked with the rest of the group as they moved toward the house.

“I have a bunch of news,” Miranda confessed.

“That’s great,” Tad commented. He didn’t have a clue about what possible news Miranda could have, but wanted to appear interested.

Tad’s ridiculous desire to be included in the ranch affairs annoyed Ethan. The guy had never had an ounce of interest before. Tad was joining forces with Ansel and Vida, giving Miranda more allies. Ethan refused to admit there was a touch of jealously that Tad’s interest also brought him closer to Miranda.

Miranda skipped up the steps of the old house as if she’d been there all her life. This family had made her feel so welcomed, and their support for her passion was remarkable. Now, it seemed, even Ethan was bringing a better attitude.

This morning, watching Ethan working with the horse gave Miranda hope that the two of them had put the negative vibes between them to rest. Today’s contact could reveal more common grounds upon which they could build a better working relationship.

Tad raced past Miranda and held open the door for her, and Ethan was first at the table to hold out a chair. Tad sat down next to the chair Ethan held out, but Miranda didn't sit.

"Ah-hum," Ansel cleared his throat in warning to the boys, then to Miranda he said, "Come with me. Let me show you what I have been working on with the design program on the computer."

Miranda followed Ansel into his office, but was disappointed Ethan hadn't come along. Maybe he had already seen what Ansel was showing her. Miranda could only guess, but it seemed logical he should join them. What she really wanted was Ethan's participation. She surmised he would have some beneficial ideas and wanted to include him.

Ansel sat at the keyboard, clicked some keys, scrolled and clicked the mouse and in a matter of seconds, there on the screen, was a plot plan for the arena.

"It's just a loose idea of what we had in mind," Ansel said after he explained what Miranda was looking at. "You can tweak things to suit your needs, but we thought it was a good place to start."

Miranda couldn't help the welling up of emotion seeing their plans in black and white. There on the screen was outlined the entire arena and surrounding facility. She saw the tack room and the meeting room. There was a seating area for parents and other spectators, and to the rear of the spectator area was the bathroom facility. Seeing it even in the rough draft form was akin to watching her dream be born. "I'm speechless, Ansel."

"We are really going to do this, Randi." Sensing her emotions, Ansel paused as they both stared at the screen. "It's for you, the kids, and for ourselves. This ranch has given my family so much joy. Now it's time to share that with some really deserving people."

"Oh, it's going to be wonderful, Ansel," were the only words Miranda could form.

"Well, what's next?" Ansel moved on.

"Oh, I nearly forgot." Miranda riffled through the contents of the oversized bag she had set down on the chair by the door and pulled out a packet of papers. "These are for liability. The non-profit will provide all insurance. Once you sign these contracts, it will cover all insurance for new construction during the building. All the structures built for the program will have coverage afterwards as well. As soon as these get recorded, we can start."

"Vida and I will look things over right away." Ansel flipped through the packet of documents, then set them on the desk.

Miranda's cell phone vibrated in her pocket. "Its Albert. Please excuse me, I have to take this," said Miranda.

"I'll give you some privacy. When you finish, come to the kitchen. Vida made a buttermilk tea cake. We have a reason to celebrate," Ansel smiled and stepped out.

Miranda leaned on Ansel's desk, facing away from the door as she conversed with her attorney. Albert wanted to check if the envelope he mailed with all the documents had arrived. It thrilled Miranda to report that everything was being reviewed for signing. Albert filled Miranda in on some other details and reminded her they needed a name for their fledgling operation in order to confirm the partnership and apply for a license.

"Oh, that's right. I forgot about the business name. We don't have one yet. I will ask Ansel and Vida for their ideas. Do you need it right away?" Albert answered, 'no'. The conversation continued for another minute and then came the goodbyes.

Miranda slipped her cell phone into her pocket and stayed for a moment in place to let it sink in. "This is happening so fast. Am I dreaming?" She said to herself, shaking her head. When Miranda turned to exit the office and join Ansel and Vida in the kitchen, there was Ethan leaning against the doorframe.

Doorways seem to be his comfortable spot, Miranda mused, then teased, "Do you always go around spying on people?"

"I don't consider coming into my office to be spying." Ethan was not teasing when he replied. Gone was the open and enthusiastic Ethan Miranda had seen in the paddock.

"I was joking. Of course, you weren't spying," Miranda laughed nervously, realizing she may have misjudged Ethan's mood again.

"I find nothing funny about what's going on here, and I would like to talk to you."

"I am always available to talk. I'll answer all questions. Consider me an open book." Miranda stayed friendly and professional.

Ethan didn't know where to begin. He had questions, alright but there was too much he didn't know. He cursed his decision to ignore his parents regarding this new deal they seemed intent upon embarking.

"Ethan," Tad's voice boomed from the kitchen. "Noah is back with the feed. It's our turn to unload it."

"Guess we can talk later," said Miranda. *There goes another opportunity*, she thought, *to clear any of Ethan's misunderstandings*.

"Oh, I promise you, we will talk."

Ethan's words were innocuous enough, but Miranda got a less than warm feeling about the way he spoke them. There was more than fear behind Ethan's behavior. Miranda hoped her communication skills were up to the challenge Ethan promised to be.

Chapter 20

Noah doe-see-doed into the house shortly after Tad and Ethan retreated, took in a lung full of cooking aromas, then let the air out of his mouth with a satisfied, “Ahhhh. Just in time for tea and buttermilk cake.” Noah spun across the floor, kissed Vida on the cheek, and sat down.

“My, aren’t we in a good mood?” Ansel said.

Noah had been in a favorable spirit since the night at the club when he confessed his love for Paula, then told her good bye. Since that night, the air smelled fresher; the sun seemed brighter, and everything had an effortless quality, Noah couldn’t explain.

“Why shouldn’t I be happy? I got the simple job this morning, and those two blockheads have to unload the feed. All I had to do was drive to town and the boys at the feed store did the loading. Yee haw!”

Noah’s exuberant expression of joy caused Miranda to startle. For her, it was a work in progress getting used to the boisterous atmosphere of a real family household. But Noah’s joviality was contagious and even Miranda laughed when he let out a ‘whoop’.

“Did you buy the mare and foal feed? They are growing like weeds and eating us out of house and home.” Ansel was happy with the crop of horses this season. Magic’s babies were popular as show horses and working cow horses, too. Some not even born were already spoken for.

“Yes, yes. They loaded the truck and trailer down with enough feed for a cavalry of horses.” Noah grabbed a slice of buttermilk cake and shoved it into his mouth.

“Use a napkin,” Vida scolded. “And don’t eat too much. Save room for lunch.” Vida added. She watched with exasperation as Noah held a napkin and grabbed a second slice of tea cake. “I’ll take that as a complement to my cooking.”

"The only reason I picked this job was for your cooking, Vida." Noah continued his rowdy teasing, headed for the stove to take a whiff of what was cooking.

"Okay, okay. Let's end this admiration session." Ansel walked over to the stove where his wife had been adding onions to an enormous pot and moved Noah out of the way. "Smells good. I can already taste it."

"Of course it smells good. Now both of you go on or I'll never finish making it." Vida held up a big spoon, pretending to hit the men with it.

"Is this far enough away?" Ansel put his arms around Vida in a bear hug.

"Oomph," Vida exclaimed, as if Ansel's grip expressed the air in her lungs, but she did not free herself from the embrace.

Miranda grinned at the scene developing around her, the familiar teasing, the jockeying around the stove, the older couple's display of affection. It reminded her of the times she spent with the Ferris family. It had been a while since Miranda belonged to something more than just herself. Miranda wanted family, friends, and a relationship like the senior Baldwins had.

It must be nice to have a companion, a lover, a partner you could always count on to have your best interest at heart. Someone with whom to share your hopes and dreams, the one person you could love unconditionally. With that kind of love, who could ever fail?

"I think I'll go on out and give the boys a hand with that load." Ansel released Vida, after giving her a peck on the lips, then headed out with a wink in Miranda's direction.

"I'm going, too, but only to watch," Noah snickered, as if he had a secret. Miranda suspected she knew Noah's secret. He was going out to help. It's what family does.

Miranda stacked the dishes and teacups from the table and carried them to the sink. "That was the best tea cake I have ever had. Can I wash these dishes?"

"Leave the dishes 'til later, dear. Please help with the vegetables? I'm making chicken and dumplings for lunch and the carrots go in first. We'll let them simmer and add the dough for the dumplings last."

Vida gave instructions and Miranda moved about like an experienced sous chef. As they worked, they talked about cooking, the ranch, and family. Miranda shared the story of her childhood while Vida listened sympathetically. Vida shared stories of the good times in the old ranch house. "If these walls could talk, so they say," then Vida told Miranda about her and Ansel's challenges in having a baby and how they had stopped torturing themselves, only to conceive shortly thereafter.

While the chicken stew was simmering, Vida asked to look at the documents for her and Ansel to sign. Together, they went over the information. Vida had questions, and Miranda tried her best to answer.

"Well, now that both Ansel and I are up to speed, I don't see what there is to stop us. Congratulations, Miranda. It looks as though your dreams will come true." Vida seemed confident in Miranda.

Miranda reached out her hand to shake on it.

"Don't be silly, girl." Vida enveloped her new partner in a hug. "Men shake hands, women hug. Now let's make a meal. Those men will be hungry."

~****~

"If there's nothing planned for the rest of the day, why don't I take Randi for a ride? You know, since our tour got cut short the other day." Tad asked as soon as the once full plates of chicken and dumplings were almost empty. He had been working on building up the courage to talk. He had little experience with women like Randi and was out of practice asking a girl on a date.

"There is never nothing planned, Tad. There is always work to be done. We'll be weaning the foals soon and the creepers need repairs." Ethan spoke with authority; not happy Tad was arranging the time during the workday to be with Miranda.

"That's a really nice offer." It flattered Miranda that Tad had put a lot of thought into the invitation, but she declined. "I'm not dressed for a trail ride and I didn't bring my boots. I have to return to town to mail the non-profit papers."

"That's right partner." Vida stood up and asked, "Does anybody want a second helping?"

"Non-profit papers? Partners? What do you mean?" His mother's words were bullets zinging by too fast to process. Ethan had missed too much while in a state of denial. He needed to act today. His plan was to talk to Miranda while slowing his folks down before they did something rash. Was it too late already? Ethan felt his heart rate increase and a shortness of breath. "Can you please catch me up before this goes any further?" Ethan demanded.

Tad bowed out after his plan to escort Miranda on a trail ride failed. Based on the rising tension he noticed between the Baldwins, Tad decided it was an opportune moment to step aside from the family's new endeavor. He would find another subject in which to interact with Randi.

Ethan's reaction no longer surprised Miranda. It was obvious he was quite out of the loop and the lack of information adversely affected his fears. Conversely, she did not wish to waste time filling him in. That was up to his parents to decide.

"In other news," Miranda announced when no one else answered Ethan's question, "I got the green light from Jonelle at the community center. With her expertise in grant writing and fundraising, she promises to be a big help."

"Jonelle?" Ethan's focus shifted. "How do you know Jonelle?"

"You know Jonelle, don't you?" Miranda answered the question with a question.

Ethan went to school with Jonelle. They were in the same graduating class. He wondered how Miranda knew everyone so quickly. Had she infiltrated the entire community? What did Jonelle have to do with the Alma Soñada Ranch? Ethan's confusion grew.

"Ansel, let's sign those papers so Miranda can get on with the show." Vida and Ansel left the kitchen, with Ethan on their heels, leaving Miranda and Noah sitting at a table of empty lunch dishes.

"I'm gonna make myself useful while I wait." Miranda gathered the plates, glasses and silverware, brought them to the sink and began washing.

Ansel and Vida sat together at the desk taking one last glance at the paperwork and it all seemed in order to them. They trusted Randi, and her lawyer and Ansel's cousin in law, Albert. There was nothing more to do but sign. Ansel showed Vida the brightly colored tabs, and they signed where showed.

"Mom, Dad. Are you really going through with this? Why don't we give it more thought? What do we know about Miranda Dunn and her business, whatever it is? We are ranchers, successful ranchers. Isn't that enough?" Ethan could not hide his desperation.

"Ethan, your mother and I are sure of this. We have been thinking about it, investigating the feasibility, for a while, and we feel it is time for action. Randi has experience with this business, she has successfully worked in multiple aspects and has good instincts. She has already lined up many partners and has gained investors. We understand and appreciate your concerns. Before we turn these papers in, let's bring Randi in. We will all four sit down and talk. I'm sure Randi will gladly answer questions." Ansel wished his son wasn't so resistant. He hoped Ethan would have been interested from the start.

"Ansel!" Tad yelled into the house from the vestibule. "Magic has a loose front shoe. I was bringing him in from his pasture and noticed it."

"Okay," Ansel said. He finished signing the last page, much to Ethan's dismay.

"Tad. Get the shoe pullers." Ansel instructed. "Magic must have clipped the front heel with his rear toe when we pulled that tree out by the roots. We need to remove the shoe completely so he doesn't catch a wire. Vida?" Ansel called over his shoulder on his way out, "will you please give Bartleson Farriers a call?" Ansel followed Tad outside.

Vida said to Miranda, who was still cleaning up the lunch table. "Thank you, dear. I'll finish the dishes. The papers are all signed and waiting on the desk in the office for you."

Miranda dried her hands from the dishwashing and went to collect the signed documents. She intended to drop the contracts in the mail to Albert for filing.

"Oh, I guess it's my turn to sneak up on you," Miranda said when she came upon Ethan in the office and he was thumbing through the papers. Miranda was happy to see Ethan taking an interest. Ansel and Vida must have given him an overview. Now they could all move forward together with no more misunderstandings. "Great, you have the papers. Did you have any more questions?"

"Just one," Ethan paused and picked up the packet of documents, "do you prefer to watch me shred these?"

"Wh… huh?" Miranda searched Ethan's face, waiting for the punchline. He remained silent and held the pages as if for Miranda to have a last look.

"Do you think I will allow you to submit these documents? You may have my parents hoodwinked, but your charm won't work on me."

"Oh boy," Miranda quickly realized Ethan's parents must not have talked to him after all. He was still acting confused. Or was he? Maybe there was no confusion at all? Maybe he was a selfish man, preferred to keep the ranch to himself. That was a different story. Miranda reformulated her evaluation of him. His resistance might not be coming from fear, it might come from greed. Miranda changed her strategy. "So you think I'm charming?"

"What? NO!... What?"

As she'd hoped, it threw Ethan off guard. "Oh, you think I'm not charming?"

"No, stop changing the subject. I said your charms WON'T work on me." Ethan couldn't believe how this woman could so easily confuse him. He was getting more angry with each word.

Miranda knew she had to deescalate things quickly. "No worries, Ethan. You keep the papers. They don't have to be submitted today. You and your folks can manage it and get back to me."

Her diplomacy irked Ethan even more. He realized his threat to shred the packet was hollow. His folks would not cotton to him unilaterally, deciding to cancel a contract they had willingly signed. Not only would his parents be angry, but they would just have Miranda's attorney print another copy. Ethan was up against a wall.

"Shredded or not, these papers will not be submitted if I have any say." Ethan threw the documents onto the desk. "How dare you to think you can come in here, gain my folks trust and fill their head with your ideas? This is a working ranch, not some commercial property for you to exploit, capitalize on for your little program. You have no morals, no values. I may have misjudged you when I thought you were a realtor, but between you and those agents, I'd rather deal with them any day. At least realtors are honest about their intentions, unlike you pretending to be a friend to our face while you screw us behind our backs."

Ethan's comments baffled Miranda, and the personal attack hurt her. This animosity was wholly out of line. "I've let you speak your mind. It's good to know where you stand. But remember this: I won't let you insult me and question my motives, let alone my morals and values." Miranda stepped toward her antagonist, eye to eye. There would be no recovering her dignity if she backed down.

Ethan realized things had gotten out of control, he hadn't intended to insult her but Miranda brought out in him emotions he could not figure out. Her face was so close to his, he detected the anger on her wrinkled brow. In her eyes, he saw pain, and he recognized his hurtful comments were responsible.

Unwilling to move away from her, his hand reached up to smooth the lines on Miranda's forehead.

The tender touch of Ethan's hands confused Miranda after the lashing of his words. Not clear what was going to happen next, Miranda remained immobilized. The energy between them had nowhere to go. Ethan reached up with his other hand and pulled Miranda's head forward, planting a kiss on her defensive lips.

The sensation he found was a paradox of sweetness and rancor. She was responding, so he didn't stop. When he felt satisfied with the kiss, he moved slightly off and looked at her.

Miranda had momentarily lost perception and was thinking with only one part of her brain; the part that enjoyed being kissed. Miranda liked the feeling it left her with after the kiss and liked the thought of kissing Ethan again. Slowly, she regained rationality. Miranda's other thoughts demanded to be recognized. She felt her blood pulsing in her neck and was indignant about the liberty Ethan took. If she were a less stable person, she might've hauled off with her arm and slapped him.

"It was… I… you…" Ethan stumbled back, shocked by what happened, and judging by the expression on Miranda's face, Ethan thought her mind might be in the same condition. Not sure whose move it was in this game they were playing, Ethan waited.

"I am not sure why you are so adversarial. Perhaps you are not fully aware of why I am here. If you are, then based on your behavior, you might be the most self-centered and egotistical person I know. You will not drive me out, no matter how uncomfortable you make me feel. I am supported by your parents, who share my dream of helping others less fortunate than ourselves. I have found people in this community whose generosity makes up for your lack of it, and with them, I am inspired." Miranda and Ethan were still nose to nose, and Miranda didn't wish to stop talking for fear she might look down at Ethan's lips and her mind would drift back to the kiss.

"You make it sound like charity except you are a fraud. You take advantage of others 'generosity for your own gain. And you call me self-centered? You don't even know me. If it's selfish to want to protect this land from wolves and scavengers the likes of you, then so be it. But you are worse. You are the wolf in sheep's clothing. You are unscrupulous. I would hold a dime-store hooker in higher regard."

Ethan's rant left Miranda unable to respond. She couldn't follow his line of thinking, didn't know where to begin to further explain, and she was tired of trying. Ethan was clinging to his misconceptions relentlessly and trying to enlighten him only drove him farther in opposition. When cornered, he resorted to personal attacks after which there was no room to negotiate.

Taking a deep breath, and with her voice calm and low, Miranda spoke slowly, "Now it's my turn to speak, and this is the last time I talk to you on this subject. Your parents and I are partners. They have invested as much energy as have I, and we will continue to move together for as long as this partnership brings goodness and promise to those who struggle. Your unfounded accusations and name-calling, although unpleasant, will not deter me. My interactions with you will be limited to the absolute minimum. I will conduct my business through your folks alone. For the times in which we must work together, I will show you respect and I expect the same in return."

Before Ethan could say anything, Miranda turned and walked away. In her desire to leave, she forgot to grab the documentation, but she had no intention of going back in there until Ethan was gone. Miranda wanted to stay far away from Ethan for a while. She walked into the kitchen and Vida appeared, holding a basket.

"The shoer is coming. Perhaps you should meet him," Vida said. "He might be interested in doing business with us. We could get your string of therapy horses on a routine schedule. He'd be guaranteed the work and may offer a discount in return." Vida set the basket on the table.

Miranda focused on Vida's enthusiasm and commended her initiative. "Look at you, already thinking like a non-profit owner. And what, may I ask, is the basket for?"

"You said we need a name for the business, right?" Vida collected the basket she had brought in. "I thought, let's do this diplomatically. We'll each anonymously scratch a few name ideas on these slips of paper, put them in this basket and randomly draw them out, then we'll read off the names and vote." Vida was so thrilled with her idea; she didn't notice the strained expression on her guest's face.

"That sounds like fun." Miranda words didn't match how she felt after the scene that had just taken place in the office. She was determined to keep things positive. It might use all her energy, but Miranda would not let Ethan suck the joy out of her life. She had worked too hard to have her dreams tainted by one man's negativity. Picking herself up by the bootstraps, Miranda pulled a square off the rainbow colored post-it note pad, and with the pen poised, announced, "Here's my contribution."

Miranda finished writing her idea on the scrap of paper. Then Tad came in and announced, "Doug Bartleson is here to look after Magic's loose shoe."

"Come, Randi. Let's introduce you to the shoer." Vida took the pen and paper from Miranda's hand and led her out the door.

Chapter 21

Ethan came into the now empty kitchen and looked out the window to watch his mother, Tad and Miranda, walking toward the farrier's rig. He felt like an outsider looking in. His attempt to speak honestly with Miranda had blown up in his face. Ethan was at a loss on how to proceed. What does a man do when he is witnessing a train wreck, but every attempt to derail it, instead of making things better, only increases the level of disaster?

And what of Miranda, and that kiss? It was completely out of context, inappropriate, and by some definitions, an assault. Ethan couldn't say it was involuntary. One doesn't just become lip to lip by accident, but it wasn't something he chose, either. Driven by a primal urge, Ethan had made a move that may have been the biggest blunder and he couldn't help but wonder if, under different circumstances, it wouldn't have been a mistake at all. If he and Miranda met as regular people, say at the bar one night, would there be positive chemistry between them?

Differences aside, Ethan was attracted to Miranda, and based on the natural response he felt during the kiss, unless he was wrong, Miranda was into him, too. But now, too much had happened, Ethan lamented. Miranda made it clear she was done talking to him. Even if they could have come to some agreeable understanding, the chance of finding a language in which they could establish respectable communication had slipped away.

Backing away from the window, Ethan didn't want to watch as Miranda cordially greeted the blacksmith. Everyone was smiling. They had things to discuss and Ethan felt he hadn't the right to impose his negativity now. On his way out of the kitchen, Ethan noticed his mother's basket with a handwritten sign on it that said, "The name-game." Seeing there were already three pieces of notepaper folded up and laying at the bottom of the basket, Ethan picked up the pen and jotted down a few words, his contribution to the drawing.

The meeting with the farrier went well. Doug Bartleson offered to provide shoeing for Miranda's therapy horses at his cost in exchange for riding therapy for his nephew, Colby, who was recently diagnosed with autism. Doug was excited about the prospects of having a therapy program so near.

"We are heading to the meadow in a few minutes. Would you like to look at our covered arena project? The blueprints are being drafted by me," Ansel paused. "I know what you are gonna say. I am not an architect, nor a designer, but have you seen these programs you can get on the computer?"

While the shoer straitened and reset Magic's right front shoe, Ansel shared with Doug how he was creating plans with a software app he had installed and how the program did all the work for them with just a few measurements and parameters entered. Doug shared his ideas on the methods to prepare the ground of the arena floor and the type of footing to best serve the horses.

Ansel listened with interest as Doug explained the different arena floor materials. Both men were still chatting as the group walked from the barn, through the pasture and on to the meadow. Miranda hung back while Vida and Ansel told Doug their further plans; a separate driveway, space for parking, a viewing area and so on.

As the Baldwins described what they were building, Miranda felt the weight of responsibility to make it happen. What if she had bitten off more than she could chew? This was a large undertaking, and she had no experience with anything of this magnitude. Was it crazy to be just boldly moving forward? Drawing on instinct and sound advice where she could get it was Miranda's modus operandi. But was she making the right choices? Was she tricking the Baldwins into believing in her, only to let them down when she failed? Maybe Ethan was right, this meadow was teeming with life, beauty, it was fragile and because of her, there would be major disruption to the environment.

The grassland was gloriously alive, from the grasshopper leaping from blade to blade to the warbler swooping in to catch an unsuspecting butterfly. Miranda heard Ethan's words in her head and felt the pressure of his judgement. She stopped walking to listen as if the meadow itself were pleading its case. The stand of aspens on the western boundary quaked like a unified jury, and the old oak tree near the swimming hole sat on the bench to judge.

Ansel was pointing out the details to Doug, Vida was contentedly confirming, while Tad just took in the sights. Miranda felt disconnected, like she was above the scene looking down.

"You seem distracted, Randi. Is everything okay?" Vida noticed Miranda had stopped walking.

"I was just thinking… all these plans… I mean… I don't know…" Miranda's stammering turned Ansel and Doug around to look questioningly.

"What is it, Randi? Is it the arena plans? We can still make changes." Ansel coaxed her for clarification, but Miranda couldn't explain.

"It's not that…" Miranda couldn't tell them she was having second thoughts. Ethan's words had gotten into her mind, and there they were, now echoing like a broken record. Maybe she was using everyone, capitalizing on their generosity, promising things she couldn't do, asking people to take a chance with no guarantee she could deliver. Ethan was thinking of the environment. He understood the impact this project would have and, as steward of the land, he was speaking on behalf of the flora and fauna that had no voice.

Miranda started walking away with her fists clenched, trying to silence one man's voice and focus on the voices that cheered her on. Where were the voices that offered their help and expertise? Where were those that confidently invested their money hoping to donate to a good cause? She wanted to listen to those voices. How could all those people be wrong? How could those people trust her if she herself had doubts? She had doubts only because Ethan planted them there and it was up to her to evict those doubts like weeding a garden. Her confidence sells it, but her past success keeps them invested. That is what Miranda would focus on. She wasn't about to give up. That would be only letting herself down. She would not do that, nor was she about to let down anyone else.

Miranda stopped and turned to rejoin the group with renewed energy and ran smack into Tad, who was following close behind her. The hit knocked her off balance, but Tad caught her hand and supported her on unstable feet.

"Oh, sorry. I didn't know you were behind me." Miranda apologized then, with her free hand, grabbed Tad's hand that was still holding hers and asked, "What do you think about all this?"

The intensity with which Randi demanded was too much for Tad to process so quickly. Randi's steady, dark eyes stunned him into silence. Tad couldn't answer, couldn't remember the question, couldn't look away.

Miranda tried again. "Do you understand why the Baldwins want to do this?"

"Randi, why are you asking me? That is a strange question. You and Ansel and Vida have been working on this for a long time, right? You should know how they feel."

Miranda let go of Tad's hand, and he shook it as if he had held the handle of a hot griddle.

"Of course, of course," Miranda said. Nothing had changed. She just had a slight lapse in faith, but that was over now. The Baldwins were working with her on their own accord. They were willing and had ideas they wanted to share. Together, they were creating something greater than themselves.

"Tad?" Ansel called, standing where the rest of the group had stayed when Miranda walked away. "We're heading back to the complex. Doug's gotta get back to work."

Tad nodded and waved, showing he heard the message, and turned back to Miranda, who was now walking toward the river bank. When he caught up with her, Miranda was staring contemplatively into the crystal-clear water, slipping steadily down the stream.

"The river knows exactly what to do. The water just flows along and conforms to the banks. It doesn't question the shore, it simply adjusts." Miranda spoke almost inaudibly, and Tad did not know what she was talking about. To him, her contemplative face looked sad.

Miranda continued, slowly sharing with Tad a memory. "When I was sixteen, I took lessons and rode at a training facility in Torrington. This stable let me work with the beginning riders. I've always loved kids, and the kids liked me, too."

Tad found it difficult to concentrate on what Miranda was saying when the deep lines and down-turned eyes made him want to run his fingers gently across the curve of her soft cheek to erase the furrows and bring back a smile. Tad forced himself to focus.

"There was a little girl named Carrie who rode every day at eleven in the morning. Her father would bring her in and leave. I wasn't sure why her father didn't stay, but I could see it bothered Carrie. One day, Carrie arrived very excited to tell me her father and her brother, Jason, were going to stick around and watch her ride."

"I discovered her father usually dropped Carrie off at the stable, then left to pick up Jason from physical therapy, where he was treated for cerebral palsy, but on this day, both Jason and Carrie's father were there to see her ride. It thrilled Jason to watch his sister going around the arena. Carrie's father noticed how much joy it brought to both his kids and from that day on Jason got to stay and watch."

"It was then that I developed this idea of physical therapy on horseback. I thought about how much fun it could be for Jason to ride with his sister. I thought they both could benefit from riding together. It turned out equine therapy was a thing. There were many such programs across the country. I convinced Jason's doctors to go with the trainer, and we got permission from the stable owners to allow the therapist, who also volunteered to come out, to oversee the safety aspects. We got the horses familiar with the wheelchair and Jason learned how to groom them and I was teaching him about the bridle and saddle." Miranda stopped talking and tried to clear her throat, which had suddenly become dry. The moisture turned up in her eyes, which filled with tears.

Tad wondered why Miranda was crying and waited for her to regain composure.

"Jason slowly progressed with his relationship with one horse in particular. The horse was not shy of Jason's wheelchair and would stand like a statue so Jason could safely maneuver around. Patience and understanding were the key factors in the relationship. I remember there was a bond between human and equine I had never seen before."

"The doctors loved how Jason responded to just being around the horses, and after some time, the physical therapist felt confident that with a spotter on each side, and someone to lead the horse, Jason could ride. Though the cerebral palsy and other co-conditions severely impaired Jason's mobility, we wanted to see if we could safely perch Jason on the horse. I tried to convince the stable owner to allow it, but there were insurance and liability risks to consider. I was only a kid with a generous heart and the adults didn't take me too seriously." Miranda dropped her head, remembering how hard she tried.

"But the CETO? And your non-profit?" Tad questioned. "You were a kid back then, but now? You are so successful now."

"Yes," Miranda answered, "but it never happened for Jason. He died of heart failure. He was nineteen. I wanted so badly to give him the chance to ride, to feel the power of the horse, the liberation of movement. On top of failing to get Jason on a horse, I felt the pain of loss. The spot in my heart where Jason had been was now an empty space. I barely knew him for a year, but he became very dear to me. Jason had been coming to the stable for therapy for six and a half months, but the emptiness left in his absence was painful."

"I am so sorry, Randi." Tad reached into his pocket for his container of chew. Randi's situation with Jason was hard for him to understand. Was she in love with him? Or were they just friends? Her emotions confused Tad. Then, when he saw the look on Randi's face as he inserted the pinch of pungent snuff between his cheeks, he quickly explained, "I'm gonna quit chewing, Randi. Vida has been hassling me for a while now."

Miranda watched Tad say one thing, then do the opposite.

"Continue with your story, Randi." It irritated him when women judged him. Why did they always want men to stop chewing?

After a momentary pause, Miranda continued, "They formed the CETO a year later when Carrie's father, the doctors, and the physical therapists who were all inspired by Jason got organized. I continued to help every summer and stayed involved throughout college, then started my non-profit after graduation. Now, when I see a new child come into the program, when I find another stable owner I can bring into the fold, every time I put people together to do great things, I feel good about it but I never forget that Jason ran out of time. I want this to happen here at the Alma Soñada. The kids and families should have the chance. I don't want anyone to miss out like Jason and Carrie did."

"Everything is on track here, Randi. You don't need to worry." Tad offered a comforting arm around Miranda. With the point of her shoulder jabbing him in the armpit, Tad pondered how he would have preferred a full-on frontal hug, but he would take what he could get.

Miranda knew Tad probably couldn't understand the complexities that pushed her strongly toward her goals, the energy that drove her to help as many families as she could, but she appreciated his offer of sympathy. Tad's arm felt protective wrapped around her and Miranda welcomed the comfort. She didn't think to move away.

The inner voice spoke again in positive tones as Miranda's spirit lifted. When she and Tad walked back up to the homestead buildings, Miranda was again thinking ahead, making plans, and imagining all the good things together they were going to do.

Chapter 22

"Where are Tad and Miranda?" Ethan asked when the others returned from the meadow that afternoon.

"They'll be along shortly," Ansel answered Ethan, who was saddling Winston.

"They're walking?" Ethan knew it was a stupid question, and what he really wanted to ask was, 'you left them alone together?'

"Yes, they are walking." Ansel chuckled and teased his son. "I believe they are capable."

Ethan glared at his father, not at all in the mood for frivolity.

"Lighten up, son. I was just teasing. Randi seemed a little stressed, and Tad stayed a while with her in the meadow. They took a walk along the river."

"Oh, no," Ethan groaned, remembering his last interaction with Miranda.

"Do you know why Miranda might have been upset?" Ansel looked at Ethan with suspicion.

"I don't know, maybe." Ethan wasn't ready to spill all the beans.

"Care to elaborate?"

"I kissed Miranda, Dad." Ethan blurted out, starting the story in the middle.

Ansel chuckled, but it didn't surprise him. He had been sensing the tension between his son and his new partner. "Well, now, that is an interesting development. Your mother will be happy you are finally taking an interest in women, but with Randi? That seems inappropriate. We are her business partners. What on earth made you do that?"

"There's more," Ethan gritted his teeth.

Ansel's eyebrow lifted. "Go on."

"It's just all this business with the ranch. It scares me. I've seen city folk and how they are when they pretend to be cowboys. How many horses have come to us for retraining after being mistreated by some fool who doesn't know what they are doing? And all the horses need is to be treated with kindness and understanding from the start. That is what those city dudes do to horses."

"I have a hard time sending those poor animals back time and time again. But what can we do? I can't stop the city slickers from doing what they do and they won't listen to any riding advice either. It is heartbreaking to be part of the cycle, but it would be worse for the horses not to be. It is the horses who suffer either way. Dad, do you want to associate our family name with that type of business? What will the folks think when they see our ranch contributing to the town's problems?" There was a quiver in Ethan's voice.

Ansel listened to Ethan with admiration for his son's compassion, but he wasn't sure about the context. "Is this another misunderstanding? Your mom and I are not contributing to a problem, son. There are no city slickers coming to our ranch. There will be no mistreating of any horses. Randi's program does not create or encourage people who mistreat animals, and she is providing opportunities for those less fortunate to see what we have, and to experience the joy of ranch life."

"I told Randi that under no circumstances was I going to let her turn our place into a dude ranch." There. It was out. Ethan had spoken the truth, knowing he was running out of time to make his dad understand what would happen if they allowed this business venture to continue.

"A dude ranch? You think we are setting up a dude ranch?" Ansel was stunned by Ethan's theory.

"I know that's not what you are calling it, but a skunk by any other name will never be a rose. I've seen Miranda in action and she is very convincing. She has many people believing this is some sort of community minded thing. She has people in town eating out of her hands, and she plans to recruit even more. And it's all about the profit. I heard her talking about raising money, Dad," Ethan spoke as his exasperation spilled over.

"Listen, Ethan," Ansel tried to start at the beginning, in order to clear up the many misconceptions.

"Dad, I know how much you guys want this. I mean, you have been planning for months, but I think you got too caught up to think things through. I just don't think you and Mom understand how you will contribute to the spread of tourism, to the further demise of Rambletap Springs."

"Now hold on a minute." Ansel needed Ethan to let him speak. "Before you insult your mother and my intelligence with these inaccurate claims, please listen."

Ansel waited a moment to be sure Ethan was listening, then explained. "First, we are not caught up in anything. We are very aware of what we are doing. Alma Soñada Ranch will become the home of Randi's riding program and there is nothing more to be decided."

"Second, Randi is not manipulating anyone. She is the hardest working person I have ever met outside the ranching industry, and she is not looking to capitalize on anything. Miranda is the Miranda Howarth-Dunn, heiress to the vast financial empire of the automobile industry family. Her late father was Gordon Howarth-Dunn. She doesn't need to raise money for herself. In fact, Miranda's estate is the largest donor of funds to her non-profit. She matches the annual donations with her own money. She also sponsors scholarships so that the kids whose families can't afford the program can take part."

"And last, we are not opening a ranch resort for greenhorns. We are creating an equine therapy program for physically and mentally challenged youth. A place where people can come as a family, spend some time in the beauty we selfishly take for granted. It is time we give back a little. It's good for us, good for the Alma Soñada, and helps others." Ansel held his head and chest high with the noble explanation.

"An equine therapy program?" Ethan said, still in disbelief.

"Randi has worked with kids and young adults and has run her branch of the Connecticut Equine Therapy Organization in Connecticut that provides horseback riding for children with disabilities. Ethan, these are kids who can't walk, children with autism and other mental challenges. All the funding to start the program here at our ranch is being supplied by Randi personally from her late father's empire."

"Bringing this kind of facility to Rambletap Springs will help folks in our own community foremost. All we are providing is our permission to use this ranch. We will do all we can to help and will contribute beyond that, too. We will only charge for expenses incurred to run the program, with complete consideration for preserving this ranch as a cattle ranch. There is nothing in the works to the detriment of the Alma Soñada Ranch."

When Ansel stopped talking, Ethan just stood silently, contemplating all his father had just revealed. How could he have let his imagination run so wild?

He had been wrong about everything. Not a dude ranch at all, but an equine healing program. And Miranda wasn't running a con game. She was wealthy. Ethan was familiar with the Howarth-Dunn empire. Miranda probably had more money than some small countries. Ethan realized there were bound to be ramifications for his actions toward his parent's new partner. Ethan ran his fingers through the loose curls on his head ferociously. "What have I done? The hurtful things I said, Dad."

"I don't know what you said, but no use fretting about it. Randi is not only generous, but I imagine she is also a forgiving person." Ansel encouraged Ethan not to dwell on it.

"If I were her, I wouldn't be so quick to forgive me," Ethan said, dejectedly. *I'll be lucky if she doesn't press charges*, he thought. "I hope I can fix this."

"You can start by apologizing first to me and your mother," Ansel advised. "You will get the chance to apologize to Randi, as well. Right now, you got a horse to look after."

"I am very sorry, Dad, to you and Mom." Ethan followed orders. He knew his father was right. The opportunity to speak to Miranda would present itself, and he could ask for forgiveness, but that didn't set his mind at ease.

Ethan's thoughts were zig-zagging like the swarm of mosquitos on the meadow at dusk. He wished to find Miranda Dunn right away and apologize. Time would intensify the asperity of the words he spoke to her. But he couldn't go running off like a lost puppy looking for its mother. Miranda was with Tad, and Ethan needed to talk to her in private. Ethan threw himself into the tasks at hand and set about his chores. It was not a good distracter, but it was all he had.

~****~

The sun was setting and provided little warmth as Tad walked Miranda out of the meadow. Miranda silently enjoyed the peaceful beauty around her. The peak to the west was casting its shadow hungrily across the wild flowers that had closed for the night, as if that would protect them from the darkness. The shadow would continue its path through the meadow until even the aspens were in the dark. Tad glanced at Randi as she surveyed the meadow.

"It's a beautiful place, isn't it?" Tad followed her gaze.

“Hmmm,” Miranda responded, as she savored the view, then she turned to Tad, “Thank you, Tad.”

“Of course.” Tad liked to be appreciated. “But what did I do?”

“I needed someone to talk to, and you were there for me. I really appreciate it. You made me feel at ease. The Baldwins are so supportive.” Then Miranda remembered Ethan, his harsh words and inappropriate behavior, and corrected herself in her mind, *the Baldwins, not including Ethan*.

“I just saw you were upset and didn’t like it, is all.”

“Well, it felt good.” Miranda confessed. Feeling the support of others was something Miranda’s soul hungered for.

The mountain shadow had completely dimmed the meadow. The sun bathed only the crown of the magnificent oak with the last weak rays of light. Standing like a sentinel, nature’s lighthouse, guiding birds and squirrels to its branches for shelter, the oak tree provided a landmark for the deer and elk, foxes and rabbits, leading them to the life-sustaining waters on the river’s banks.

The tree’s massive roots gave stability to the banks, redirecting the river’s meandering flow, and created a safe habitat for the fish and frogs, salamanders and snakes. And now the tree provided Miranda with the answers she needed, gave her a glimpse of symbiosis, and permission to proceed and become a part of its family, too. Miranda silently promised the tree she would take care of and act responsibly in consideration of all the life in the meadow. She would see that this little piece of heaven remained as pristine as possible.

Reluctantly, Miranda turned to walk back to the building complex and as she and Tad rounded the last bend on the path, the house and barn came into full view. Miranda noticed someone riding in the arena doing fast paced maneuvers. She was positive it was Ethan on Winston.

“What is he doing?” Miranda asked as she watched Ethan moving Winston about.

“Reining patterns,” Tad answered passively.

Miranda went to the side of the arena for a better look and it amazed her to see Ethan taking the horse through intricate moves, seemingly without effort. First, Ethan galloped Winston across the arena, then he would sit back slightly and the horse would slide to a stop with his haunches nearly on the dirt, his hind legs tucked under his belly.

Then the horse gathered himself and stood up square on his legs before Ethan put him in a spin, making one and a half revolutions, followed by a bolt forward and a gallop into a simple figure eight where Winston did a change of balance at the intersections without losing stride. Ethan and Winston repeated this pattern a few times and appeared to move as if from the same brain. The rider's cues were indiscernible. The horse's moves gave the illusion he was deciding on his own.

"I did not know Winston could move like that. He looks so different, so smooth and athletic."

"Humph." Tad grunted. He knew Ethan was a better rider than he, that fact never bothered him until now. Tad looked at Randi, watching the other cowboy putting the little cutting horse through some more moves. Ethan had strayed from official reining patterns used in competitions, opting for unofficial patterns he was inventing on the fly. The horse and rider team were doing a choreographed dance, and the jealously seeped into Tad's heart.

Not only was Ethan a better rider, he was simply a genius with training, giving the horse cues in a sequence the horse had never done before, and making it look like they'd practiced for hours. Ethan could make a horse look better trained than he actually was, and Tad knew he could not compete. He had to get Randi away from the arena.

"Randi," Tad asked. "Wanna come with me to the barn? I need to see if the stalls got cleaned."

"Hmm?" Miranda murmured, but her eyes never left the action in the arena.

"Shoot," Tad pressed his lips around the curse.

Miranda pulled her eyes away to look at her friend. "I'm sorry, what?"

"Never mind, I've got some chores to do. You stay and watch. I'll see you later."

"Thanks, Tad." Miranda flashed a smile.

"Shucks," Tad smiled back, his thin mustache curling with his silly grin. As he turned to walk away, he reached for the canister of smokeless tobacco.

~****~

Ethan had seen Tad and Miranda coming from the meadow, and he thought it almost looked like they were walking hand in hand. He had been riding

Winston for nearly 20 minutes to warm the horse up. Ethan would have ridden out to meet them, but by the looks of it, he decided Tad might not wish to be interrupted. It pleasantly surprised Ethan when the next time he glanced up, he saw Miranda watching him, and Tad was pouting beside her. Ethan smiled inside, then concentrated on Winston as he worked the horse off the rail. He needed to show Miranda what a horse like Winston could do, and the little horse rose to the occasion.

"Ho!" Ethan asked, with his weight deep in the saddle, and Winston came to a sliding stop. The horse stood still, waiting for his next cue, and Ethan leaned forward and patted Winston's neck, then urged him into a walk for a cool-down. Ethan looked up, and it delighted Ethan to see Miranda standing alone.

"What do you think of little Winston now?" Ethan asked as he came to a stop by the arena fence.

"He is quite athletic. I can now see why he went over that creek with nary an afterthought. He obviously trusts his rider. I bet with some time I could have him doing well in the dressage arena, too." Miranda professed.

"Dressage!" Ethan snorted, and Winston's head bobbled when he felt his rider tense up. "I don't think we'd waste a talented horse like Winston on dressage."

Not wanting to begin another battle in the war of wills against him, Miranda simply said to Ethan, "Don't knock it till you've tried it."

Based on Ethan's dismissive reaction to Miranda's idea concerning Winston's talent, it convinced her he didn't understand that the word dressage in French means training, schooling. Simply defined, dressage means riding a horse through specific movements that displayed strength, fluidity, and style of movement. It was supposed to look like horse and rider were dancing. With emphasis on harmony and communication, it was exactly what Ethan and Winston had been doing.

Ethan let the subject drop, remembering he already had enough for which to apologize. He didn't need to add to the script by arguing with Miranda the pros and cons of English and Western riding. Ethan continued walking Winston in a large circle. As the hardworking horse caught his breath, Ethan tried gathering the courage to begin his apology, but every time the apex of his circular orbit brought him closest to Miranda, his voice headed for the hills.

Miranda stayed by the arena watching for a while. It seemed like Ethan might have something to say, and she wanted to welcome any opportunity to have a decent conversation.

Winston was almost cooled down from his workout when Ethan decided what to do. He would offer a lesson, and while Miranda was up on the horse, her lips a very safe distance away from his, Ethan would offer his amends. With the previously scattered leaves of his courage now raked into a workable pile, Ethan turned to the arena side. But Miranda was already walking toward the house. He noted she had her slender arms cradled around her front, probably to preserve body heat, for the sun had long since completed its descent from the sky, taking with it the last bit of warmth. Ethan would have to wait to offer Miranda a lesson on Winston. Tomorrow is another day.

Chapter 23

The ringing of the telephone awakened Miranda, and she stretched across the bed to end its intrusive racket.

"Hello?" Miranda held the receiver away so she could clear her sleep raspy throat.

"Good morning, this is Vida."

"Good morning."

"Ansel hooked your car up to the charger last night, and this morning it started up fine."

Miranda greased the wheels of her mind by rubbing the sleep from her eyes, and she remembered the events from the evening of the day before. Tad had to give her a ride from the ranch to the Dinmont hotel after Miranda discovered her Range Rover wouldn't start. Vida had invited her to stay as a guest in the house, but Miranda really wanted to get to the hotel and Tad volunteered to drive her.

"I am relieved it is just a dead battery. I can get a new one right away." Miranda examined the alarm app on her cell phone to see why it hadn't gone off and noticed she hadn't activated it. Her olfactory system told her the coffee maker hadn't suffered the same fate as the smell of coffee drifted through her hotel room.

"Ansel is bringing your car to the shop this morning to get a replacement battery."

"Oh, you are too kind, but that isn't necessary. I will grab an Uber and come for the car this afternoon," Miranda protested.

"Grab an Uber?" Vida chuckled. "Nonsense, you have enough to do. Will you be at the new office site?"

"Yes, I'll be at the office." Miranda didn't argue. In the city, 'grabbing an Uber' was Miranda's go-to response when she needed a ride. She had an active account and the app on her phone. There was an app for everything from hiring a dog walker to grocery delivery. Out here in the sticks, there weren't quite the same options. There was one taxi service with two cars. "Thank you, Vida."

"Okay, dear. I'll let Ansel know, and we'll see you later."

"I will be in town all day," Miranda answered. "Thanks, again."

Miranda jumped into the shower to expedite the wake-up process, grabbed her to-go coffee cup, and headed out on foot toward down town. Miranda ran across the street and saw Alisha Conrad, the staff member sent by Jonelle from the community center, walking up to the stairway outside the two-story building. The two women exchanged a greeting, then Alisha announced, "Have I got a surprise for you?" She opened the office door with glee.

"Oh, my gosh," Miranda let out a gasp as she beheld a room completely set up for business. "You have been hard at work, Alisha."

There was only enough money in the budget for one full-time staff member, and Miranda was pleased it was to be Alisha. For a youngster just graduated from high school, she was already proving to be indispensable.

"And looky here," Alisha picked up the phone that sat on what was to be Miranda's desk, "A landline. You are physically and officially on the map."

"I don't know what to say. You are wonderful, and I am eternally grateful."

"The volunteer crew was out yesterday to set up the internet, too. You are online and ready for action." Alisha beamed.

"Well, I suppose there is nothing left to do but unpack supplies and organize. Let's get started."

Miranda had delivered a few boxes filled with essentials after she got the keys to the place, and it was now time for organizing. The morning slipped by as Alisha and Miranda worked and the conversation flowed. It turned out they had more in common than just their desire to serve the people in the community and help others. They were both adopted, grew up around horses, and both loved the outdoors.

It was almost noon when Miranda and Alisha stepped back to survey their progress. "Now we are really ready for work," Alisha said with satisfaction, "Let's get this show on the road."

"Not before you gals have had lunch."

Miranda spun around, startled by the voice from behind her. Tad and Ansel had found the place.

"Here are your car keys." Tad reached out his arm. "We picked up a new battery, and the car is good as new."

"Ansel, Tad, Alisha," Miranda introduced, just in case. "I believe you all know each other?"

"Hi, Alisha, good to see you," Tad said. Alisha was the youngest sibling of a pal Tad had hung around with when they were in high school.

"So?" Ansel rubbed his hands together. "How 'bout lunch?"

"We thought we'd treat you to lunch." It had been Ansel's idea, but Tad spoke first as if to take credit hoping it would impress Miranda.

"I won't say no to that," Alisha enthusiastically offered a suggestion. "Why don't we go to the Paradise Grill? I absolutely love their Greek Salad; the caramelized walnuts and feta cheese taste so good together."

"Sounds good," Miranda agreed. "But only if you let me treat. You have all done so much to help me already. I also need to reimburse you for the battery. How much do I owe you?"

"No charge. I made a deal with the mechanic. His horse needs a tune-up, so we made a trade. Ethan will ride his horse for a few days and we get the battery." Ansel was proud of his bartering skills.

"Oh," Miranda wasn't sure Ethan would appreciate being volunteered to exchange his time for her benefit.

"Don't worry, Randi. Ethan needs to have work, or he gets bored." It annoyed Tad that even when Ethan wasn't around, he was still something to compete with.

"Shall we go?" Ansel held open the door for the ladies.

The Paradise Grill was owned by a couple, Richard and Lisa Campbell, who came to Montana from California. Hoping to find a community that danced to a slower beating drum than the high velocity pace of Southern California, the couple chose Rambletap Springs. The native Montanans in Rambletap Springs predicted the Campbells wouldn't last one season, and even Richard and Lisa themselves are not embarrassed to admit they nearly didn't. There were two strikes against their success.

The first winter was a cold one, and the locals were not immediately drawn to the foods on the menu, which was entirely West Coast Cuisine. Richard learned to shovel snow, and slowly, after a few brave individuals ventured forth to try their fare, the feedback was good enough to bring in others to enjoy such unusual oddities as hummus and tofu. It turns out there are enough people in the area who embraced a minor change and the place caught on.

Miranda enjoyed the lunch; she daringly ordered the Quinoa Tabbouleh salad, and it didn't surprise her when her friends were not afraid to order something unique as well. Ansel and Tad had broadened their palates thanks to Vida, and Alisha had an adventurous side. Because the food had been so tasty, and Miranda had skipped breakfast, she had eaten too much and she was glad for the walk back to work. Tad and Ansel said goodbye at the Paradise Grill and headed in the opposite direction. After an enjoyable morning away from the normal routine, it was time to go home to the never-ending responsibilities of ranching.

"Kudos on the choice for lunch," Miranda congratulated Alisha's suggestion. She liked the Paradise Grill and the Campbells. "And what a friendly couple they are."

"It is good food, and they are lucky to have become successful. It took them a while, but they finally made it. Adapt and overcome." Alisha summed up Miranda's own motto.

Miranda and Alisha headed down the main street of Rambletap Springs mindful of the traffic, which, even at the heaviest, wasn't anywhere near what Miranda considered a lot compared to that of Torrington.

"Oh, there's Paula Mariano and Suzanne Mitchell," Alisha recognized the girls her older brother had gone to school with whom were stepping into a bridal shop down the street. "I didn't know Suzanne was back home. Rumor has it she is getting married…"

Miranda started up the steps to the second floor, allotting only half her attention to Alisha as the story continued. The people Alisha was gossiping about weren't that important to Miranda.

"You know Paula, of course," Alisha opened the door.

"We were introduced, but we didn't say more than a few words to each other. She seems nice, though," Miranda confessed. "I haven't noticed her around the ranch much, but I guess she lives there?"

"Yes, she lives there. You haven't seen her?" Alisha's curiosity was piqued. "She is usually always around if Ethan is around."

"I believe Paula is staying with a friend." Miranda didn't enjoy telling someone else's story.

"Paula must stay with Suzanne. She is probably helping with wedding plans." Alisha surmised. "That makes sense, but I am still surprised that Paula would stay in town, and not at home. She likes to keep close tabs on Ethan."

Miranda continued to focus on her computer screen, but she had to admit she was a little curious how much more Alisha would tell.

"They were dating, you know," Alisha chattered on as she worked on the list from which she was creating a database of potential equine therapy providers. Alisha saw if Miranda would respond, then continued, "Maybe you don't know."

"I'm new here, remember?" Miranda teased. "I know very little about anyone or anything."

"Well, I guess I can tell you. Or at least I will tell you what I know," Alisha stopped typing. "The story changes, and depending on who's telling it, I'm not sure the actual truth."

Miranda could see the animated way Alisha spoke and deduced that she enjoyed knowing things about others, and liked to talk about it, too. Not a terminal character flaw, Miranda thought, provided the gossip was relatively benign. Miranda was relieved to know this about her new co-worker sooner rather than later. She would have to give careful consideration to what she would share with Alisha.

"Well, it all began when we were kids. I found all this out from my brother and sisters who were friends with them." Alisha began with gusto. "Everyone in school knew Paula liked Ethan. She was popular with all the boys, but only had eyes for him. If I recall, they were all part of a group of friends and Paula and Ethan didn't start dating until Paula was a senior in high school and Ethan was already at the university. They were soon engaged but never got married. Gossip has it Ethan caught Paula cheating the night before the wedding. When Paula's folks died in a tragic car accident not long after the wedding got canceled, Paula went to live with the Baldwins and it appeared Ethan and she were back together."

"Now it has always seemed strange to me. It's been like a year, and there never was a wedding. It appalled some folks they might live together in sin. Others say the couple eloped and are living happily ever after. But I reject both those theories."

Miranda considered the two theories. Both were plausible, except Ethan and Paula had separate rooms in the main house. Miranda remembered the rainy day she had returned Paula's sweat pants to her room. It was not Ethan's room, too.

Alisha explained her own theory. "I don't think they eloped. I don't believe they are even still together. They are never at church together. We never see them together. Of course, Ethan hardly ever leaves the ranch. I wouldn't mind seeing him around. I had the biggest crush on Ethan in grade school. Older men have always been my thing. Ethan was cute then and has only gotten better looking with time."

"Hmmm," Miranda gave an obligatory half laugh at the mention of Ethan's looks. "Not something I noticed."

"Yah, right?" Alisha smiled but shook her head, knowing Miranda had noticed though she claimed otherwise. "Well, you and Tad seem to have a connection. You two would make a cute couple."

"We are not a couple, and why is it required that everyone be coupled up?" Miranda rolled her eyes derisively. Alisha may have a work ethic beyond her age, but she was a kid just out of high school mentally.

Alisha let the question wither and die as the two women fell silent. Miranda contemplated her friendship with Tad. He was certainly a nice guy, happy and easygoing, and seemed to pay her a lot of attention. Though she and he had only connected as friends, if she were dating, and Tad asked her out, she thought she might not decline.

Chapter 24

Ethan looked out of the guest house window he was cleaning to see a car he didn't recognize turning around in the driveway. Ethan considered who it might be. His dad and Tad had come home from town a while ago, and the collection of personnel coming to the ranch on business usually went straight to the meadow and not up here to the houses.

As planned, the contractor from the Whitley company had delivered the ground-breaking equipment for the modest earth moving needed at the sight that was to be an arena. Even though his father had assured him they were doing things with the utmost concern for the environment, Ethan felt compelled to keep tabs on the construction. Ethan couldn't bear to think of the monstrous machines raping the land and assaulting the meadow dwellers.

Thankful for the distraction of all his chores and duties, Ethan stayed focused on other things, including the fillies brought in for training. He already had them accustomed to the feel of the saddle. He had introduced them to the bridle, and was teaching them ground driving; moving them around him in an arching circle and communicating with them through the long lines.

When Tad and Ansel had left for Rambletap Springs to get Miranda's car battery replaced, Ethan couldn't ignore the jealousy he had felt. He hoped he would have had more chances to speak to Miranda alone and apologize, but that hadn't happened. Figuring the sooner Miranda settled in at the ranch, the more likely the possibility he could quickly deliver explanations for his behavior, Ethan adopted a new plan. Ethan found time to ready the cottage for Miranda's arrival. He had been cleaning windows when the strange car pulled up.

Ethan saw Paula emerge from the car and his mother came from the house, so he continued cleaning. After the windows were crystal clear, Ethan went to work removing the ashes from the little fireplace and tried to remember the last time there had been wood burning there. Maybe his mother and father came to the cottage for privacy from the busy activity of the main house, or maybe Noah had been out here on occasions to get some space from his brother. The twins often squabbled about silly things and once in a while needed some distance. Whatever the case, the fireplace needed sweeping.

Ethan understood how Noah might feel. Lately, he thought it'd be nice to have some time away from Tad, too. The guy was becoming quite annoying. When Miranda's car refused to start the other evening, Ethan realized Miranda might stay the night as a guest, giving him a chance to talk to her, but Tad quickly volunteered to drive her to town. Miranda climbed into Tad's truck and off they went, together.

Ethan had told himself he wasn't jealous; it was just eagerness to clear the air between him and Miranda. But the envy Ethan tried to reason away didn't resolve and reared up again when Tad went off to town to help with the battery replacement.

The resentment Ethan felt toward Tad was difficult to reason with. For Ethan, it was a jumble of conflicting emotions. Mixed in were the emotions brought out when Ethan remembered how he had kissed Miranda. There was embarrassment but also excitement. The softness of her lips, the way she kissed him back, Ethan couldn't recall ever feeling like that. The way Miranda had responded showed there was something there on her end, too.

Ethan thought not only about apologizing for the misunderstandings since the day they met, but also thought about how to reveal to Miranda the feelings she brought out in him. The courage he needed to do the first and Miranda's response would decide if he could do the second. "The opportunity will present itself." Ethan repeated the phrase, hoping it would manifest.

"Opportunity for what?" Paula had silently opened the door, catching Ethan off guard.

"Paula! You startled me."

"I know. You were talking to yourself." Paula came in the rest of the way and plopped down on the drop cloth that covered the sofa, which nearly took up the entire room.

Ethan stopped cleaning and watched Paula sit down. He braced himself, not sure what she wanted, and he wondered how much thinking out loud he had done. How much of his inner thoughts had Paula heard?

"Relax, Ethan. I am not here to throw myself at you. I will not do that anymore. That's a pattern I intend to change. I need to talk to you. Is now a good time?" It hurt Paula that Ethan was shying from her like a suspicious colt, punished too hard and for no reason.

"Sure, let's talk." Ethan wasn't ready to let go of his suspicions, but he wanted to hear Paula out.

"I am releasing you, Ethan."

"Paula, we haven't been together since... well, you know." Ethan spoke guardedly.

"Yes, I know..." Paula's eyes dropped. "I am so sorry that what happened between me and Noah hurt you in the most unforgivable way. There is nothing I can do now to take it back. The past is the past and I apologize for what I did."

This was the first time Paula admitted out loud that she and Noah had been together. Paula hadn't acknowledged her mistake in the past, nor had she apologized. Ethan speculated maybe this wasn't another of Paula's schemes.

"I am asking for forgiveness. I need to do this so we can both move on." Paula's eyes darkened with emotion and Ethan felt the familiar twang of guilt whenever Paula got emotional and cried.

"My time away gave me a chance to think. Seeing Suzanne and her fiancé, how they act with each other and look at each other, has been an eye opener. What they have is how love should look. We never had that, Ethan."

On autopilot and motivated by Paula's tears, Ethan sat down beside her and put his arm over her shoulder.

"I realize we have always been such a big part of each other's lives, but I no longer picture us as a couple, husband and wife." The words came reluctantly from Paula, "I am going to miss you. This is goodbye."

"Good bye? You'll miss me? Where are you going?" Ethan was not expecting this.

"I am moving back to town. It is where I belong. I'm not cut out for the ranching lifestyle. The isolation... and all the dust..." Paula joked.

Ethan nodded his understanding. He appreciated how hard this time of change had been for his dear friend and, in retrospect, wished he'd been more helpful as she navigated the mourning process after losing her parents.

Paula went on, "Your parents have been so kind. It breaks my heart to leave you all. I am truly grateful for everything. I hope we can all still be like family."

Ethan took Paula's hand in his, "We are family, Paula, geography will not change that. You will always have a home on this ranch and we will be there to support you wherever you go."

Looking into Ethan's eyes, Paula saw love. The sincerity she saw behind the words he spoke moved her from sadness to joy. She had been longing to see this look on Ethan's face for so many years and had finally got from him what she needed. The overwhelming relief made Paula laugh.

"Are you laughing at me?" It surprised Ethan that Paula was laughing.

"Not at you, Ethan, at us. I'm laughing 'cause I'm happy." Paula stood up.

Ethan stood up, too, and pulled Paula into a brotherly hug. "I am so happy to hear you say that, Paula. All I've ever wanted was for you to be happy."

"I really love you," Paula hugged him back.

"I love you, too," Ethan laughed. It felt so good to say it and mean it.

After their warm embrace, Paula reached down and pulled the rumpled covering off the sofa and folded it. Helping Ethan clean the cottage seemed like the thing a sister would do for her brother, and Ethan returned to sweeping the cinders from the hearth. It looked like the place would be ready for its new occupant soon.

Chapter 25

The early birds were making quite a racket as Miranda jogged through the waking streets of Rambletap Springs. Their racket had been so loud, there was no point in listening to her music. Miranda left her iPod behind and listen to the songbirds instead.

Dissected by the great Missouri River, Rambletap Springs had two parts to the town. On the east side was the new section. Recently built super markets anchoring the ends of shopping centers with little shops in between were sprinkled throughout. There were also the sprawling developments of new houses with planned community features like pocket parks for the kids, and recreation centers. For every acre of land used for housing, there were equal resources set aside for health and medical facilities to be built.

The town leaders had mixed feelings, some supported expansion, others were adamant about keeping Rambletap Springs small. In between lay compromise, the growth was slow and deliberate. Soon there would be a hotel, and a complex for businesses to grow. The goal was to encourage people to come, but only with careful planning.

On her run this morning, Miranda headed across the bridge to the old section of town and found a lot to be desired in the neighborhoods there. The residents were friendly; the streets were narrow and lined with shade trees. The houses were small and the yards were tidy.

As she continued up the main street, Miranda caught sight of Mr. Greyson Woods and his Rottweiler walking the other way. When the dog drew near Miranda, he stopped and sat down. Miranda greeted Mr. Woods and his Rottie, Spencer, whom she had officially met the night before on her walk home from Delightful Decadence, the ice cream and frozen yogurt shop on the west side.

After the big lunch with Alisha, Tad, and Ansel, so late in the day, Miranda hadn't been hungry for dinner, but she always had room for frozen yogurt. Strolling through the old part of town was her favorite evening activity. Main street, which was also the highway, was renovated as stipulated by the plan to let the city grow.

First, they reduced the travel lanes to two, one in each direction, and used the space previously set for traffic as parking. To further encourage folks to shop the small businesses, the sidewalks were improved; they added benches and vegetation beautification projects. They invited community artists to submit plans for murals, and planter boxes added color on each corner. Hanging from the vintage street lights lining the main road and a couple blocks up each side road were color spot flower pots.

"I guess Spencer thinks we should stop and chat every time we see you now that we are friends," Mr. Woods confessed.

"We have the same walking schedule." Miranda spoke to Mr. Woods while looking at Spencer.

Mr. Woods turned to his dog and said, "Spencer, say hello to Ms. Dunn."

The dog faced Miranda and stared up with his mesmerizing brown eyes.

"Mr. Woods, I believe you have trained this dog so you can meet people." Miranda smiled and gave Spencer a pat on his broad head

"Spencer is an excellent judge of character, and a great icebreaker, too. He only stops in front of people he sees worth knowing."

"Well, I am flattered, Spencer." Miranda gave a slight bow forward. "A compliment like that from a dog of your status could only be a boost to my self-esteem."

Spencer lifted his head and expelled a muffled woof, which startled Miranda, and the two humans laughed.

"I'm sorry, Ms. Dunn, if he gave you a start." Mr. Woods scolded Spencer for barking.

"It's okay. I love animals, and Spencer was just expressing himself. I appreciate his honesty."

"Is that so?" Mr. Woods rose to stand taller on his feet. "Well, to keep it honest, and based on Spencer's good judgement record, may I be so bold as to ask you to dinner?"

Miranda hadn't expected the invitation. It caught her off guard, but Mr. Woods continued to speak.

"I've seen you every day since last week and I know you have been staying at the Dinmont Motel. I thought a home cooked meal would do you some good and I don't know how much longer you'll be around. Spencer would never forgive me if we missed out on getting to know you."

"Eating in restaurants is getting a little redundant." Miranda was hesitant to accept, but talking herself into it seemed easy.

Mr. Woods could see the trepidation. "I must admit, I have a selfish motive. I understand you are involved in some sort of project that will bring an equine therapy program to the good folks in my town. That interests me and I would like to learn more about it."

The confession made Miranda less suspicious. She didn't know if Mr. Woods was in favor of the project or against it. Either way, Miranda could use the opportunity to share the facts and perhaps secure another supporter.

"I will accept the invitation for dinner and would love to tell you about what brings me to this beautiful town." Miranda met Mr. Woods with an equal amount of directness.

"Excellent, excellent," said Mr. Woods.

They exchanged contact information, and Mr. Woods gave Miranda his address. "See you at seven." Miranda waved with a confident smile, which was gratefully received. Then Mr. Woods and Spencer carried on with their morning walk and Miranda jogged off in the other direction.

~****~

"What were you and Paula doing in the guest house?" Noah growled when he caught Ethan alone in the barn doing the morning chores early the next day.

Noah had been hoping to see Paula again since the night at the club when, after professing his feelings for her, he strode away and hitchhiked back to the ranch. It had irked him to see Ethan and Paula together in the cottage. Noah had run into Paula at the feed store in town and they talked casually at first, then a little deeper about their feelings.

Paula admitted she had been too hung up on Ethan to even notice Noah, but since their conversation on the front steps of the nightclub, she hadn't been able to get him off her mind. Noah was hopeful Paula would start noticing him now, but wasn't about to push it. She had to come to that conclusion on her own. The casual meeting established some neutral ground upon which to move forward, where ever forward might lead.

When Noah saw Paula climb out of the car the evening before, he had hoped she was coming to see him. He was about to intercept her in the driveway, ask her out on a proper date, but Paula went straight to the cottage to see Ethan. Spying from across the driveway, Noah could see them talking. Their interaction played like a movie through the picture window, and when the two figures embraced, he couldn't watch another minute more.

Noah went to the bunkhouse he shared with his twin, hoping Paula would come to see him and have a good explanation for her encounter with Ethan. When he saw Paula and Ethan walking to the main house, his heart turned to stone. Noah needed to get out of this triangle of pain once and for all. Far away wasn't even far enough.

"I'm going to tell the Baldwins I'm quitting. Things are quiet, and you and Ethan can handle the work." Noah explained when Tad found him packing his things.

"You should talk to Ethan first." Tad had advised, but that hadn't convinced Noah.

"Hmm… I don't think so." Noah had lost a little faith in his brother's wisdom as of late when it was Tad who recommended his brother tell Paula how he felt. That advice, when followed, had brought Noah more pain, along with an uncomfortable vulnerability Noah had never expected.

Tad's relentlessness pushed through his brother's resolve to leave, and Noah promised to settle things with Ethan in the morning. Morning came and Noah was seeing his promise through.

"Paula wanted to talk to me," Ethan answered Noah's question carefully, sensing the tension in his friend's voice.

"Talk?" Noah hissed. "About what?"

"Nothing that concerns you." Ethan continued to move the recently delivered bags of manna for the foals from the palate upon which they sat and into the feed room. He felt his conversation with Paula was a private matter and nothing Noah, who had violated their privacy before, needed to know.

"I think you don't recognize what concerns whom. What I need to know is…?" Noah hesitated.

"Not that you deserve answers to questions regarding myself and Paula, Noah, but get to the point. What do you want to know? I ain't got all day and these bags of feed will not move themselves." Ethan would not tip-toe around his friend any longer.

“I’ll tell you something you don’t know. I’m leaving this place.” Noah sensed the change in energy.

“So go,” Ethan cut in sharply.

“You would like that, wouldn’t you? Then Paula would have nobody to turn to. You’d go on pushing her around like a dirty ol’rag, punishing her and destroying her spirit.”

“Why don’t you stop with the unfounded accusations? What about how you treat her? If you were concerned about Paula, you would have never…?” Ethan lost his desire to air the laundry and concentrated on ignoring Noah’s false allegations of mistreatment. “Besides, didn’t you say you are going? The door’s that way.”

“Oh, I’m leaving alright, but not before I get a few things out of my system.” Noah was finding strength he didn’t know he had to confront his adversary. “I need to know. Did anything happen between you and Paula last night?”

Noah had inadvertently stomped on Ethan’s last ounce of restraint, the anger, hurt and betrayal he thought he had put behind him came rushing forth. The actions Noah had taken in sleeping with Ethan’s fiancée might as well have just happened based on Ethan’s current feelings.

“I don’t owe you an answer to that question. It’s none of your business. Why does it matter anyway whether Paula and I have relations? You didn’t mind having relations with her when she was my fiancée.” Ethan lashed out.

Noah’s face turned crimson. He got as close to Ethan’s face as he could without touching. “You bastard. How dare you speak about Paula that way? You make her sound like some kind of floosy.”

“You certainly treated her like one.” Ethan did not back down as Noah’s hot breath hit him squarely. Noah didn’t back down, either.

Face to face, in a dual where neither combatant wanted to make the first move, the two men stayed within inches of each other. Ethan thought of how easily he could reach up and take hold of Noah’s throat and squeeze until his anger dissipated. Only then would he feel he could be even with the man who had been his boyhood best friend but had betrayed him in the worst way.

Noah’s energy waned. He moved away first and seemed to shrink back, vulnerable and shaking. “How did we get here?” Noah’s hurt seeped around the edges of his anger, leaving him exposed. “How did it come to this?”

"You committed one of the most egregious of acts a man can do to another." Ethan softened a little.

"I am not proud of what I did. My actions hurt you, Paula, and everyone. I didn't mean for it to happen." Noah bowed his head.

"You make it seem like an accident. How do you explain an accident when it happened on more than one occasion? You can't accidentally sleep with another man's girl, Noah. You allowed this to happen." Ethan looked at the guy he had known all his life, the person he hated for the transgressions and the subsequent insults and wise cracks Ethan had had to endure since their false peace treaty. But Noah, in his shrunken, lovelorn state, didn't seem worthy of any more of Ethan's energy. Ethan could feel himself release all emotions. Pity took the place of rage. Mercy was what Ethan offered today. He turned away knowing Noah could no more answer the questions than explain anything else when it came to Paula.

"I gotta go…" Noah's words trailed behind him as he fled through the barn door.

"What are you doing?" It surprised Tad to see Noah grabbing the duffel he had packed the night before. "Did you speak to Ethan?"

"I did." Noah slid the long zipper up, shoving in parts of clothing that tried to escape from the bag that used to carry his baseball and football equipment to high school and home.

"And…?"

"And I'm leaving." Noah was too anxious to explain the story to his brother.

"Will you at least talk to Ansel and Vida?" Tad pleaded.

"No more talk, Brother." Noah was building his autonomy. "You will tell them thank you for everything and I'll be in touch."

"What about Paula?"

Noah stopped the shoving and zipping, and looked out the window in thought. "When you see her, tell her I'm doing fine."

Noah swung the bag on his shoulder and stepped over the threshold of the bunkhouse. Head held high; he could feel dignity returning with each stride that took him away.

Tad stood frozen in shock, then hurried out after his brother. "Wait a minute," he yelled.

Noah slowly turned, wishing they didn't have to drag out this painful farewell.

Tad caught up and held out his hand. "Good luck, bro, and take care."

"See you 'round, man. I'll let you know where I land." Noah grabbed his brother's hand and shook it vigorously.

Tad pursed his lips and stepped forward, pulling his brother into a one-armed hug, then quickly stepped away.

Noah turned and walked down the driveway, away from the rising sun.

~****~

"You have a date with Mr. Woods?" Alisha repeated Miranda's confession. "Oh, that is just too weird. He was my high school teacher." Alisha was making files for new students coming into the program when she and Miranda began talking during their work time that morning. Miranda was following up, answering emails. Alisha usually did most of the talking, but today she was enjoying the fodder Miranda was providing for the grape vines.

"If I'd have known you would get such a shock, I would have never said a word," Miranda teased, not really minding her friend's amusement at her expense.

"So," Alisha fished for more information. "Are you attracted to older men? I guess Greyson Woods is not a terrible choice if you want that father-figure type."

"It's not a date, and though Mr. Woods is not unattractive, I already told you I am not looking for a mate." Miranda was direct, hoping to close the subject.

"Let me get this straight. I'm trying to nail down the facts." Alisha summed up what she knew so far. "You are unattached and having a non-date with my high-school teacher. You may be interested in dating Tad, and you claim Ethan is not attractive..." Alisha paused, resting her pencil on her lips.

"I never said Ethan isn't attractive," Miranda corrected, falling into Alisha's trap. "At the moment, Tad is just a friend. Greyson Woods is a potential client or donor, and that's that. I am simply not in the market for a man. I am too busy for anything more, including this conversation."

"So, you think Ethan is attractive?" Alisha asked. Maybe Miranda was interested in Ethan after all.

“I think this conversation is over.” Miranda was firm.

Alisha would not find out the answer today, and she didn’t pursue the subject. There would be time for the juicy tidbits to fall as they may, gossip-wise, and it would draw out the entertainment value.

Alisha’s quest for information had Miranda thinking again about the possibility of dating, specifically Tad. This was the second time Alisha had alluded to Tad and Miranda being a couple. Miranda tried to picture what that would look like. She thought about the two of them in some romantic restaurant, with candlelight, soft music, sipping a delicate glass of wine. Though it didn’t seem preposterous at first, she couldn’t imagine having a deep conversation with Tad.

As Miranda’s daydream continued, Tad morphed into Ethan, who was reaching across the table to touch her hand, his fingers gently caressing. The day dream evaporated into a memory of the kiss in the office. Miranda felt again the heat of Ethan’s nearness, the gentle yet demanding pressure of his lips. A shiver went up her spine. Miranda jumped to reality with the buzzing of her vibrating cell phone.

“This is Miranda Dunn,” she said, feeling the warmth of redness on her face as if caught in her wakeful musing. It was Tad calling.

“I was just thinking about you.” Miranda recognized his voice but was surprised Tad had her cell number. She grimaced and clamped her eyelids tight wishing she hadn’t mentioned what she was thinking. Alisha was watching and listening, trying to find out who Miranda was thinking about when she had observed her boss daydreaming.

“You were thinking of me?” Tad asked, like a child who got permission to go to the movies on a school night, and Miranda could only imagine the look on his face.

Again, Miranda squeezed her eyelids shut and struck herself lightly and repeatedly on the forehead, in a ‘kill-me-now’ gesture. She was grateful Alisha could only hear one side of the phone conversation. “What can I do for you?” Miranda was careful not to mention the name of the caller for the primed ears of her co-worker.

“I wanted to invite you out to dinner. Can I pick you up at six?”

“I’m so sorry I can’t make dinner plans with you. I have other plans,” Miranda replied.

“Of course,” Tad said.

"But I'll see you tomorrow. I'll be moving in tomorrow afternoon." Miranda hoped she didn't sound insulting to Tad by patronizing him, but to her surprise and relief, it worked.

"Okay, so, I'll be thinking about you until tomorrow?" Tad perked up.

"Um-bye," Miranda ended the conversation.

"Two invitations on the same day, my aren't we popular?" Alisha guessed the context of the conversation and couldn't resist teasing. Based on what Miranda had said, Alisha also surmised that the call was from someone at the ranch.

"You have a mean streak, don't you?" Miranda could tell Alisha was a jokester and liked to solve mysteries. She was glad Alisha wasn't focusing on Miranda's day dreaming right before the phone.

The two women fell back to work. Miranda unclenched her nerves, grateful the conversation seemed closed. The day went by quickly, and without any further gossip. Miranda began to relax as she looked forward to her evening plans. She knew dinner with Greyson Woods would be drama-free.

Chapter 26

"Good morning, Mrs. Arthur," Miranda handed her motel room key over the counter to the older woman. "Thank you for everything." Today was the day Miranda was to move to the Alma Soñada.

Her dinner with Greyson Woods the previous evening was a delightful way to spend the last night. Greyson, who had insisted they address each other by first names, had so many interesting tales to tell of his adventures traveling during summer breaks from teaching. He had traveled to such exotic places as India and China, and his stories had mesmerized Miranda.

The evening had progressed and, as promised, Miranda told Greyson about CETO and the work she had done with them since she was a teen. She then explained how she started her own non-profit that brought together therapists and professionals to form equine therapy programs on a smaller scale. The intimate nature of Miranda's business model promised to make the programs more malleable than the general programs in which some patients fell through the cracks. By narrowing the brushstroke, the unique and individual needs of each client were considered.

Greyson had listened with genuine interest, and then, toward the end of the meal, he announced he had an agenda. His mom had recently passed away and had left a sizable trust. Greyson explained how he had started a college scholarship program for deserving students in her name and now wanted to expand his philanthropy. His mother loved horses, had been an accomplished rider among her peers. Greyson thought his mother would have been happy to give to such a good cause. Greyson's generosity and his unsolicited offer humbled Miranda.

"I am doing this of my volition, and with complete confidence." Greyson had walked Miranda to her car, shook her hand, and she was on her way.

All the generosity Miranda was receiving, most recently from Greyson Woods, was overwhelming. As she packed her vehicle with her belongings for the move to the ranch, Miranda couldn't hide the elation. Everything seemed to fall into place nicely.

And to top it off, Miranda said to herself as she drove to the ranch that morning, *another beautiful sunny day.* Miranda sang out loud with the tune playing on the radio.

~****~

"I'm sure going to miss Noah," Vida said at breakfast the morning after Noah's departure with the emotion one would expect from a mother missing her child, "I hope he is okay. Tad, did you call your parents? Maybe he went there."

Vida and Ansel were both still shocked at Noah's leaving the ranch the day before, with no explanation other than a brief message from his brother. Then Ethan took off on horseback as he often did, but there had been no preparations or discussions leading up to it this time. The two cowboys skipping town on the same day could have been a coincidence, but even after they interrogated Tad for more information, the two parental figures were not satisfied.

Ansel found it nearly impossible to keep Vida from worrying about the inexplicably disappearing cowboys. Ansel told his wife Ethan had gone to the cabin in the high country to check on the cattle, though he wasn't certain of that. It was not unusual for any of the men that worked the ranch to spend time away while tending to the grazing stock.

Tad had no update on his brother' whereabouts to comfort Vida. He was having enough trouble of his own with his brother's absence. The twins had never been apart for an extended period like this separation promised to be. That Ethan was also gone would have been a blessing for Tad regarding Miranda if it hadn't meant more work for him. It cut like a two-edged knife that Tad would have Miranda to himself, but had triple the chores with both his brother and Ethan gone.

"No sense worrying about things that are out of our hands." Ansel stood up from the breakfast table, rubbed his hands together and declared, "Thank you, my beautiful wife, for the delicious and nutritious breakfast. I'm going to get some work done before Randi comes."

Vida acknowledged her husband's compliment and volunteered to pick up some extra chores. With both Ethan and Noah away, there would be more work for the senior Baldwin and he was still not 100% recovered from his bout with diverticulitis. With more work falling on Ansel's shoulders, too, it would be impossible for Vida to insist he follow doctor's orders to take it easy, but he couldn't stop her from helping.

As if reading Vida's mind, Tad picked up on her concerned expression. "I'm on it, Vida. You needn't worry about Ansel. I'll see to it he doesn't do too much. We will get through this like always."

"Thank you, dear," Vida said with two-part relief; she didn't need to explain to Tad how much they needed him and she hadn't had to ask for his extra efforts. "You are my hero."

"Of course." Tad's offer was genuine, but his enthusiasm was forced.

Tad followed Ansel out to start the chores, feeling the weight of the work plus the responsibility of keeping track of his boss who shouldn't overdo it. What a mess this all had turned out to be. Thinking about when he and his brother were kids, Tad remembered how Noah had always come to his older by twelve minutes brother for advice on everything. Noah would ask, should I play basketball or baseball? Should I take Biology or woodshop class? Should we go to the movies or to the club? Tad had given his brother advice, for decisions large and small, and Noah always took it. Tad had never realized how much of Noah's decisions were based solely on his advice.

Somewhere along the line, the decisions Noah left up to his brother became more important. In the advice he gave to his brother regarding Paula, Tad misjudged Noah's feelings for Paula. Tad had discouraged Noah from the beginning, thinking broadly of the friendships.

Now, Tad thought, the way things had turned out, it was all messed up, and he wished he'd never gotten in the middle. From coaching his brother about his love life, to running interference between the Noah and Ethan when Paula became the wedge, Tad had been involved in too many aspects of everyone else's lives. His attempts to keep everyone together peacefully resulted in the group of once best friends torn apart. Tad's efforts were for naught.

"A fat lot of good it did me," Tad exclaimed, as he spat and tossed forkfuls of manure from Magic's extra-large stall. "All I got is triple the chores."

"Tad?"

Tad stopped talking to himself when he heard Randi's voice.

"Oh, here you are." Miranda came into the barn and saw Tad standing with his weight on the handle of the pitchfork like it was propping him up. "Good morning."

"I didn't hear you drive up. Did you just get here?" Tad leaned the tool up against the stall wall and as he walked toward Randi, he couldn't help staring at her shapely figure. Dressed in jeans, a blouse and boots, her clothing was appropriate. Tad thought Randi had a way of making the simplest of attire look sexy.

"I've been here for about ten minutes." Miranda felt embarrassed by Tad's uninhibited gaze.

"Do you need help to get settled in?" Tad offered.

"No, I don't have a lot to unpack. I came to help you out here."

"Don't be silly, this is hard work." Tad was trying to show Randi he valued men doing men's work.

"Why don't you tell me what needs to be done, and if I can't handle it, I will tell you." Miranda grabbed a rake and waited for direction.

Tad showed his displeasure with a grunt. He didn't like such an independent woman. He delegated undemanding jobs he believed would satisfy Randi, but though she didn't want to press the issue, she saw through his manipulative ploy to protect his own ego. The two worked side by side.

Miranda was no stranger to the work required to keep a barn clean and the horses comfortable. After cleaning the stalls, they straightened up the tack room, then swept the breezeway. Tad took Miranda outside to help with turnouts. First to be led out from the paddocks were the three fillies Ethan wouldn't be there to exercise.

When Miranda asked about Ethan, Tad stuck to the story Ansel had relayed about him being up in the summer valley checking on the herd. Miranda watched the three young horses frolic and play in the liberating freedom of the pasture and wondered when Ethan would return and why he would leave during their training.

"It's a shame all the time lost if the horses don't get worked consistently," Tad commented as he and Randi cleaned the paddocks.

Miranda noticed Tad was sucking on the wad in his cheek but held back her disgust. She thought it strange. Tad's comment wasn't entirely accurate. Young horses rarely regressed during lapses in training. They never forgot what they had learned, they just didn't progress. Tad's statement also made

Miranda suspicious of Ethan's absence. It seemed more likely to have been unplanned, and she hoped all was well with the cattle herd.

Tad continued, "I could keep the horses in training, but Ansel won't let me. I am just as good a rider as Ethan." Tad bragged with a touch of bitterness.

Miranda didn't respond when she detected the ill feelings and wondered about the reason Tad expressed animosity toward Ethan, who was supposed to be his friend.

"All done with this one." Tad announced when he picked up the last pile of manure in the paddock.

"Time flies when you're having fun." Miranda hadn't minded the job; it was a good workout.

"I made it clear you didn't have to help." Tad decided Miranda was being sarcastic. Perhaps she was unhappy she'd volunteered. Before she could respond otherwise, Tad lifted his nose to the air. "It's lunchtime. Beef pot pies, cucumber salad, and chocolate chips cookie bars for dessert."

"You can tell all that with your sense of smell?"

"Nah," Tad teased, and motioned for Miranda to walk with him, "I peeked this morning during breakfast and saw the fixin's."

"Better loose the chew," Miranda advised. She noticed Tad's cheek was less pouchy, but she could tell he was still chewing, even though he spat when he thought she wasn't looking. Tad ducked around the corner and Miranda continued to the house.

"It's such a nice day. We thought we'd eat out here." Ansel was sitting at the table on the veranda. Miranda pulled out a chair and Ansel asked her, "So, how do you like mucking up after horses?"

"It's not so bad. If there is one thing you can count on, its where there are horses, there will be poop," Miranda laughed.

"Try doing it day after day." Tad huffed when he joined the two at the table. Holding a bottle of Fanta, he poured the orange drink into the glasses, then sat down beside Miranda. Tad wanted it to be known mucking horse poop wasn't his favorite thing.

Miranda didn't bother telling Tad she had racked up many consecutive days of stall mucking at barns that housed dozens of horses. If they did the math, the time they had each spent cleaning up after horses was probably comparable.

After lunch, and after Miranda had let Tad carry a few things in from the car, Ansel suggested they all give Randi a little time to get settled in the guest house.

"The chicken yard fence needs mending, the tractor needs tending. There is much still to do before sundown," Ansel said, then laughed. "Hey, that sounded like the words to a country song."

Though Tad did not appreciate the orders or Ansel's sense of humor, he reluctantly obeyed, and left Miranda alone to unpack. How was he supposed to spend time with Randi when his boss kept piling on the work?

Relieved to be left to her own devices, Miranda began moving in. Finding her new accommodations to be more than adequate, the guest house was much larger than the little hotel room she had been in for the better part of a week. There was a practical kitchen, a roomy living area, and one full bedroom, as well as an equally sized open-floor space upstairs.

There was a phone line running from the wall into the loft and to Miranda's relief, it was live and had internet connectivity. Though dial-up was not the latest and greatest in technology, it thrilled Miranda to have the line. The loft, which made a nice home-office space, was where she immediately began setting up her work space using the antique vanity as a desk. Her laptop whispered and hummed the usual start-up noises.

First Miranda caught herself up on emails, then she drafted a letter to send to her best friend, Amanda Ferris, letting her and the family know her new address. The Ferris family were eager to know all the news about Miranda's adventures out west, and in the brief phone call she had made when she first arrived, Miranda had promised a long letter and pictures would be forthcoming.

Miranda longed for the camaraderie of her soul sister and surrogate family. She needed someone she could trust to talk to; she had things she needed to confide, and it was nothing she wanted to share with her new friends and partners. Miranda really hoped Amanda could come out to visit soon. By the time Miranda finished the email and pressed send, she noticed the time. Finishing the unpacking quickly, it was time to get cleaned up for dinner after her morning chores left her less than fresh.

Chapter 27

The Baldwins had given Miranda a standing invitation to take meals with the family, leaving her the option to use the kitchen in the cottage as she pleased for meals on her own. Having dinner with people was the obvious choice, and Miranda wanted to go to the main house in time to help Vida prepare the meal. As Miranda stepped out of the shower, she decided she would dress up a little. It would present a respectful gesture, and perhaps Ethan will have returned from the mountains.

"That would liven things up at the dinner table," Miranda said to herself. She took extra care in getting ready; eye make-up, curled hair secured on each side with pearl combs, a simple a-line wrap around dress with bell sleeves in a deep red floral print, and sandals. Looking for her sweater, Miranda decided not to waste too much time trying to find it.

The coolness of late afternoon was creeping in, but she only had to go across the driveway. The lightweight fabric of the dress would provide little protection from the elements, but after dinner, if the need arose, Miranda could borrow something from the plethora of outdoor wear in the mudroom off the kitchen if she needed to.

Tad had been anxiously hoping Miranda would show up at the main house for dinner. Mealtimes were quiet since Paula, Noah and Ethan were away. Tad felt like a third wheel, but for tonight there was an alternative if Miranda showed. Tad had more on his mind than eating, and his having gotten cleaned up and wearing his Sunday clothes was the first clue.

Vida had kept Tad busy chopping vegetables for the stir-fry, and when she finished that, she had him setting the table. He grumbled a little at the instructions Vida threw over her shoulder. Tad wasn't familiar with the tasks, but he hoped Miranda would soon appear for mealtime and the evening could begin. In his opinion, this evening was a double date. Finally, when dinner was ready, and Tad was about to burst with trepidation, Randi might not show. There was a soft knock at the door.

"Come on in, Randi," Ansel said. Tad's hovering behavior annoyed him and Ansel was relieved that, with Randi's arrival, the mealtime could progress. "You don't have to knock."

Miranda came in cheerfully and with a respectful apology. "I hope I didn't keep you all waiting. I had intended to arrive early, but time got away from me."

Vida was placing a bowl of steamed rice on the kitchen table. "We were just sitting down. Come. Let's eat."

"It all smells wonderful." Miranda lifted her chin and breathed in the sweet savory aroma of deliciously seasoned beef strips that were simmering among vegetables in a ginger tahini sauce in the wok on the stove.

While Miranda was complimenting the chef, she was unaware of Tad's reaction when she entered the room, but Ansel noticed. To him, Tad looked like a dog expecting a treat, and by the direction of his drooling stare, Randi was on the menu.

Tad lost his breath, watching Randi come into the room and devoured her beauty. He loved the way her cotton dress lightly hugged her curves, and he decided she had dressed that way for him alone. Tad held a chair for Randi and breathed again when she sank gracefully on to the seat.

"Vida, you did it again. You are a wonderful chef. The meals you prepare can take us around the world. Asian is one of my favorite foods, and this is the best I have ever tasted," Miranda said, after everyone had fully enjoyed their plate full of home cooked goodness.

"Thank you for the compliment. I have gotten no complaints so far," Vida said, then winked at her husband.

It warmed Miranda's soul to see the love, the obvious connection between Ansel and Vida. She hoped she would have what they had, and it surprised her that her next thought was of Ethan. Miranda didn't want to admit it had disappointed her when she first arrived and, after taking a quick count of the settings, she realized Ethan would not be there for dinner.

Miranda thought it was odd that Ethan was away. It seemed irresponsible of him. In her opinion, he broke his commitment when he left high and dry the three fillies in the middle of training, not to mention all the other duties.

Miranda also noticed no one seemed concerned about Ethan's absence. Apparently, this was not unusual. Everyone seemed to take it in stride.

"Dinner was superb, Vida." Miranda voiced her appreciation for the meal served family style. The group had lingered, savoring the food and the atmosphere, and then they all chipped in with the clean-up. It was time for Miranda to head out. "It's been a busy day. I'll be making my way back now. G'nite, all."

"Goodnight, Randi. We wish you a peaceful rest for your first night here on the ranch," Vida said.

Tad awkwardly offered an invitation to walk Miranda home, but the front door to her new living quarters was less than fifty feet away. Even more awkward was when they got to her doorstep and Tad asked permission to kiss her, but before she could even answer, she got not an innocent peck on the cheek, but on the lips.

Without consent, Tad had driven in for a juicy kiss, tongue and all. He may or may not have been a good kisser. Miranda, having been taken by surprise, wasn't about to make an assessment. As soon as her mouth was free, Miranda spoke a hurried good night, then slipped through her door, closing it quickly behind her. She knew without a doubt, while wiping saliva off her lips, she would have a talk with Tad tomorrow.

~****~

Ethan had been gone for two nights now, and he knew he could stay only one extra night without compromising his obligations at home. He almost envied Noah the total freedom to up and leave, but he knew the minute he'd leave he'd want to be back. The ranch was an anchor of security not a weight that brought him down.

The time spent in the high country always gave him what he needed. His parents were understanding, within reason, about his need to escape. This behavior was something he had done since he was a child, though as an adult the time away grew in distance and in duration.

Ethan had found Carmen's cabin to be as welcoming as always. Everything was in its place since the last time he had found sanctuary from life's strife within the four rustic walls. Ethan spent his time looking in on the herds, checking fences, and when he wasn't foraging for edible flora; berries, herbs, root vegetables. He was reflecting on life.

Among the many topics that mulled around during this down time was the situation between himself and Paula and Noah. Ethan realized what a waste of time it had been to dwell on the past. His holding on to the wrongs and not forgiving his best friends for their trespasses was only hurting himself. All the anger and drama were only impeding the things that really mattered; love of family and friends and the simpler things in life. Actively pondering about Noah and Paula, visualizing their happiness whether they end up together or on some other path, assisted Ethan in building a better outlook for his own future.

Ethan also thought about Tad with guilt that it had been his and Noah's absurd fight that had pushed Noah into leaving. Ethan was sorry Noah was gone. He knew the separation must be difficult for the brothers. Considering Tad's feelings, too, Ethan hoped he and Noah could one day really and truthfully put the past away, for everyone's sake.

The time alone at the camp with no one else but his horse and the cows to talk to had also cleared Ethan's thoughts on Miranda. He solidly admitted there was an attraction, and he figured he was not mistaken that it was mutual. He could understand if, given the circumstances of their interactions, Miranda wanted nothing to do with him other than what might be necessary. Ethan hoped that once he explained, and apologized completely, maybe with time, Miranda would come around.

Ethan planned to circle the herd another time tomorrow morning for one last visual before heading back down the mountain. Before turning in for the night, Ethan stepped outside the cabin door to gather enough wood to stockpile for the next stay. He took a last glance at Heart to make sure the gelding was still securely staked and happily munching on grass, then settled in for a good night's sleep.

Upon waking early the next day, Ethan made good on his plan. Traversing the valley floor, the cattle were spread, peacefully grazing. Ethan rode through the shadow of the eastern slope with the rising sun still tucked behind the mountain. The rays that broke over the ridge were bouncing off the western slope, creating a picture beyond words. The gently tapering valley floor was covered with wild flowers that bloomed later at the higher elevations.

Running steady and clear, the river meandered past the aspen stands, eventually feeding into a large pond at the southernmost point where an outcropping of granite formed a natural dam. The water then spilled over the rocks in a picturesque fall that begged to be played in on warm summer afternoons. After the falls, the valley dropped off sharply, and the terrain became difficult for a human and impossible for a horse to traverse.

As Ethan guided Heart through the herd from small bunch to small bunch. The calves ran to their mothers, but the cows, with their instinctive wisdom, knew one man on a horse was not a reason to get excited and barely raised their heads up from the rich grass. Ethan made his way in a large zig-zagging pattern and an hour later, he and Heart were ascending the trail that had brought them in.

When he reached the rim, Ethan stopped and turned for one last look. The gentle breezes rising with the warming air ruffled Heart's forelock and played with Ethan's neckline curls as they both watched the scene below. It was moments like this that reminded Ethan of how precious was life and how much was to be lost by the encroaching march of development. Reluctantly, Ethan turned around, leaving the serenity and facing the reality of changes that were all part of life.

Chapter 28

Tad was feeling slightly used, what with the responsibility of chores falling mostly on his shoulders. He was anxious that he hadn't spent a moment alone with Randi for over twenty-four hours. Adding to his frustrations, this morning at breakfast, Randi hadn't given him any attention, and there was no proper occasion for talking about their kiss. He hadn't been able to stop thinking about her and wondered if she thought of him, too.

Miranda had stayed in the house with Ansel and Vida all morning and after lunch, Ansel and Miranda saddled up Winston and Magic and went for a ride. It had killed Tad to be stuck doing work when all along he had only wanted to ride off with Randi himself. Tad was running out of time. Ethan could come back home soon. Ansel and Vida expected he'd be back today. Whether Ethan came home today, tomorrow was Tad's day off and other than the most essential chores, he intended to have his time with Randi.

Tad had seen Ansel and Randi return from their afternoon ride a while before he finished up with the last of the day's work and, with energy anew, he got cleaned up and dressed for dinner. Tad aimed to salvage the little time left in the day to focus on Randi. He was looking forward to tonight, and he was determined to be open and honest without shyness or reserve. He resolved to eat some good food and then, with Randi, he would have whatever might be available for dessert.

"We have a surprise, and a reason to celebrate. Randi and I have an announcement," Ansel proclaimed when Tad, Miranda, and Vida had all sat down to eat dinner.

"Enough with the drama. What is the surprise?" Vida asked.

"Yeah, Ansel, spill." Tad could tell it was good news by the way Randi was smiling.

"I bought Winston." Miranda could not contain her excitement.

“You bought Winston?” Vida looked at Miranda. “Why would she have to buy him?” Vida turned her head to face Ansel. “Randi, you can have the use of our stock anytime.”

“What’s the big deal? A horse is a horse.” Tad couldn’t understand the hype.

“I have always had horses available whenever I wanted to ride. There has never been a time in my life since Gordon adopted me that there weren’t horses, but I never had one of my own. It feels right to call Winston mine. After our wild ride and the way we took care of each other, we just seem to fit. We are a team,” Miranda explained to Tad and Vida the same things she had said to Ansel on their trail ride that afternoon.

“That seems logical, Randi. I am glad you and Winston found such a connection. Winston is a superb horse. Congratulations,” Vida said with complete understanding.

Tad still didn’t get it. He was a cowboy, just a rider, and to him, a horse was a tool. Randi wasn’t a cowboy. What did she need with a horse? When she rode for pleasure, she had the choice to take any horse on the ranch. His mind switched gears as he recognized the opportunity for time alone with his love interest. “Randi, how would you like me to take you on a trail ride to the summit? You can have another excuse to connect with your horse,” and me, Tad added in his head.

“Maybe not up to the peak, but a ride around the meadow?” Miranda answered. “I have a lot of work to do at the office, but if I get back from town in time, a quick ride sounds nice.” Miranda didn’t want to give Tad any false signals, but a brief ride would give her an opportunity to set things straight and she could avoid any more awkward good night kissing. She wanted to make it clear to him, she and Tad were just friends.

Ansel noted the exchange and wished Randi hadn’t been so quick to accept the invitation. He and Vida had noticed Tad’s attempts to engage Randi at a personal level. They had talked about it and concluded there were times it appeared to make Randi uncomfortable.

“A short trail ride? I’ll take it.” Tad jumped on the chance. “It’s a date.”

“Not a date,” Miranda corrected, but Tad hadn’t heard. He was busy celebrating.

Ansel felt the need to say something. Tad’s annoying persistence was making everyone uncomfortable. Though it probably wasn’t his place, Ansel would have a chat with Tad and bring up the subject without too much suspicion. Ansel hoped he could instill in Tad the need to treat Randi with respect, get the guy to calm down some.

After dinner, Miranda helped Vida in the kitchen while Ansel and Tad discussed the ranch work coming up on the agenda. When the kitchen was back to perfect order, Miranda thanked Vida and Ansel, "Good night," she said to the group.

"I'll walk you home," Tad pounced.

"I think she can find her way, Tad," Ansel advised.

Miranda went out into the cool evening air after saying goodnight to everyone, and despite Ansel's comment, Tad followed her.

Ansel and Vida watched the two younger folks head out, then exchanged glances.

"Tad is sure smitten with Randi," Vida spoke first. "What do you think about it?"

"Do you think it's okay?" Ansel asked.

"It is what it is. As always, we have to let it play out."

"I remember being that age, and I know what Tad has on his mind," Ansel reasoned. "I know little about Randi's experiences, but I suspect she doesn't take to men pawing and mauling her for attention."

"I can see your point of view. You are a good papa-bear, but let's not worry. Randi seems like she can take care of herself quite well."

"Okay, my dear. But let's keep an eye on things."

The couple retired to the comfort of the family room. Sitting together on the sofa, Ansel snuggled his wife in to lean on him and turned on the TV.

"Ethan comes home tomorrow, and everything on the ranch will be back to balance again. You'll see." Vida switched off the TV and moved in closer to her husband.

Ansel smiled when he realized his wife's intentions and turned off the lamp above his head. He trusted Vida's intuition completely about the kids. It was time to forget about other people for a while and focus on each other. Their time alone in the big ranch house was limited. The moon shone through the full framed window and filled the room with romantic shadows as Ansel and Vida replenished their bond of intimacy.

~****~

"Isn't it a beautiful night?" Tad gazed at the sky as he hurried to catch up with Miranda.

"Oh," It surprised Miranda that Tad had followed her. Before she could react further, Tad took hold of her arm and pulled her in for a kiss.

Miranda strait-armed his attempt with a hand on his chest. "We need to talk." Miranda had no chance to say another word as Tad's strength buckled her arm at the elbow, his lips closed in.

Knowing she could not out power him, Miranda waited for the kiss to end. Tad finally released her and whispered, "I know what you are going to say, and I agree. Things are moving fast. I feel it, too, but I like it."

"That's not even close, Tad," Miranda began, but stopped when up from the meadow gate came Ethan riding Heart.

"What the heck…?" Tad exclaimed. "Ethan?"

Using Tad's startled lapse of attention to her advantage, Miranda escaped through her own doorway. Mad at Tad's rudeness, frustrated she hadn't the chance to put him in his place, it also embarrassed Miranda at what the situation must have looked like to Ethan as he rode up in the darkness. Miranda bid her hasty retreat, leaving the two cowboys outside.

Ethan couldn't be sure what he saw. If his time alone on this last trip to the high country had taught him anything, it was not to jump to conclusions, but looking at Tad's triumphant face was a lot to bear.

"You're back late." Tad stated the obvious and didn't hide the irritation Ethan's return caused.

Ethan turned his horse to walk past Tad and up to the barn.

"Do you need some help?" Tad followed Ethan.

"No, thanks, but I could use the company." Ethan had been alone for three days.

Tad began excitedly to tell all about his and Miranda's growing relationship, even though Ethan hadn't asked. As Tad spoke, Ethan busied himself in Heart's stall, giving the horse extra care and a decent dinner for the hard work the little quarter horse had done. It was painful, but Ethan listened to Tad with postured interest, trying to decide if there was anything more than friendship going on. He would concede if it seemed Miranda had made her choice.

"Any news from your brother?" Ethan changed the subject after he felt he'd listened to enough about Miranda.

"Not yet. I left a message with the folks letting them know he might come their way, but haven't heard."

"Has anyone heard from Paula?"

"Why?" Tad bristled, feeling sympathetic to his brother's departure knowing the direct link to the love triangle.

Ethan looked up into the corner of the barn as if studying the darkness and then said, "Paula is like my little sister, Tad. I care about her. Your brother's absence may have come as a surprise to Paula. Someone should just check in with her, at the least." Ethan stepped out, ending the conversation there, and headed to the house for a bite to eat, a shower, and then a good night's sleep in a soft, warm bed.

Chapter 29

Ethan had gone to town right after breakfast the next day to get some dietary supplements for his father. After returning home late the day before, he would have preferred staying at the ranch. Ansel offered the job to Tad, thinking maybe the cowboy would like a trip to town for a break from the grind. It would have been an undemanding job, but Tad turned it down.

Vida had placed her product order from Walgreens online. The chain store was another sign of corporate encroachment upon Rambletap Springs. Ethan would have much preferred using the Rexall. Frequenting the family-owned old-fashioned pharmacy was like visiting friends.

The Rexall had survived the divesting process when, in the 1970s, the Rexall company folded under the incessant attacks by corporate discount chains, and had remained an independent business, Goodman's Goods. The Goodman family closed their operation doors for the final time two years ago.

As he entered the bright new store, Ethan was assaulted by piped in music. There was no smiling face behind the counter to greet him, only kiosks of self-checkout machines.

Ethan made his way to the back of the store trying to ignore the dizzying effect of the overabundance of products on the shelves. At Goodman's, there wasn't a million choices of shampoo, lotions or toothpaste, but the store always had what was needed.

Ethan inspected the contents of Vida's remote order to verify it was all there. "Psyllium?" he asked the pharmacy tech. "For people? I'm gonna have to give my Pops a hard time about this."

It struck him funny his dad would use the same ingredient they frequently gave to their equine stock when they showed signs of colic. Ethan found it amusing, but the cashier wasn't in on the joke. Ethan grabbed the bag of goods and exited, leaving the clerk wondering why Ethan was laughing.

While walking to his truck, Ethan was surprised to see Noah. And with Noah was Paula. For a moment, the three friends were silent, but Noah broke first, erasing any trace of awkwardness. Without being asked, Noah explained he had gone to Helena to visit his parents and while he was there, he and Paula talked for hours by phone. Noah had a lot of thinking to do. He and Paula worked it out and agreed to date.

Over the next few days, and many conversations later, they decided they didn't want to date. Noah couldn't wait any longer. He agreed to return to Rambletap Springs only if Paula would accept an engagement ring. She had not only agreed, but upped the ante. They met at the courthouse where they got a license. They were man and wife. Ethan was the first to congratulate them.

"I got a job at Willoughby's Feed and Grain. Lord knows I spend so much time there, anyway," Noah said, nervously reading Ethan's response to the news.

"And I'll be starting my job at the bridal shop," Paula added. "We are going to live here in town." As Paula spoke, she never took her eyes off her betrothed.

"Can I buy you guys a cup of coffee? Let's celebrate," Ethan offered. It pleased him to hear his friends were happy. Despite their rocky past, Ethan wanted to show both Paula and Noah there were no more hard feelings.

Over coffee, the three friends chatted, touching on the past only long enough to put it to rest. They talked about the future. Noah offered to be available to help at the ranch any time the Baldwins needed an extra hand, and Paula confessed she'd be visiting as often as she could manage. After all, they were family.

"Vida will insist there be a standing invitation to dinner," Ethan felt comfortable speaking on his mother's behalf. He knew his mother all too well.

"That means a lot to us." Noah beamed at his bride with pride. "Right, honey?"

"I am so happy for you two. I really mean it." Ethan felt his words. "I wish you the best."

"Thanks, man." Noah shook Ethan's hand with visible relief as the negativity that had separated them for too long disappeared.

"Yes, thanks, Ethan." Paula gave him a sisterly hug.

"And remember, Noah," Ethan said as the group finished their beverages, "when you tire of working in town, you will always have a permanent job waiting for you at the Alma Soñada."

Paula winked at Ethan, thanking him with her eyes. "If the feed store idea doesn't pan out, Noah can commute." Paula didn't want her desire to live in town to prevent her new husband from pursuing the work that was truly in his heart.

"We will work it all out later, darling." Noah kissed Paula's forehead, touched by her considerate idea. "First, we need a honeymoon."

Ethan left the newlyweds on that note with a wave and a nod. "Go on now and have a great time. You two deserve it."

The news that Noah was back in town and of the marriage was a relief to Vida and Ansel, "All's well that ends well," Ansel had said, and Tad's response was positive with a hint of resentment, "Noah didn't even tell me a thing about this," he had exclaimed.

Tad hadn't dwelled on the subject too long as he began looking forward to his upcoming trail ride with Miranda later that afternoon.

~****~

As promised, Miranda found time to meet with Tad and, by mid-day, the two were riding across the meadow. It was comfortably warm, almost summer, and a perfect time to be outdoors. The stillness augmented the music from the birds chirping and bees humming. The very air even seemed to relax the tension in Miranda's tight neck and shoulder muscles. The rhythmic plunk-plunk of Winston's hooves played like a lullaby. Her thoughts drifted away skyward.

Miranda thought of how good Ethan had looked riding Winston in the arena the other day. In remembering, she saw again the smile on Ethan's face when he felt her watching and wondered if he knew how impressed she had been. Ethan had smiled the same way when Miranda watched him working the fillies.

Then Miranda remembered she hadn't been able to observe Ethan's face last night when he rode out of the darkness and came upon the awkward scene in the dimly lit driveway. Tad's unsolicited advances had placed them in an embarrassing position. Miranda resolved to set the record straight with Ethan as quickly as she could. But first she had to deal with Tad.

"Penny for your thoughts." Tad noticed Miranda's contemplative expression.

"Just enjoying the ride," Miranda lied, even though it was the perfect opening to say what she needed to say. Miranda decided telling Tad she didn't have romantic feelings for him would be better if done near the end of the outing.

"Over the next ridge, the one we climbed before, and at the crest is the trail that will bring us to the valley and Carmen's Camp." Tad wanted to engage in conversation and didn't want Randi wrapped up in her own thoughts the entire ride.

"Wait," Miranda said. "I agreed to a quick ride around the meadow. Why are we going to the ridge?"

"It's not too much farther. There is still plenty of daylight and I wanted to surprise you," Tad said, delighted in his cleverness. "I have vittles in my saddlebags. We can have a snack and be down before nightfall."

"That is not the arrangement we had." Miranda was about to turn Winston around.

"Are you angry with me?"

"I'm not happy."

Despite her better judgement, Miranda kept pace with her trail companion. The look of disappointment on Tad's face was irritating. Winston continued forward, and within minutes, Miranda resigned herself to a longer ride. It was a beautiful day, no rain in sight, and she wasn't sure when she would have the time in the near future to make the trip up.

"Fine, Tad. It's fine," Miranda acquiesced and committed to enjoying the rest of the afternoon.

Carmen's Camp was as lovely as Vida had described it and it hadn't taken them very long to get up there. The cabin was in excellent repair and Miranda stood for a while to admire the monument that had been erected with a brief history written to share with any passers-by. The sign let it be known the place was a treasure to be treated respectfully.

Tad offered Miranda to have a look inside while he secured the horses on a hitching post in front of the rustic log fence constructed in spilt-rail fashion.

As Miranda pulled the cord that switched the latch open and pushed in the door, a familiar scent that tickled her nostrils welcomed her. She recognized the smell of clean soap, the smell she quickly identified as the one she encountered when she literally ran into Ethan in the hallway after he had showered. As her eyes took in the cozy cabin scene of the table and two chairs next to the fireplace with a cast-iron cauldron hanging on a tri-pod that swung in and out of the flames like a hinge, Miranda imagined Ethan being there.

Her gaze moved around the room to the rocking chair on the other side of the hearth and then to the bed with a colorful quilt folded neatly at the foot and a lofty down blanket covering everything except the two pillows that overlapped each other on the tiny bed. Then Miranda caught sight of a small dresser with an antique pitcher and bowl, and hanging on a hook on the wall beside it was the source of the scent that begged Miranda to breathe deeper. There hung a towel Ethan, having been the most recent occupant, had probably used.

Miranda could easily see Ethan standing bare chested over the bowl full of clean water poured from the matching pitcher. She imagined his well-fitting Wrangler Jeans were once again unbuttoned on top, and the muscles on his back would have undoubtedly twitched and flexed as he bent forward to wash his face.

"What's going on? You gonna stay in here?" Tad poked his head in, his features undistinguishable because of the strong back-lighting.

"Just looking around. I'm coming out." Miranda moved toward the door and into the bright mid-day sun, leaving her secret vision behind in the shadows.

"You look like you saw a ghost," Tad said, as he tried to evaluate her expression. "The place has quite a history, but it ain't haunted."

Tad's mocking tone would make it easier to tell him the truth. Miranda was ready to tell Tad right here and now they were way too different. They weren't right for each other and she knew they could be nothing more than friends.

"We may as well rest up, take our time eating our late lunch and skip the trip to the rim after all." Tad was having a hard time connecting with Miranda. They had barely had a conversation, and he was getting frustrated. He changed the plans again to suit his agenda.

Tad unpacked the lunch he had put together; Vida's seasoned, roasted chicken, potato salad, fresh carrots and zucchini sticks, and for dessert, two apple tarts. There were also two apples, "One for Winston and one for Sonnet," Tad explained.

Miranda smiled at the sentiment. Tad liked to see this expression on her face and sat down on the blanket he had spread over the course meadow grass, inviting Miranda to join him. "What a glorious day!" he exclaimed.

Once Tad had finished eating, he laid back propping up his head with a bended elbow and stretching his legs in front of Miranda. His thigh was casually touching her knee, his boots were resting unbeknownst to him on the star-shaped petals of a bitterroot flower.

"I can see why you and Noah didn't go with your folks when they moved to the city. You are so lucky to appreciate what you have here." Miranda drank in the surrounding beauty, trying to ignore the bright pink flowers being crushed by Tad's clumsy boots.

"Oh, I consider myself very lucky, indeed." Tad took Miranda by the arm and pulled her toward his face.

Miranda resisted, but Tad was stronger. He rose to sitting, locking his lips on hers as she tried to pull away. Then he pushed her until she was the one reclining back.

Tad performed the task in one movement, all the while never ending the kiss, and Miranda would have been impressed if not for her distress at the situation. "Tad, s-s-stop!" Miranda stuttered into Tad's pressing lips.

Tad sighed and sat up. "This slowing down will not be easy, Randi. I really like you."

"Slowing down?" Miranda realized she was experiencing another misunderstanding. "Slowing down from what, Tad? We are not starting a relationship." Miranda saw the confusion immediately in Tad's eyes. "At least not a romantic one. I thought you understood. I am not looking for a boyfriend."

Tad couldn't believe his ears. Randi must feel what he was feeling. How could she not? Tad focused on the specks of pollen from the bent and broken flower that had stuck to the leather boots, trying to make sense of what he had just been told. The only conclusion he could come up with is Randi was just too busy right now. That had to be it. He would have to try harder to avoid putting any pressure on her until she was ready.

“We better get a move on.” Tad gathered the remnants of the lunch and shoved them carelessly into the saddlebags. “Might as well shoot for the ridge.”

The riders were soon back in the saddles and left Carmen’s Camp behind as they headed for the summit. The trail was a steady rise to the top. It became rocky, and the horses had to concentrate with every step. Soon, Miranda saw patches of snow in the shady spots under trees and bushes and as they climbed, the size of the patches grew bigger and more frequent until they were traversing large sections too big to go around.

This was the first time Miranda had ridden in the snow and you’d have thought it was Winston’s as well by the way he was handling it. With each patch they had to cross, Winston balked and sidestepped, trying not to step from the ground to the white stuff until Miranda, with steady hands and leg pressure, convinced the horse to trust her.

Then, when it was time to leave the frozen patch and return to terra firma, the process had to be repeated. Miranda couldn’t help but laugh at the gelding’s silly antics and soon, with the passing of each patch, Winston’s game brought Tad out of his grumpy mood. He joined in the entertainment when he couldn’t resist Miranda’s infectious laughter.

When they got to the peak, Miranda let out a gasp as she absorbed the view, scanning all there was to behold. From their vantage point, she could see not only the summer valley and the ranch beyond but also the town’s namesake, Rambletap Springs, and the great plains to the south. “This is breath-taking. Beyond description, like nothing I could’ve imagined.”

“I’m glad to be the one to show you.” Tad allowed Miranda to take it in.

After a time, Tad broke the silence, and the words flowed from him like the river’s waters. “The old wagon trains used to come through and they sometimes got stuck in storms…”

Miranda listened with half an ear as the view before her took up most of the space in her consciousness. The massiveness of what she saw from this lofty station was giving Miranda a new perspective on life. She realized what she was doing here with the Baldwins on the Alma Soñada Ranch, though important within itself, was not the only thing to think about.

Surrounded by so much space full of life, Miranda knew one was only bound by limitations based on the world they see, or chose not to see. Suddenly, standing there on the top of the world, Miranda felt insignificant.

When she noticed Tad had stopped talking, she was still not ready to stop admiring the splendor. Its humbling lessons were cleansing. She had no sense of time or place.

Finally, Tad announced they had better be heading down. Miranda made no move to cue the horse, so Tad repeated, with a little more intensity. "We need to head back."

Evaluating Miranda, Tad could see she was far away in thought, almost sad or scared, and he couldn't understand why. He wished she would join him in the present. What a romantic moment they could share. It was all Tad could think about. All he wanted was to help her, to hold her and, yes, to love her. She was not willing to let him, and it saddened him. Tad lowered his head and waited.

Miranda had never been so overcome by emotion that she simply could not move or talk or even think. She felt the vastness close in around her and fill her up. The empty feeling she always had when she saw a mother and child seemed so minuscule now. The loneliness she felt from not having a hometown, never belonging to a family, not knowing her ancestry, seemed so trivial from up here. She belonged. On this ridge at this moment, she belonged.

To the spirits that danced all around her, she belonged, and there was no place else for her to be. The Lord had a plan, and he was carrying it out. She was but a grain of sand on the beach of life. Her existence was equally insignificant and monumentally important at the same time.

Dismounting in a spurt that startled her horse, Miranda ran to the edge of the cliff with her arms open as if to embrace the harmony that surrounded her. Everything in nature had its purpose. It all worked in symmetry, in cycles that had no beginning and no end. Things were always happening, the equine therapy program was going to happen, and Miranda was for once able to let go of the pressure.

She threw her chin forward and laughed as the self-inflicted burden of responsibility gushed out of her and into the atmosphere. Miranda hollered from the depths of her lungs, "Take it. Take it all. It is yours." Pumping her arms, Miranda released the energy she was holding in and gave it to the universe. She no longer had to carry the burdens on her own. The spirits that circled rejoiced with her as Miranda joined the realm of the faithful.

"She's losing her mind." Tad muttered as he leaped off Sonnet and ran after Miranda. "Are you crazy?" Tad grabbed Miranda and yanked her away from the edge, snatching her from the precipice, saving her from what he perceived as an attempt to jump.

With the spell broken, Miranda staggered over to lean against Winston, breathlessly smiling, still reveling in the magnitude of joy, the exhilaration of what she had just experienced. "I wasn't gonna fall off," she said when she noticed Tad's look of condemnation. She lifted herself up onto Winston, who had stood patiently waiting where she had left him. Tad didn't understand, and she knew she could never explain.

Chapter 30

Ethan had made good progress with the training. He picked up where he left off and the three young horses were learning fast despite their vacation from daily training. At least with these three, it proved Ethan's theory that if there was an established working relationship from the ground with open communications, the rest of the training was easy. Reading each horse's personality and adjusting his method to suit her, he spoke to the horses in actions that conveyed intentions. There was no dominance necessary, no need for forcefulness.

When asking the horse for something, Ethan made anything else the horse did seem like an uncomfortable option, so when the horse found what was easiest, it was her decision as well. Instinctively, all a horse wanted was to be in harmony. Most horses went along with no drama. The occasional circumstances when a horse balked, the rider could, if they have a good understanding and mutual respect, work the horse through it, and arrive harmonious in the end.

Ethan finished with the fillies for the day and began unsaddling them when he realized the sun was soon to be extinguished as it slipped ever closer to the ridge. He couldn't help it, but found his eyes searching the meadow periodically, looking for Tad and Miranda to return from their ride. To his frustration, they didn't come, and he started in on the evening chores, fed the stock horses and the dogs, then went inside, still wondering where the wayward riders were.

It had been dark for nearly a half an hour when Ethan heard Vida announce the riders had returned. Ethan set down the book he had been reading and figured he'd go out to help with the stock.

"I'll go, Ethan," Ansel said. "I'll send Randi in and take care of Winston for her." Ansel needed an opportunity to speak with Tad. He didn't like that

Tad and Randi had obviously gone on a much longer trail ride than originally agreed upon.

A few minutes after his dad left, Ethan heard someone come in and wash up in the little bathroom off the service porch. Ethan guessed it was Miranda and was glad she hadn't gone straight to the guest house, possibly skipping the family meal altogether this evening.

"Sorry we are late for dinner." Miranda apologized when she came in.

"We weren't waiting," Ethan answered, then approached Vida, who was putting the finishing touches on the meal she was preparing.

"Dinner will be ready in a minute." Vida handed her son a bowl full of fresh vegetables and mixed greens. Then Vida turned to Miranda. "You were away too long for a loop around the meadow. How far did you go?"

Ethan plunked the bowl down harder than necessary on the table set for dinner and cringed at his mother's choice of words. He didn't want to think how far Tad may have gone with Miranda.

Before Miranda could answer the first question, Vida continued the onslaught. "Did you see Carmen's Camp? Do you not love the cabin? Did you make it to the ridge? What did you think of that view?"

Miranda didn't know which question to answer first. "The ride was great. Carmen's Camp was as pretty as you described, and the cabin is cute and cozy. The ridge was spectacular, and this was the first time I have ever ridden in the snow."

Miranda responded to Vida's next questions, but Ethan's thoughts had stopped on how she described the cabin. She had said it was cozy. Cozy? The thought of Randi and Tad getting 'cozy' in the cabin conjured up an image his mind couldn't handle. "I've heard enough… I mean, had enough." Ethan stuttered, then grabbed his plate from the table as if he were done eating.

"We haven't even had dinner yet. Aren't you hungry?" Vida asked.

"I've got work to do."

"Ethan!" Vida frowned, but could not stop her son from leaving the kitchen. "That boy has always been a mystery to me. I love him to the moon, but man can he be a challenge."

Miranda had only known Ethan less than a month and had to agree with his mother, only she felt he was more rude than mysterious. She wondered, as she had in the past when experiencing his surliness, had he always been so unpredictably moody, or was he just this way around her? It was odd that a guy who seem to have so much going for him could be so miserable.

Miranda continued telling Vida about her ride that day; the sights, smells and sounds, Winston and his comical reaction to the patches of snow, the beautiful visual contrast of black cattle grazing on green fields, and even her spiritual experience.

Vida listened to everything and nodded with understanding. She shared with Miranda her own encounters with the energy that surrounded the peaks and valleys of her ranch, but even with all the sharing, Miranda felt flat. She'd like to have shared the conversations with Ethan, too.

Ethan stormed away and tucked himself in the family room, holding his book but not reading it. He was in turmoil as reality set in. Miranda had chosen Tad, and why wouldn't she? Tad was a nice guy. Women seemed to like his company when they all hung out at the Bronze Spittoon. He was supportive and sensitive and had never been rude to or called Miranda names. He was the obvious choice, but rationalizing didn't ease Ethan's angst. "Stupid, stupid, stupid." Ethan rapped himself gently on the head with the closed book in his hand.

"You won't learn anything from the book that way." Ansel walked in and caught Ethan punishing himself, literarily speaking.

"Ugh," On top of his frustrations, Ethan was also embarrassed. "I can never say the right thing around her."

Ethan didn't need to explain. His father could see the apprehension. Ansel noticed how his son acted around Miranda and wished there was something he could say to help, some advice on the matter, but all he expressed was, "don't worry," which was no consolation.

The truth is Ansel himself was worried. He had specifically gone out when the riders returned so he could warn Tad about inappropriate behavior. They now had a business relationship with Randi, and there were lines that couldn't be crossed.

After his conversation with Tad, Ansel wasn't completely satisfied, but he concluded Randi could handle things. When asked specifically about his intentions, Tad confessed Randi wasn't interested in a relationship right now. When Ansel asked how he knew, Tad was purposefully vague, which lead Ansel to suspect something untoward may have transpired, but it was only speculations.

The worrisome aspect was that Tad may not have accepted the crystal-clear warnings from Ansel to cool it. Ansel was going to pay close attention, for Randi's sake and the sake of their budding business partnership. Keeping Tad busy with ranch work would be the easiest way to give Randi the break she needed.

Chapter 31

Ethan's opportunity to apologize to Miranda came about in his most comfortable of environments, the arena with horses nearby, thanks to his father. Ansel had included riding lessons with Ethan in the package deal Miranda got when she purchased Winston from the ranch. Ethan agreed to show Miranda a few things about riding the young horse, some tips on riding Western, and a little about quarter horses, as he knew her previous experience was extensive, but she had always ridden English.

Tad was not happy with Ansel's lessons arrangement. He thought it should have been he who was given the job and not Ethan. After all, it was he and not Ethan who Miranda considered a friend. From the shadows of the barn, cleaning stalls, Tad watched with envy the activity in the arena.

"Let's start with mounting." Ethan instructed, as Miranda stood beside him.

"Come on, Ethan, I know how to get on the horse." Miranda thought he must be joking.

"I know that. Please humor me. I want to show you some things I do in my approach to green horses or horses with an unknown background. I plan to work the fillies while you ride Winston. Please, just copy what I do." Ethan stepped over to the little bay filly for a demonstration.

Keeping his eyes on her ears, Ethan took hold of the stirrup and wiggled it. The ears of the filly twitched quickly back and forth. The more Ethan pulled and rattled the stirrup, the less the horse's ears twitched until finally, when the ears were not moving at all, in one smooth motion, Ethan was no longer standing on the ground. With grace, Ethan had lifted himself up and was leaning over the horse's back.

When she realized the human was hovering over her like a predator, the little horse snorted and dropped low as if preparing to buck but before she could act instinctively, Ethan was once again standing beside her, whispering, too softly for Miranda to understand, soothing words that broke her need to respond defensively.

"The trick is not to break the horse's instinct, but rewire a new response to certain stimulation in specific situations," Ethan explained and repeated the process until the horse wasn't reacting to the jiggling, his weight in the stirrup, or his bending over her back. Then he did the same process on the horse's other side.

Miranda watched intently. Ethan's method fascinated her, and his knowledge and skill impressed her. More than that, it intrigued Miranda to see how easily Ethan could mount from either side of the horse.

"In horseback riding of any discipline, the rider is most vulnerable getting on and getting off. It is easiest for the horse to unseat the rider before the rider actually gets seated. The reason I don't get completely on is I don't want the horse to buck. If she never tries to buck, she might never discover she can. That's not saying a horse that doesn't buck during initial training will never buck. Unpredictability is the only thing you can count on with horses."

After Ethan finished standing up in the stirrups on both sides and the filly was steady and unflinching, he swung his leg over, hoping the horse wouldn't buck, but ready just in case. When the filly initially felt the full weight of a rider, her eyes widened and she looked as though she was about to erupt. Ethan once again spoke to her in the low, soothing tone. The only movement was the ears twitching back and forth to catch the sound of the rider's gently words.

"Right now, with the procedure I have done, the filly's response is to freeze. She has been standing still through this whole lesson, and doesn't know she can even take a step. With this process, I hope to have convinced her that, regardless of instinct, it is safest to stand still." Ethan was careful not to move a muscle as the filly relaxed under him. "Now, go to the center and try the process with Winston."

Miranda did as she was told. "This feels silly," she commented. Though Winston hadn't had a lot of hours under saddle to date, he was a fully broke horse.

"I am sharing with you my best kept training secrets, here." Ethan spoke low and slow, so as not to startle his mount, but the teasing words were effective.

"Now Winston won't do much when you wiggle the stirrups because he's been through this game, but this is a good way to approach the horse, any horse, especially those with whom you are not familiar, so you have an idea their mindset and personality before you even get on. You'll reduce the risk of getting hurt drastically. I promise."

Miranda nodded, copied everything she had seen Ethan do, but still felt silly doing this with a horse she had been riding for several weeks.

"Watch his ears," Ethan reminded her. "Now, find your stirrup and lift yourself up, but don't swing over. I want you to feel how to balance quietly, hovering over the saddle."

Miranda followed the instructions and concentrated, not wanting to make a mistake. It was more difficult than she thought as Miranda lifted her weight off the ground to stand in the saddle with only her left foot. She needed to balance using her leg, and she needed core strength to bend forward over the saddle. Miranda was taking this exercise seriously, as she realized it wasn't so silly. She wished to do it right. And she felt pressure to please her instructor.

While Miranda practiced with Winston, Ethan dismounted and started the process over again. Miranda forgot what she was doing and swung up to sitting in the saddle so she could watch. Ethan stepped back up after following the beginning routine, but this time when he hovered over the horse, without taking his eyes off her ears, he reached down with his hand and patted her flank and barrel, jiggled the other stirrup and once again the filly had a bit of fear in her eyes but the soothing speak quickly erased it. When the filly relaxed with him leaning over, touching her and patting and wiggling the stirrup, Ethan swiftly lifted his leg and swung over.

He committed to staying on and inserted his foot in the other stirrup. Ethan barely sat, his weight wasn't in the stirrups either, he seemed to float above the saddle and when the horse took a few steps forward, Ethan leaned over her wither for her to step ahead as if she was catching his weight. The feel of the rider was surprising to the filly, but she moved forward anyway. Her first steps were choppy as she discovered she could balance her rider.

Ethan smiled and continued to communicate with his body and when they had crossed the arena, without turning her, he simply leaned back at the time she got to the rail, and she stopped walking. Ethan waited for the filly to turn her head in either direction, and when she did, he leaned forward again and she had to step to the side to keep him balanced. Now she was walking along the rail. Ethan had gotten on and in a matter of minutes had taught her to walk forward, stop, and turn using shifts of his body.

Miranda was still sitting on Winston in the center of the ring, as if in a trance. It amazed her to see a first ride on a horse with zero experience, and all with no drama.

"Nothing to it," Ethan said as he leaned back and flashed a shining grin at Miranda. The filly stopped and Ethan stepped down. "That's it for you today, little girl." Ethan turned his attention back to the bay.

"I'm going to put this horse away and get another. While I'm away, do the mounting process on Winston from the other side." Ethan led the horse from the arena, leaving Miranda alone to practice mounting from Winston's right side, the off-side.

Miranda dismounted and moved to Winston's other side. She wasn't sure why Ethan wanted her to get on and off from the right side. A rider always mounted on the left, no matter the style of the riding. Miranda quickly discovered how awkward it was to mount Winston. She lifted her left leg up, but quickly realized that was wrong. She switched legs, but her right leg muscle trembled when she stepped up, and when she was standing in the stirrup, she found it difficult to swing her left leg over. Winston stood patiently all the while.

When Ethan returned with the next horse, Miranda walked Winston along the rail and watched him work the second filly. Ethan followed the same routine, and the horse responded in much the same way until the part where she discovered the rider's legs on both sides. Her response came much quicker.

Before Ethan could soothe her with his voice, the horse bolted forward, rounded her back, and bucked. Ethan stayed with her, using his magic floating technique, and after two little hops, the bucking became a choppy lope. The horse's ears twitched as she and her rider circled the arena, but soon her gait steadied, her ears quieted and when Ethan leaned back, she slowed to a walk. Miranda fell in beside Ethan and they walked together.

"Every horse reacts differently," Ethan explained, as the two horses stepped in sync.

"The bay did seem more relaxed," Miranda said.

"The bay did well, but the second filly will progress quicker."

"How do you know?"

"Her quick response shows she'll be a fast learner. If I'm fast enough to intercept the automatic instinctive response often enough, she'll learn to trust."

"The bay seemed to trust you. Wouldn't it be the opposite?" Miranda asked.

"My predictions are not foolproof, but I have an excellent track record. With the bay, there'll be less opportunity to work through problems because she goes with the flow. When she balks at something in the future, when she gets surprised, it'll be a bigger reaction."

"She'll rely on her instinct to flee?" Miranda speculated.

"That's right, and she won't be so quick to rely on her rider. The rider won't have had as many times to intercept her reaction, and she won't have had as many opportunities to learn to circumvent her instincts."

"Remember your wild ride on Winston?" Ethan continued. "He relied on instinct, and so did you, but you weren't in sync. Winston is like the first filly. He goes along easily but responds deeper when surprised. It's not a bad thing. The bay and Winston will be splendid horses, dependable, but it'll take more time for them to get used to new riders, unlike this horse," Ethan pointed to his mount. "Horses like her will easily go from one rider to another. She'll be called a term I'm sure you are familiar with, bomb proof."

"I feel very in sync with Winston," Miranda defended her relationship with her newly purchased horse.

"You and Winston didn't start out on the same page, though, remember?"

"Yes," Miranda recalled the first part of their first ride and admitted. "It felt like we weren't even in the same book."

"And then, when Winston spooked, he reacted instinctively until you intercepted. When you saw the danger and your instinct kicked in to make him jump, he responded. Winston had never experienced a creek crossing. He is still quite green."

"Hmmm," Miranda thought about what Ethan said, and it made sense. Miranda understood why some horses seemed so dependable and others were spooky all the time. Then Miranda's train of thoughts jumped over to another track.

"Wait a minute," Miranda turned in the saddle to face Ethan. "That means you set me up. You knew Winston might not connect with me quickly. Were you trying to see if I'd fail?"

"For the sake of honesty, yes," Ethan admitted. "I figured you wouldn't even make it to the meadow gate. You impressed me with how you handled

Winston. You rode well, kept him in control using your skills. I figured you and he'd be fine after that."

Miranda reacted to this confession at first with anger, but then she thought what Ethan said was almost a compliment. It irked Miranda that she acted as though she needed Ethan's approval. A strong desire normally motivated her to be appreciated for her knowledge and skills in business. Now she knew she sought the same recognition with horsemanship. "Well, I guess I was fine. Winston and I worked it out."

"You did more than that. You got to find out for yourself how it feels to be in total harmony with the horse, not that you hadn't experienced that before." Ethan was trying to choose the right words. "But when you connect with a horse deeper than the surface relationship..."

"It feels like magic," Miranda interrupted.

"I guess it does." Ethan and Miranda stared at each other. They were communicating well, for the first time since they met, and neither broke the spell.

Ethan could not remember someone understanding his philosophy the way Miranda did. Ethan could hear his mother's voice as he remembered her telling of kindred spirits. Vida explained it as an indelible connection between two people. Ethan only knew this kind of connection with animals, but perhaps Miranda and he were kindred spirits. This sensation with a human was new. The energy evoked within was unfamiliar, but he liked it. It was exciting.

"So what's next, teach?" Miranda broke the silence without letting go the eye contact.

"I have to put a first ride on the third filly. You and Winston are finished for today." Ethan thought he saw disappointment from Miranda and quickly added, "But you are welcome to stay while I work on the last one."

Miranda put Winston away while Ethan readied the last horse, then she climbed on the top rail of the arena fence to watch. Ethan started the same way he had with the first two horses, and other than a few subtle differences, the filly responded favorably.

It amazed Miranda at how much energy Ethan gave to the horse in order that she feel comfortable with everything he was doing. She was his only concern, and it made Miranda a touch envious. As she had seen before, Ethan's handling and riding looked like he and the horse were dancing, moving as a single creature, two hearts beating as one.

Miranda recognized by now when it looked like Ethan was wrapping up the last ride of the morning, she jumped off the rail. It was lunchtime, and she wanted to check if Vida wanted company in the kitchen.

"Miranda," Ethan called, "before you go, I want to talk to you about something." Ethan dismounted and lead the filly through the gate to the barn to unsaddle her and turn her back out with the other horses.

"Of course," Miranda followed Ethan. "What's up?"

"I really want to apologize, finally and officially, for my behavior lately. There is no excuse. I barely can even come up with a reason." Ethan selected the exact words to say. "I made assumptions based on no information. I was suspicious without cause, and I was rude."

Miranda couldn't argue with his facts, so she nodded and stood by to hear if Ethan had more to say. When no more words came, she spoke, "I appreciate your admissions, and I, too, will admit I didn't do all I could to clear things up. I knew you had questions and concerns, and I should have handled it much differently, too."

"So, we're okay, then? We can start fresh?" Ethan held his breath, set the saddle on its rack, and waited for her answer.

"I'll accept your apology if you will accept mine."

"Consider it done." Ethan held eye contact with Miranda and noticed again the simpatico he experienced before when he and Miranda were talking in the arena.

"Consider it done? What's done?" From out of nowhere, Tad came around the breezeway from the back slider doors of the barn.

"Tad, hi," Miranda greeted the other cowboy wondering if he had been in the barn all along.

"Hey, Tad." Emphasizing his friend's name, Ethan felt irate when his connection with Miranda was cut short.

"Ethan just finished up with the last ride," Miranda said.

"Good, Randi, 'cause lunch is about ready. Shall we?" Tad crooked his elbow in front of Miranda's chest, a gesture Miranda had seen when people square dance. Miranda did not accept the invitation to take hold. She didn't wish to dance with Tad.

"Thanks for today, and for the lesson, Ethan." Miranda recognized what Ethan was sharing with her was so much more than riding lessons. He was showing her his training methods. "Same time tomorrow?"

"See you then." Ethan smiled.

Ethan gathered the rest of the tack to hang it up in the tack room, taking time to place the leather gear properly on the right hooks for easy retrieval the next time it was needed. He wanted to give Tad and Miranda time to get ahead of him. From the corner of his eye, he noticed Miranda hadn't taken hold of the arm Tad presented, and there seemed to be an awkward distance between them as they walked to the house, clues that gave Ethan hope Miranda and Tad were still only friends.

Tad rather abruptly took hold of Miranda when she didn't lock arms with him as soon as he presented his bended elbow. Miranda insisted on talking to Ethan, even though the lesson was obviously over. Irritated that Miranda and Ethan had way too much fun at their lessons, Tad released his anger by practically dragging his girl away.

Tad had been watching his boyhood friend and Randi riding in the arena and, to him, it looked like there wasn't much teaching. It looked like Ethan was just showing off. The arrangement was a ploy, Ethan had managed it, so he had Randi as a captive audience. Tad saw right through Ethan's tricks, even if Randi did not.

"Well, that looked like a waste of your time. Was that supposed to be a riding lesson?" Tad said venomously. Miranda freed herself from Tad's hold on her arm as they transected past the Maple in the center of the complex.

Miranda had grown weary of Tad's little tantrums. Even after their trail ride talk, Tad wouldn't accept they were not dating. His behavior had now escalated to possessiveness, and Miranda didn't appreciate it. "It was a great lesson. I learned so much. Ethan is an excellent teacher," Miranda replied.

Is that what you think he's doing? Well, I have much to teach you, too. Tad thought, but stopped himself from saying it. He had to be cautious. He knew he needed to tred lightly. Miranda was not like the women he'd had in the past. Those women had been ridden hard and put away wet. They were broken in and put up very little fight. Miranda would be one with whom more effort was required. Tad readied himself for the challenge.

Chapter 32

Over the next few days, the ranch experienced unsettled weather, not unusual for springtime in Montana, as storms from the Pacific moved regularly through. There was much to accomplish, work they could do indoors. As soon as the skies cleared, the tractors broke ground on the arena that would be home to Miranda's riding therapy program. Ethan watched from across the driveway as his family piled into the Suburban and headed out to the build site where construction had begun.

Despite the weather, Ethan had continued training the McGuire horses working through the stormy days. After some finishing touches, the fillies were ready to leave the ranch. Keeping himself busy, Ethan had been masterfully avoiding situations that involved Tad and Miranda, but his best friend's ridiculous behavior was wearing thin on everyone. Tad weaseled his way into every situation, sometimes having to compromise his chores and responsibilities. And Ethan kept stepping aside, preferring to spend a limited time with Miranda when it was just the two of them.

Together, Miranda and Ethan continued to work with the horses. Miranda was a fast learner and quite helpful, and she and Ethan found they had more in common regarding the horses. Whenever they were in mixed company with Tad, Tad fawned and pawed over Miranda, and Ethan believed it made her uncomfortable. He hoped that in his absence, maybe Tad was less inclined to feel competitive. Maybe then Tad would end the obnoxious behavior. Ethan was willing to do what he could to make things easier on Miranda. He wished Miranda would set Tad in his place if she didn't want his attentions.

What Ethan hadn't noticed was the exhaustive effort Miranda was putting in to keep Tad at arm's length. While Miranda was avoiding Tad, Ethan went to great lengths to avoid both Miranda and Tad. It was a silly game with no winners.

Ethan smiled and nodded in response to the wave Miranda sent his way before she stepped into the vehicle to drive with the others to the meadow. The governing agencies had fully approved the plans for the facility. Miranda had poured her heart and soul into it and, Ethan thought with pride, she was getting it done. He longed to go with her, to share in the celebration, but it was easier to remain on the outside of those dealings, alone and uninvolved. It was a lonely proposition.

Finding excuses for staying away from the little things was easy. Not showing up for the Mitchell-Rhodes nuptial exchange was another story. Suzanne Mitchell's wedding was an event Ethan sought to avoid, but Ansel and Vida were pushing hard. Paula and Noah were also insisting Ethan be there. Everyone in the community was automatically invited to a Rambletap Springs weddings. They considered attendance non-optional.

Tad had been talking at length about what he planned to do at the reception. It was being held at Villa De Leon, Suzanne's uncle's place, and one of the nicer restaurants in town. There was to be live music and an open bar, which guaranteed there would be much merriment. Tad confessed his plan to take advantage of how sentimental women get at weddings and hoped to make his and Randi's relationship official.

Ethan dropped a wheelbarrow full of manure in the barn aisle upon hearing Tad's plan of action, but Tad saw no connection. Instead, he rattled on about what Randi did at breakfast, and what Randi had said the other day. Randi this and Randi that. Ethan wanted to stuff the manure into Tad's mouth to stop him from speaking. It appeared to Ethan that Tad's relationship with Miranda wasn't heading in the direction Tad assumed it was. In Ethan's opinion, Miranda wasn't that into him, but it was none of Ethan's business.

Bumping along in the Suburban over the unpaved road, Miranda said to herself, "I sure wish Ethan could've joined us." then realized she had spoken out loud. They sandwiched her in-between Tad and Vida in the middle seat of the Suburban. The back of the SUV was full of the celebratory fanfare Vida had prepared, and Ansel, along with the contractor and his wife, sat on the bench seat in front.

"Oh, forget about that party pooper," Tad bristled. It baffled him that Randi had brought Ethan along wherever she went, even when Ethan wasn't physically present. It bothered Tad that Randi had stuck to her convictions, keeping him in the friend zone. Tad wanted romance. He expected to be the only thing on Randi's mind, but though Ethan was never there in person, he was always present in Randi's thoughts. Tad hoped his relentlessness would quickly wear down her resolve, but lately it seemed to have the opposite effect than what he desired.

The small party of people tumbled out of the vehicle when they parked near the new buildings. The groundwork and grading were done, and the skeletal structure that would be the sides was in process. There was a picnic table Ansel had set out where the big group area would soon be built. Miranda's office assistant, Alisha, and Greyson Woods, were sitting at the table waiting.

As Miranda panned around the area, she imagined what it would look like when finished. The feeling was both terrifying and exhilarating. The group area tables were to be built by wood donated to the cabinet shop. Greyson Woods 'donation was paying for the roofing. Miranda's foundation was providing the steel for the framing, the arena walls, and the pipe pens to hold the horses. The tack room, grooming area, and the observation deck would be finished last once the funding from other benefactors Albert had line up started coming in. Today, they were having another drawing to choose the arena's name.

"I've got the basket," Miranda held up the container with bits of paper in it for all to see. Vida finished filling the glasses of champagne as Ansel began handing one to each guest.

"Will you do the honors?" Miranda held the basket in front of Greyson.

"With pleasure," The retired school teacher reached in for a folded strip.

"Shuffle them up good, Greyson," Ansel coached. "And remember, the creator of the name is to remain anonymous."

Greyson unfolded the paper and studied what was written.

"Well, what is it?" the crowd grew impatient.

"Sunrise Arena."

"Sunrise Arena," Miranda rolled the words off her tongue. "I like it. It goes well with the name Riding High Stables."

When they had drawn a name to be entered on the permits and non-profit documents, Vida had pulled out the paper that said, "Riding High Stables at Alma Soñada Ranch." Now the arena was to be called Sunrise Arena. Miranda didn't know whose contribution to the drawing it had been that brought the name to the stables, but Sunrise Arena was hers.

"To Sunrise Arena." Ansel raised his glass.

"Sunrise Arena it shall be," Miranda added, keeping the secret.

"Here, here," said Tad, raising his glass in a toast. He was trying to appear supportive, but it had disappointed him that Miranda had asked Greyson Woods to do the drawing. Tad's dissatisfaction continued when the paper Greyson chose wasn't Tad's own contribution.

"Cheers," said the group, clinking their glasses, then taking a sip of champagne.

"So, Miranda, when do we start the first session at Sunrise Arena?" Greyson inquired after he had savored the champagne.

"We are hoping to have clients, the beta test group, in August, but there is still a lot to be done. We have made progress with lining up some doctors who want to provide support, and we are proceeding with the training of a few therapists willing to come up from Helena. After the test run, I hope we will run an official session this fall."

Tad enjoyed watching Randi talk about the program, but he found Mr. Woods 'presence annoying. The old man was monopolizing Randi with his endless questions. Randi was explaining to Greyson what specific training the horses were getting so they could be good therapy horses, and Tad scowled when it reminded him how much time Randi was spending with Ethan picking out horses for her string.

Tad's frustration simmered inside. Ethan, Mr. Woods, the horse training, and on and on. Randi always found something to focus on other than him. When would Randi ever have space for him on her busy schedule? All Miranda could think about was her program. Everything revolved around it. Could there really be that much to it? Randi made room for Ethan, Mr. Woods, Ansel and the contractors. When was she going to make time for him?

Tad's thoughts were interrupted when he heard Ansel inviting Greyson to stay for dinner.

"I'd love to stay," Greyson accepted as he stepped into his pickup. "See y'all at the house. Oh, Miranda," Greyson continued. "You haven't forgotten about our date, have you?"

Miranda glanced at Tad, who had been wearing a scowl since they drove over, and saw his quills rise like an antagonized porcupine at Greyson's mention of a date. "You mean Suzanne's wedding?" Miranda made it a point to say it loud enough for Tad to hear. "I haven't forgotten. It will be my pleasure to accompany you."

Tad couldn't believe his ears. *That's great*, he thought, watching his plans fall apart before his eyes. It would be impossible to move his relationship forward with Randi if his high school teacher was hanging about. How dare the old man act this way with Randi? He was making a fool of himself. She was young enough to be his daughter. Tad realized he would have to be more assertive. He needed to convince Randi to break her plans with ol'man Woods and go with him to the wedding instead.

"Can I come in for a few minutes?" Tad asked after Miranda got out of the truck and headed to the cottage door.

"I need to get cleaned up for dinner tonight with Greyson." Miranda continued walking toward the cottage.

Greyson, Greyson, Greyson, Tad fumed inside. If it wasn't Ethan, it was someone else. Why couldn't she forget about them and give her attention to him? "Stop walking away when I'm talking to you." Tad demanded.

Miranda spun around at the man who was firing off an order. "Excuse me?"

"Never mind. I'll see you at dinner with the rest of them." Tad gave a smile to hide his annoyance. It was a weak façade.

Miranda shivered her shoulders and went inside alone. There was something sinister in Tad's smile that left her feeling unsettled. It was unnatural. The way the corners of his mouth curled up in an arch around the ends of his mustache reminded Miranda of the villains in a wax museum. That was not Tad's normal smile.

Tad walked away from Miranda as if in a trance. He was at a loss about what to do. Miranda made him feel out of control. He knew he was acting the fool, but wasn't sure how to stop himself. The situation frustrated him and also made him hate how he was acting. He wanted to quit embarrassing himself.

All he needed was attention from Randi. He yearned to take her in his arms and feel her warm, feminine ways. If she would just let him love her, he could stop all this foolish behavior. For so many times already, he resolved to being patient only to push forward like a bull through a barbed wire fence. This time, he had to make good on his promise to himself to let Randi come to him. Even the bull grew tired of being cut by a thousand barbs.

Chapter 33

From the arena, Ethan had seen the troops returning from the meadow following the name-drawing celebration, and hoped Miranda would come over and sit on the fence while he worked as she had done most evenings. Ethan was sharpening the skills of one of the regular riding stock horses to see if the four-year-old had enough athleticism to be a good cutting horse.

The cutters had to be small and quick, with a strong instinctive reflex to work cattle. Noah had been riding this young horse during the roundup because Ethan thought the gelding had potential, but by the end of the week, after watching the gelding work, Ethan had changed his mind. He wanted to give the horse one more chance. He was certain he recognized some cutting instincts. Ethan was seldom wrong.

For Ethan, the best part of the day was the time he and Miranda spent working together, training and riding. He and Miranda were hand-picking the most suitable mounts to be in the string for the therapy program. As good an eye as Ethan had for cow ponies, Miranda was equally skilled at choosing the right horses for therapy.

The horses had to be gentle and confident, tolerant and with a long space between stimulus and response, the opposite of a cutting horse. Ethan grew to respect Miranda's methods of evaluation and was confident in her opinions, and Miranda showed the same to Ethan for his expertise.

When Ethan saw Tad follow Miranda up the short path to the guest house, he figured she wouldn't be joining him for the evening training. It burned him up to think they would both be going inside, but it was none of his business. He tried to resign to the fact Tad and Miranda might soon be a couple. He wanted it to be him.

Ethan gathered what relief he could muster that despite what Tad said, it was obvious he and Miranda didn't seem to be that close. He was patiently waiting, knowing that most of what Tad had relayed through shameless bragging was wishful thinking. To Ethan's relief, he watched as Tad came back up the driveway toward the bunkhouse. Miranda must have turned him away at her door.

Miranda was excited to see Ethan still working horses when they all returned from the naming ceremony. Miranda seemed compelled to sit by while Ethan rode. It was the most pleasant part of her day. It was calming and enlightening, and Ethan's riding was unexpected of how a cow puncher or bronc buster should look.

Miranda had been learning so much from Ethan; he was a tremendous help to her with selecting the string of horses she needed for her program, but it was during the times it was just him riding a horse that Miranda found the most pleasure while watching.

Ethan seemed to enjoy their time, too, Miranda decided. He was open to her ideas about horses and receptive to her advice. She even helped him with some horses he was training for the ranch stock. It was both amazing and frustrating to work with Ethan. When they were working horses, it seemed to draw them closer, but with any other interaction, Ethan backed away. It was such a conundrum. Miranda didn't know how they could have such a strong connection one minute that would simply evaporate the next.

When Miranda got back with the others, all she wanted was to put on her boots and head over to Ethan. When Tad followed Miranda, she hadn't wanted him to go with her to the arena, too, so she told him a lie. Now she had no choice but to change her clothes and head to the main house to help with meal preparations. After getting cleaned up, on the way out the door, Miranda noticed the ring was empty.

On the off-chance Ethan would still be in the barn, Miranda grabbed a few carrots, thinking it would not be a lie if she didn't go straight to the house, but was only going to check on Winston. It disappointed Miranda to discover the interior lights were off. The building appeared empty of humans. In the twilight, Miranda saw well enough, so she left the lights off. She brought a couple of brushes to Winston's stall and groomed the gelding as he happily munched on the carrots.

As she ran the curry comb in small circles across the horse's back, shoulders and haunches, she let her imagination run to a place where she and Ethan were honest with themselves and each other, a place where they got along inside the horse arena and out. Miranda allowed the peaceful feeling to run down her arm and through her hand, and Winston even stopped chewing to enjoy the energy exchange.

Miranda was deep in syncopated thought when she heard from behind her, "Boy, I sure wish I was that horse."

She spun around and caught sight of a human silhouette leaning against the support beam pole with his arms folded across his chest. From the aura rather than her sight, Miranda recognized Ethan. His mere presence caused a tingle inside, leaving her without a clever comeback.

"That is one back rub I wouldn't mind being on the receiving end of." Ethan stepped in and the horse fidgeted, maybe because he felt crowded having more than one person in his stall. Or maybe Winston was reacting to Miranda's energy shift. Ethan patted the gelding on the neck without standing too close to Miranda, who had yet to say a word. Then Ethan said, looking straight into her eyes, "One lucky horse."

Ethan's unexpected appearance had robbed Miranda of the ability to speak. His proximity threatened to take away her air, and she stood as if frozen with the grooming tool in hand, resting motionless on the horse's rounded hip.

Ethan reached for Miranda's hand, covered it with his and said, "How were you doing it? Like this?"

Miranda's fingers held the brush, Ethan's fingers held Miranda's, and moved both her hand and the curry in a circular motion. When Ethan stopped their hands from moving, the brush fell from Miranda's grip. Distracted by the brush which was now laying in the shavings on the floor, Miranda next found Ethan was holding her fingers against his lips.

"These must be magic," Ethan said with a huskiness in his voice that she felt rather than heard.

Ethan looked directly at Miranda, from deep beyond the surface of his eyes, and she felt a safe, warm comforting of power when his thumb pressed the inside of her palm as if he was rubbing a worry stone. She didn't resist as he invited her into an embrace. From there, they were kissing, their lips fitting as if they had practiced.

Miranda received the soothing warmth of Ethan's body through the cotton fabric of the dress she had put on for dinner. Losing her presence of mind while they kissed, Miranda was only aware of Ethan. His essence and hers were two wisps of fog atop the mountain, whose tendrils swirled around the highest peaks, then collectively floated down the slope.

Like the shutting of a faucet, the imagery trickled away. Miranda heard the blood whooshing in her ears, and her senses returned. When she opened her eyes, there she was, in Ethan's arms, as he looked down at her assuredly.

"Can you stand?" Ethan was talking, but the words went into Miranda's ears, sounding like a recorded tape dragging too slowly across the heads. Before Miranda could process what he said, Ethan was gone.

Leaning against Winston, Miranda finally found her voice. "Of course I can stand." By that time, Winston had grown impatient and stepped away from her weight.

As Miranda realized she was falling, the barn became flooded with light and Tad came in as if from out of nowhere. "Randi!" he exclaimed. "Are you alright?"

Miranda struggled to clear her head. "Ethan?" she asked.

"No, it's me, Tad." Disgruntled that even in a semi-conscious state, Randi thought of Ethan first, Tad forced himself to be more concerned for her. "Did you faint?"

Tad helped Randi to her feet, "I guess the champagne we had at the meadow went to your head." He teased when he could see the color returning to Randi's cheeks. "Let's get you inside."

Tad, with his arm around her shoulders, pulled Miranda out of the stall.

"I'm okay, now." Miranda wiggled away from Tad. She turned to search the area, but only saw Winston. Where had Ethan gone so quickly? She couldn't have imagined it. He had been there with her and Winston, in that stall.

"What are you looking for?" Tad asked.

"I, I… don't know."

Miranda let Tad lead her away from the barn and to the back steps of the house, but she stopped short of going up. She was still trying to make sense of what had happened. "You go on, I'll be there in a minute." Miranda sat down on the bottom step.

"I'll stay with you."

"I need a moment, Tad," Miranda was firm. "Go inside."

"You certainly are a hard one to figure, Randi." Tad stomped past her and let the screen door slam hard behind him.

Miranda breathed deeply and rested her forehead on her palms. Trying to sort out the strange sequence of events. Had she imagined that moment with

Ethan in Winston's stall? An experience that powerful couldn't have been only in her mind. So where had he gone and why had he fled? Was it because he heard Tad coming?

If Tad had seen them together, it could have ended Tad's endless unwanted advances. She wanted that. But maybe Ethan did not. Was Ethan just playing a game? Was he toying with her in some kind of power struggle? Miranda needed to find out. Taking in a deep breath of fresh air, Miranda decided she would act normal. She would go inside and take back control of it all; the situation with Tad, and whatever this was between her and Ethan, both things needed to be resolved.

Chapter 34

"Ethan, do you want some scrambled eggs?" Vida offered. She had gotten up early to make breakfast for Ethan, who lately had been up and out the door before the breaking dawn.

"No thanks, Mom." Ethan sat in the almost dark kitchen with his hands wrapped around a mug of steaming coffee. "You go back to bed. I didn't mean to wake you."

"It's no bother. Porridge is okay, but you should eat a full meal, too." Vida set about fixing some eggs for Ethan. She was worried about her son. She pondered over his current behavior, which was new and not part of Ethan's regular habits, even when something was upsetting him.

Every morning, Ethan woke up before anyone else, did all his chores before the rest of them had finished eating, then spent most of his time out on the range. Ethan would sneak in for lunch only when no one else was hanging around the house and he wasn't joining them for evening meal times, either.

He would turn in after lights were out, grab some cold cuts and cheese or leftovers and head to his room. Ansel and Vida had always talked to Ethan when he was in his moods, but this seemed different, and it hadn't taken Vida long to see it was especially obvious Ethan was avoiding Miranda.

The smell of bacon reminded Ethan of what he had been missing, and he waited for his mother to finish cooking. Since the night in Winston's stall with Miranda, Ethan had been in turmoil, but there had been no one in which to confide, so he had distanced himself from everybody. That was no help, either. Ethan could not seem to find relief from the confusion he experienced in the aftermath of the kiss.

Miranda walking out of the stall with Tad that night after the moment Ethan shared with her, was a punch in the gut. The connection they made had seemed so real. The power behind it made him confident she felt it, too. When their hands melted together on the curry comb, Ethan noticed the electricity, and when their lips touched, he lost all concern for everything except Miranda. He was certain of Miranda's response to him, too. If someone hadn't come into the barn, he and Miranda could have lingered in the closeness of an afterglow of the kiss.

Upon realizing another person was approaching Winston's stall, Ethan considered Miranda's reputation. The implications of being caught in each other's arms were unseemly. So, with quick reflexes, he slipped through the small space above the mangier and into the stall next door.

When he realized it was Tad who had entered, he decided to come back over and deal with the situation head on. It was at the same moment Miranda lost her balance and fell to the soft bedding that, out of concern, Ethan jumped through the opening. Tad reached Miranda first and didn't notice Ethan standing there. By the time Miranda was on her feet, Ethan had slipped into the shadows unseen.

As Ethan watched Miranda gather her wits, he figured she would get rid of Tad somehow and stay in the barn, so he waited. When Miranda didn't come back, he worried maybe her loss of balance was something serious, so he went to the house but found everyone in the kitchen. Miranda and his father and Tad were chatting casually like all was normal. His mother greeted Ethan when he entered. Ethan made eye contact with Miranda but saw no emotion there, so he excused himself to get cleaned up before dinner.

Ethan understood Miranda's intentions for the ranch were honest and benevolent. He was on board with her and interested. Now, he realized that maybe that was all there ever was for her here. It was all just business. Maybe it embarrassed her what happened in Winston's stall and, for her, the best way to handle it was to ignore it. Miranda's actions brought pain and hurt to Ethan, but it was his own fault, and now, because of his impulsiveness, he didn't even have her friendship.

Ethan was sad to lose what he and Miranda shared while riding and training. He valued their time together, but that was over. Ethan still had much to distract him from his plight; there was always work to do, and he poured himself into it. The colts needed to be halter broke, and yearlings were ready to start ground work. There were fences to be mended and cattle to be checked. Ethan had avoided most everyone, including Miranda, all week, but he missed their training sessions.

“Ethan, are you sure you won’t be coming to the wedding? Kevin and Suzanne were both friends of yours since elementary school,” Vida watched Ethan eat in utter silence the breakfast she had prepared. At least he was eating, but she could see he wasn’t getting any joy out of the meal, just sustenance.

“Yes, ma’am. I’m going to sit this one out.”

“Everyone should be there. It is traditional. You are going to need a good excuse for not showing up,” Vida tried a little more pressure.

Ethan finished the last bite of food on his plate, scooted his chair away from the table, and stood up. He had no intention of making excuses.“ Please tell Dad I’ll check the fences on the north side today.” Pushing his hat down further on his head, he stepped out into the darkness before dawn. The sun would rise soon, but it would have little effect on lightening his mood.

Vida shivered from the draft that floated in as Ethan exited and wondered if her child was ever going to find peace. Being such a sensitive boy, Vida knew he thought emotionally, felt deeply and cared immensely about things he valued, but this opened him up to the hurt when he encountered folks who neither realized nor cared. The sense of relief Vida experienced when things with Paula and Noah and Ethan were resolved was short-lived, as there now seemed to be a new triangle brewing between Randi and Tad and Ethan.

Vida wondered what brought these cookie cutter situations into Ethan’s life and wished she could help him learn the lesson, but it was not her place. Ethan would have to figure things out for himself. With a mother’s instinct, Vida headed toward Miranda’s cottage when she realized there was light coming through the window. Perhaps there was something she could do after all.

“Good morning, Randi,” Vida said through the closed door, using her voice instead of a knock.

“Come in,” Miranda greeted the ranch matriarch in her warm terry robe and fussy slippers. She held open the door for Vida, who was carrying a tea tray.

“I saw you were awake, and since I was up, too, decided we should share some tea.” Vida set the tea tray on the little kitchen table that sat against the wall under the picture window that would have displayed the meadow if it were light out. Vida poured two cups.

"Thank you, Vida. That is very thoughtful. I guess you were making breakfast for the early riser in the household?" Miranda's question was more of a statement. Ethan's early morning departures hadn't gone unnoticed.

Vida's left brow lifted slightly. It interested Vida hearing Miranda seemed to keep tabs on her son. "We hardly get to talk, just you and me." Vida sat down, lifted her cup to her upper lip before setting it down again. The tea was too hot to drink.

"I'm glad we can chat. We are all so busy, but I think things'll slow down soon." Miranda sat down with Vida.

"Tad sure has been a big help," Vida said as she watched Miranda's face. She was looking for a change in Miranda's eyes. Vida wanted to set the stage for her inquiry.

"He really wants to take part and contribute. He tries to be helpful. Mostly, I think he tries too hard." Miranda spoke of Tad like a handler describing an insecure puppy.

"But you two have gotten to know each other. You have been getting pretty close."

"Tad can be intense. I notice a bit of a short fuse. He is a good guy and I feel lucky to call him a friend." Miranda sensed the conversation was not random.

"Ansel and I started out as friends, but a mutual attraction toward each other quickly grew, and as soon as we started dating, we both knew we were in love."

"You two are fortunate. I have never known that feeling," Miranda mused. "With my luck, my one true love will probably call when I'm busy and my answering machine will pick it up."

The women laughed together at Miranda's analogy. Without asking, Vida had discovered Miranda was not interested in Tad as anything more than friends, and the conversation shifted to another subject. Vida had found out what she needed to know. Randi was not in love with Tad, though Tad was obviously infatuated with her. She hoped Randi was being straight with the boy. Vida also now knew that there wasn't anything going on with Miranda and Ethan. At least not yet.

Vida stopped prying for more information. It satisfied her with what she had learned. Vida could only pray that nothing interfered with God's plan. This family couldn't weather the storm of another triangle of unrequited love.

~****~

"I wish you wouldn't have promised ol'man Woods you'd accompany him to the ceremony." Tad had been grieving since he found out Miranda planned to go with Greyson. He had whined and begged to no avail.

"We will all be there together, Tad. It's no big deal." Miranda had grown weary of Tad's tiresome pestering and wasn't sure how to get across the message they would never be more than friends.

Miranda was dressed to the nines for the occasion, a navy-blue, floor-length halter style dress, high at the neckline, backless, and pleated in the front. From the waist, the pleated skirt spread out, full and flowing. The style magnified the physically fit curve of Miranda's arms and shoulders, while the floor-length dress drew out her graceful height. Tad would have preferred Randi showed a little more of her legs. It was not a secret to anyone who knew him. Tad likes women that show off their sexy side.

"I hope you didn't promise to dance with him all night, too," Tad pouted. "Dirty old man." He added under his breath.

"I have made no promises to anyone, Tad. I will dance with whomever I please." Miranda had stopped trying to be subtle or spare Tad's feelings.

"What?" Tad suddenly felt like he had to compete with every man in town for Randi's attention. Tad was still pouting as he watched Randi drive away to town to meet up with her date. "Slut," he said to himself at the thought of her dancing with anyone who asked.

"If she were my date, I wouldn't make her drive herself to town," Tad said when he went inside to wait for a ride with the Baldwins. He was still fuming about not being Randi's date. Now the whole county would think she is single and available.

~****~

It was twenty after six when Ethan came into the kitchen to grab a bit of cold dinner. Tad and Ethan's folks had left for the evening wedding ceremony.

He had seen them drive off when he returned from his long workday on the northern fence line.

Ethan set his plate of chicken and macaroni salad on the table and noticed the invitation strategically placed right where he couldn't miss it. His mother's indirect way of saying she wished he would come. It made him wish he had gone. A Rambletap Springs matrimony celebration was not something to be missed. The image of watching Miranda enjoying Tad's company, however, was too much to bear.

While munching on a carrot stick, Ethan imagined Miranda dancing at the reception. The music was soft, a gentle breeze lifted wisps of hair around her neckline, and she was swaying ever so gracefully in his arms. It was as if he were there. With that, Ethan shoved away his nearly empty plate of leftovers and stood fast. The chair caught on his leg and toppled backward onto the floor, sending the big orange cat, who always rested under the pot-bellied stove, flying out from under.

In anguish, Ethan realized the whole point of staying away was to keep from thinking like this. He was torturing himself anyway, so he might as well be at the wedding. At least, among people, he would have a modicum of distractions.

Chapter 35

Mr. Woods held out his arm for Miranda as she stepped up and out of his Corvette at St. Gabriel's church. Miranda smiled at Greyson and thought about the men from the country clubs she had known growing up who purchased corvettes in their older age. To Miranda, a Chevy Corvette symbolized the middle-aged white man's struggle to stay young, but on Greyson, it was endearing. As the two of them walked toward the chapel, they drew more than a passing glance from other guests arriving.

"We must be quite the handsome couple," Miranda lovingly complimented her escort, as they walked arm in arm.

"It is you, dear child. You alone causing the stir. Have I told you how stunning you look?" Greyson patted Miranda's hand.

"Aye, you have, and now I'm becoming self-conscious." Miranda didn't mind the compliment, but wasn't accustomed to standing out so much in a crowd. For the events she frequented as an heiress, what she wore this evening would have been considered conservative. For this crowd, her attire was a cut above.

"Chin up, girl. Just smile and I'll try to distract you from the gawkers." Greyson rather enjoyed the attention but wanted to be there for Miranda. "Come on. Let's go inside."

St. Gabriel's church was a historical building and a place of worship. Miranda took in all of its beauty from one end to the other. The pews were intricately carved with grape leaves and doves, and the floor beneath was of cream-colored marble. The walls down each side had colorful stain-glass windows depicting different scenes from the Bible. Down in the front, on each side of the pulpit, were carved statues; the Madonna and child on one side, the Crucifix on the other.

As her eyes adjusted to the low light, Miranda's focus drew up to the ceiling which was divided by ornate golden filigree into sections wherein were hand painted pictures of angels among clouds, and every ten feet down both sides of the sanctuary were hung crystal chandeliers, twelve softly lit and twinkling bulbs in each.

Finding a spot where he knew Miranda would feel less conspicuous, Greyson sat down with her and began pointing out individuals in the crowd. "That's the senior Mr. and Mrs. Mitchell, Suzanne's grandparents, and those are the groom's parents, Mr. and Mrs. Rhodes, and two of their other three children, Kari who graduated from high school this year, and Larry who is a sophomore. The Rhodes fourth child, Steven, is the Best Man."

Greyson continued to name off more folks than Miranda could ever hope to remember, but she nodded, glad to be focused on him, grateful he was trying.

Tad had come in with Ansel and Vida and frantically waved to catch Miranda's eye, but to her relief and Tad's disdain, the usher politely steered the group of three to an empty pew.

Soon the soft music from the speakers above went silent and the pipes of the magnificent organ released their air. The congregation stood to watch the bridesmaids and groomsmen enter, three pairs in all. The bridal march played next and the hush of anticipation settled like a blanket over the audience as before their eyes appeared the bride.

Suzanne looked radiant in her boho-elegant wedding dress; a lace and chiffon, long-sleeved, V-neck, beautifully styled gown. Her Maid of honor worked tirelessly to keep the train and skirt flared out. She did an excellent job to best show the exquisitely designed alternating panels of fabric which were floor-length in front, extending three feet on the carpet in the back. The bride, escorted by her deer-in-the-headlights father, moved gently and evenly down the aisle to her nervously waiting fiancé.

The traditional ceremony went smoothly, evidence that practice went well at the rehearsal dinner. The priest strayed from the conventional when he informed the audience that by witnessing this union; they were being asked to step up and be there for the new couple if they needed help during the course of their marriage. It was up to everyone there to share their love and advice to help keep this marriage on track.

Returning to the customary format, the priest lead the bride and bridegroom through the exchanging of rings, then followed his liturgy with a prayer over the new union. Last he introduced the newlywed couple and extended an invitation for all guests so inclined to come to the reception.

All eyes followed the husband and wife as they walked together up the aisle, smiling and receiving congratulations from guests seated along the center. Miranda watched them to the door, then her attention diverted when she thought she saw a familiar figure standing in the entryway. Was that Ethan? Miranda couldn't get a second look as the congregation filled the aisles.

Greyson and Miranda stood up to leave, and Tad tried to migrate over to them, but he got caught in traffic. It forced Tad to watch Miranda walk out of the chapel without him. Gone was his opportunity to catch her in a moment of weakness under the ceremonial cloud of another couple's wedded bliss. Cursing his bad luck, Tad anxiously wanted to get to the restaurant. At least there was an open bar. He planned to get drunk tonight.

Tad left the gathering outside the church's massive doors and made his way to the Suburban to wait. From his elevated vantage point in the slightly sloping parking lot, Tad caught a fleeting glimpse of Miranda surrounded by many of the town's people.

As he watched the spectacle, he thought it was pretty rude of Randi to take away the spotlight from Suzanne. Wasn't today supposed to be about the wedding? The way everyone gathered around Randi, you'd think she was a celebrity. Did Randi ever stop schmoozing? She made every connection an opportunity for business networking. It all seemed so phony.

Tad continued to stew as he reached into his jeans pocket for the cylindrical canister of chuff. Then when he saw the Baldwins making their way from the church front into the parked cars, to his utter contempt, Ethan was with them.

"When did you get here?" Tad didn't hide his annoyance.

"They invited everyone," Ethan answered indirectly, then added, "You sure are in a cheery mood."

Ethan's sarcasm did not amuse Tad and he spat on purpose, nearly hitting Ethan's boot with the disgusting collection of saliva and tobacco juice he generated.

"I'll get my truck and meet y'all at the Villa." Ethan stepped over Tad's assaulting spit wad, but provoked the bear with words, "Cheer up, Tad. Weddings are joyous occasions."

Ethan couldn't help but feel schadenfreude. Tad's mood showed he was not happy with how things were going with Miranda. What was disappointing to Tad was a positive sign for Ethan.

~****~

The throng that gathered around them surprised and humbled Miranda as Greyson continued the introductions. The men and women she met offered donations of time and services. Some gave welcoming advice, or just expressed genuine interest in what Miranda was bringing to their tight-knit community. Highly respected by the citizenry of Rambletap Springs, the Baldwins, with shining endorsements, had gone a long way by word of mouth to establish goodwill from the residents toward Miranda.

By the time she and Greyson made it to the Corvette, it had been nearly ten minutes since the photographers had finished up their shoot at the church site and left for the reception. Miranda hadn't spotted Ethan since leaving the soft lighting inside, and it convinced her she had been looking at someone else. She had also not seen Tad and was glad about that.

When Miranda and Greyson arrived at the restaurant, the hostess led them to the private area; a grand room with a floor to ceiling wall of glass panels which slid open onto a covered ramada and the outdoors, an expanse of green lawn filled with tables and chairs. The party was in full swing already, the bride and groom were mingling and the musicians were setting up to play. The bride and groom approached the long table where some members of their court had already taken their seats, and the staff served dinner.

Miranda and Greyson found two available chairs in the middle section between the indoor room and outdoor space. "I can't thank you enough, Greyson, for your efforts to make me comfortable. I want so badly to make a decent impression on the folks whose support we need. This could have been an overwhelming experience, but for you."

"You are easy to read, Miranda. You are honest and up front. Anyone with a modicum of feelings will understand your intentions." Greyson spoke as he pointed to the two bottles of wine waiting to be poured. "Red or White?" Greyson asked. The red wine, a Sangiovese, a medium bodied estate wine from California, was Miranda's choice.

As Miranda sipped, she observed all the cheerful characters with whom Greyson conversed. She was sorry when she caught sight of Tad, who seemed to glare when their eyes met.

Tad had been one of the first to arrive. He had skipped the table wine and headed straight to the open bar. When Ethan came to the venue, he noticed Tad already indulging and, though he'd rather have gone to say hello to Kevin and Suzanne, he knew he should monitor his inebriating friend. Ethan joined Tad at the bar.

"Just look at her," Tad complained to Ethan, who did not take a seat.

"Yes, she is so beautiful, so full of life." Ethan realized who Tad was talking about.

"Didn't you see her?" Tad wanted Ethan to understand. "She is flirting and flaunting with everyone, and I can't believe Mr. Woods. The dirty ol'man!" Tad grumbled and motioned to the bartender for another drink.

"That's not how I look at it, man," Ethan explained, "As far as I can see, Mr. Woods is being the perfect gentleman, a suitable escort, introducing Miranda to people, keeping away the rude and misbehaving guys before they could make their moves. You should be thankful."

"Thankful!" Tad snorted, then slammed the liquor to the back of his throat with a gritty cough. "Why should I be thankful? He is taking up all her time and attention. So selfish." Tad swiped his sleeve across his mouth with the arm that held the shot glass, tipping it enough to allow the remaining drops to drip to the floor. "Hit me again."

The bartender glanced from Tad to Ethan. He understood when Ethan shook his head and did the open hand slash at his own neck, the universal signal to cut off Tad's consumption. The understanding barkeep knew Tad had had enough for now.

"Mind your own business, Ethan," Tad had seen the nonverbal exchange between Ethan and the server. It insulted him. "I can take care of myself. Barkeep, hit me again!"

Ethan nodded, and the bartender obliged, filling Tad's tiny glass with a small splash of liquor.

Tad looked around the room and in his altered state of mind all he saw were men, hovering around Randi like predators at the water hole, waiting for the deer to come down and drink.

"I wish the band would hurry and play. I got to ask Randi to dance before the vultures move in." Tad drained another shot, slammed his hand on the bar, and asked for another.

"There will be plenty of time to dance, Tad. You should play it cool."

"You can't tell me what to do." Then Tad grew suspicious. "Why are you sticking your nose into mine and Randi's business? Are you trying to wedge us apart so you can move in?"

There was no need to respond. Ethan knew you can't reason with belligerence. Ethan's silence speared through Tad's delicate psyche.

"You are, aren't you?" Tad accused. "You arrogant fool. You think everything should always be about you, don't you? Why can't you stand to see other people happy? You made life for Paula miserable, ruined my brother's chance at happiness, and now you are coming after me and Randi."

"Your brother and Paula are fine, Tad. Happy as can be. They are at the table with my folks. Let's go sit down and eat. They are serving dinner now." Ethan ignored Tad's insulting comment. Drunk people were obnoxious, and Tad proved to be no exception to the rule.

~****~

Ethan led his staggering friend on unstable legs to the dinner table. When Ansel saw them coming, he put some bread on a plate and set it down for Tad. "Here, son, eat this."

Tad had finally cooperated with Ethan and agreed to leave the bar and sit with the family at the circular table. Noah, Paula, and the senior Baldwins were already enjoying the dinner prepared for Suzanne and Kevin's wedding reception.

"But I love her, Ethan," Tad implored as he fell into the chair. "I have to be the only one to dance with her." Tad's determination was becoming an obsession. His condition was deteriorating.

"First you must eat." Ethan instructed as if speaking to a recalcitrant toddler.

Ansel steadied the chair that threatened to topple from the imbalanced occupant and mouthed the words, 'how many?' behind Tad as he bent forward to grab the bread. Ethan whispered a response with a questioning shrug, "at least three."

"You will have time for dancing when you've sobered up." Noah's attempt to soothe his brother's concerns was fruitless.

Tad reached for Vida's glass of wine, nearly spilling it, and Ethan took hold of Tad's hand. "You've had enough. Eat some bread." Ethan glanced around, noticing the folks sitting nearest them had witnessed the kerfuffle.

"Get your hands off me." Tad glared at Ethan and stood on wobbly legs as the band played. "I'm going to ask her now."

"You can't ask Randi to dance now, you can't even walk. You need to sober up." Ansel could see Ethan and Noah were having no luck with keeping Tad at the table. "Sit down." he ordered. There were now three sober guys trying to control one drunk.

"The hell I will. I can walk." Tad broke free. "I'm asking her now."

Tad got to Miranda's table without falling. "May I have this dance?"

"Excuse me." Mr. Woods quickly stood up and put himself between Miranda and the drunk Tad, just as Ethan and Ansel arrived.

Tad pushed his way past Greyson and half fell into Miranda. "Out of the way ol'man." He asked Miranda again. The number of people involved in the fracas had now grown and it drew the attention of more.

Miranda stood up, hoping she could take control by appeasing Tad. Tad pulled Miranda by the arm through the dancing couples with surprising agility, considering his impairment after the amount of whiskey shots he had consumed. With no rhythm, Tad jerked Miranda about to the fox-trot beat of the song, I Do by artist Colbie Caillat. Luckily, other partiers hadn't caught the scene at the table.

"You're drunk," Miranda said.

"Drunk in love." Tad slurred.

"Charming." The alcohol on his breath mixed with the faint smell of chewing tobacco made Miranda cringe.

Tad caught the sarcasm. "Mind your tongue, woman." This wasn't the romantic moment that had played out in his head. Miranda was ruining it.

"You shouldn't have drank so much." Miranda had been among drunks before, had seen the effects of alcohol that left most folks jolly and, though a little over the top, mostly fun to be with. Tad wasn't that kind of drunk. Miranda turned and walked away.

Tad caught Miranda's arm and spun her toward him, making it look like a dance move and when she got near enough, he gripped her face with his other hand and kissed her mouth. "I guess I know one way to silence you."

Miranda realized Tad was causing another scene. Miranda was about to walk away again when Greyson tapped Tad on the shoulder. "May I cut in?"

"You've had her all evening. Get your own girl, man." Tad stood his ground, no longer dancing.

Greyson led Miranda away from Tad and Noah forced his brother in the other direction.

"Let's take him toward the far end," Ansel advised.

"Look at that slut. She acts all uppity with me, but she'll let other guys touch her." Tad watched through slitted eyelids and sought to keep track of Miranda.

"Come on, Tad," Noah pleaded with his brother, "You are acting the fool."

"Let go of me!" Tad started spinning to free himself from between Ethan and Noah who were still holding his shoulders, and when he shook free, he hauled back his arm, taking aim but it wasn't a fair shot.

"Take it easy, partner." Ethan drew no offense to the failed punch meant for his face as he twisted Tad's outstretched arm and he and Noah took the brawl outside. "Time to get some fresh air."

"Knock it off, guys," Tad continued to squirm. "Why are you dragging me out here?"

"You've lost the choice. I'd rather not spend my time out here with you, but I don't want you to ruin this wedding for anyone else." Ethan knew Tad had the tendency to overindulge. Many times, during their night clubbing days, he had been there to look after his best friend. But this time Tad had carried it way too far.

The wedding reception festivities continued. Everyone seemed to forget about the disturbance. It had shaken Miranda up a little, but when everything went on as if all was normal, her nerves settled. Greyson explained this was not unusual for a Rambletap Springs celebration, there was always some drama. Miranda danced with a few of the single men. She loved to dance, and the men were all pleasant partners.

Ansel was the first to rejoin the party inside, then Noah. Miranda was grateful the situation with Tad seemed under control, but it disappointed her that Ethan was not returning to the reception. The band played a slow song and Paula and Noah seized the opportunity for a romantic dance.

When Ansel and Vida decided to cut the rug, Miranda sat beside Greyson at the table feeling envious and happy at the same time for the couples who had found their one true love. From the corner of her eye, Miranda noticed Ethan had come back inside. Making eye contact from across the room, Ethan started moving toward her. He was smiling, and Miranda gratefully assumed the issues with Tad had been handled.

"Not so fast," from behind, Tad intercepted Miranda as she started moving through the crowd to meet Ethan. "You're coming with me."

Tad's arm was around Miranda's waist, and he pulled her away from the celebration and into the shadows.

Miranda couldn't find anything to hold on to and struggled to maintain her balance in high-heeled shoes. "Let me go."

"Stop struggling. You can't fight me." Tad seemed undaunted by her defensiveness.

"You are hurting me." Tad's aggressiveness shocked Miranda.

Running out of options, Miranda felt herself acting on instinct. She raised her knee with force, aiming for the most vulnerable part of a man's anatomy, but Tad moved his leg in time to divert the attempt. His leg was now in between Miranda's and he pressed himself against her. Miranda made a fist, and swung before Tad could react, and though she landed the swing effectively, leaving Tad stunned, it didn't stop him from hitting back. Tad back handed Miranda, hitting her cheek and mouth with such force, it surprised him. As his hand made contact, he realized what he had done and let go, causing Miranda to crash to the floor.

After the hit, Miranda felt an explosion of sharp pain, and a few seconds later, a reverberating sensation in her brain when her head hit the floor. Then she felt a sense of floating before everything went black.

"Randi?" Miranda heard a faint voice that seemed to come from far away. "It's me, Vida." The older lady was on her knees, bending forward over Miranda.

"Why are we on the floor?" Miranda tried to lift herself up, but her head was spinning. "What happened?"

"Don't get up," Vida advised. "Honey, I think you took a tumble. Did you faint?"

"No, I…" Miranda struggled to remember. "I was… Tad was…" Miranda lifted her hand to the side of her face and winced.

"Oh, my gosh!" Vida exclaimed when she saw even in the low light of the darkened corner, the young woman's face was red below the eye and her cheek was swelling. Vida looked over her shoulder and saw Ansel coming toward them. Luckily, the other guests hadn't noticed the unusual activity in the shadows.

"Is she okay?"

"Someone hit her, Ansel!" Vida couldn't believe the words out of her own mouth.

"It was Tad," Ansel explained. "Ethan saw it happening, but couldn't get to Miranda fast enough. He took Tad outside." Ansel searched the crowd for Greyson, and when he saw the other man, he waved.

Greyson came over and saw Miranda. The look of deep concern on his face was evidence the injury was becoming more obvious by the second. "We need to put ice on that." He said, "Dammit! I lost sight of Miranda for one second. How did this happen so fast?"

Miranda tried again to sit up as the folks busied around her. She still couldn't remember clearly how she ended up on the floor. Vida could see Miranda still wasn't okay, and it took two people to help her up to the chair Greyson had brought over when he went for ice. The terry cloth towel containing the ice stung upon contact, and Vida soothed Miranda with a cupped hand on the face, the other side that wasn't throbbing like a drum. "It's okay, Randi, you're safe. I am right here and he's gone now." Vida held her hand tight as Miranda looked at her. Then her eyes filled with tears.

~****~

Ethan saw Tad taking Miranda into the corner against her will and zig-zagged across the room to get to them. From a distance, he watched in horror as Tad struck Miranda across the face. He couldn't catch her as Miranda fell, and when Vida came over, Ethan went after Tad, who had dropped Miranda, and ran for the door.

Once outside of the restaurant, Noah and Paula caught up with Ethan, but not before Ethan had unloaded on the drunk man until Tad wasn't able to get up and take another hit. Ethan had followed Tad outside and found Tad sitting on the pavement by the Suburban, legs sprawled in front of him, staring blankly at his hands. Ethan hauled his old friend to his feet and showed no restraint in giving Tad what he deserved.

Ansel came upon the boys engaged in a fight outside. Ethan threw his opponent against a parked car, and Tad went down for the last time. Ansel broke in and held back Ethan. They loaded the badly roughed up Tad into Paula and Noah's pickup.

"Can you take him to your apartment?" Ansel asked. Taking Tad to the ranch tonight was a bad idea. Ansel was afraid of the residual anger Ethan might experience. He had never expected such a violent display from his kind and quiet child. Ansel could wrap his mind around Ethan's response. The actions were justified. But Ansel couldn't deny it was unsettling to see such rage.

Chapter 36

Miranda tried to piece together the sequence of events as she rode through town in Greyson's Corvette. It was hazy around the edges. She remembered Vida holding an ice pack to her cheek while talking with Ansel, Ethan, and Greyson, but her focus vacillated in and out. The words they were saying made no sense. Miranda just couldn't grasp the context. Vida had walked Miranda to Greyson's car and now he was driving her to the ranch, but there were still so many holes in her recollection.

Aside from the throbbing cheek and pounding behind her eyes every time there was an oncoming vehicle, Miranda noticed her wrist and right hand were throbbing, too. Miranda furrowed her brow, forcing herself to remember. They had all been at the wedding reception. Miranda pictured the scene. In her mind, she saw the Baldwins and Paula and Noah. Ethan was there, too. Ethan had been taking care of Tad. Tad had had too much to drink.

Then, like a sleeper wave in a turbulent tide, it all came crashing down on her. Tad, the dancing and him becoming angry. She remembered his alcohol and chewing tobacco breath, and his tight arms holding her against her will. As her memory returned with painful awareness, Miranda became embarrassed. This was not the way to make a first impression on the good folks of Rambletap Springs.

Throughout the drive, Greyson tried to think of something to say to Miranda as she sat so close in the tight space of the sports car's cockpit. But he had very little experience with this sort of thing. When he heard her breath catch, he suspected she might be crying. He wanted to tell her it was okay, it would all be alright, but couldn't relate. He had no way of knowing how it felt to be dominated without mercy, forced against one's will, and then knocked around like a sack of grain. Greyson wondered if this was what a father feels for a daughter in this situation. All he wanted was to hurt Tad the way Tad had hurt Miranda. He was aware Miranda was conscious, but she could have a concussion. His idea to take her to the emergency hospital was overruled, and he now wished he'd have been more insistent.

Miranda couldn't stop shaking and wished she could slip into the foggy feeling before when she couldn't remember a thing. Her face had swollen on the one side, partially impairing her vision. She hoped Greyson wasn't looking at her, she must be a mess. As Greyson maneuvered the car up the dark ranch driveway, Miranda reached for the door handle.

"This is fine," she said, hoping the car would slow enough for her to jump out.

"Is there anything I can do?" Greyson said as Miranda had her seat belt off and bolted out the door before the transmission on the car was in park. "I'll wait out here." Greyson was at a loss when Miranda disappeared behind the closed cottage door.

Passing through and closing the cottage door behind her did nothing to stop the recurring image of Tad's angry face as his hand came crashing across her cheek. She could feel his clenching fingers gripping her chin, and taste the chewing tobacco residue on her lips left by Tad's assaulting kiss.

Miranda went to the bathroom to wash her hands and face and brush her teeth, hoping that would end the torturous memories. Disrobing seemed as though it might erase the sensation of Tad's gripping and clawing hands, but it gave her no relief. There was no comfort to be had.

Once again, feeling a strong need to get away, Miranda thought of Winston and remembered how safe she was around him ever since the first ride when they took care of each other. Miranda wanted to feel safe again and taken care of. Quickly slipping her legs into her jeans, Miranda threw a long-sleeved shirt over her bra and camisole, pulled on her socks and boots, grabbed her parka, winced when her hand pulled through the armhole, then stepped out the front door into the night.

Greyson may have gone into the house. He parked his car by the kitchen door and there was a light on inside. Miranda was relieved to get to the barn unobserved, and when she slipped through the sliding door, the familiar smells washed in to comfort her. Running on instinct, Miranda couldn't see, but she didn't need to.

Without turning on the barn light, she entered Winston's stall and heard him nicker and move toward her. She felt the horse nuzzle her pocket where there usually was a treat, and it felt like a hug. Miranda turned her face, swollen side up, into Winston's mane and wept. The violent image of Tad smacking her around was a movie that played on a continuous loop in her head.

Miranda's eyes adjusted to the darkness, and she had Winston saddled and bridled and in one step she was astride. With a spray of gravel, they sprang from the barn as the gelding obeyed his rider's squeezing legs.

"Miranda?" Greyson ran from the kitchen when he heard hoofbeats. He saw a light in the guest house and thought Miranda must be in there. He must have been hearing things, but upon inspection, he gathered the cottage was empty and the pounding of hooves could have been Miranda on horseback.

Alone in the driveway, Greyson didn't know what to do. Where were the Baldwins? He then saw two sets of headlights and waited impatiently for the cars to arrive.

"Hurry!" Greyson shouted. "Miranda just took off on horseback. I think she went down the driveway."

Ethan, who had arrived in front of his parents in the Suburban, didn't even hesitate. He hit the throttle, spun his truck around, turned the high beams on, and drove to the meadow gate. The gate was closed and secured, and the headlights shining across the expanse of grass revealed nothing moving. Ethan cursed, hit the steering wheel hard with his hand and didn't even register the self-inflicted pain. If Miranda had fled to the meadow, how had she gotten through the gate without opening it?

Ethan returned to the complex where his mother and Greyson still stood and shouted, "I'll need a horse!"

In a fast few minutes and with the help of Ansel, Ethan had Heart saddled and was off and running. Miranda had gotten a good head start, and Ethan couldn't even be sure of the direction she had taken. Ethan let his horse choose, hoping he might follow his stable mate. Heart ran straight across the meadow and headed up the trail to Carmen's Camp, a trail Winston had been on several times. Maybe Miranda was running blind, trusting her horse's instinct to pick a familiar direction.

~****~

The darkness was like water cascading down and the oppressiveness sucked the energy out of Miranda's frenzied flight. Miranda had lost track of how long they'd been on the move and she slowed Winston to a trot. She hadn't meant to run him so hard and she could feel Winston's sides heaving for breath. Where were they? Miranda wondered. This had been a stupid idea. There was no moon. Miranda couldn't see a thing. There was no point in turning around. She couldn't tell what direction would get them home. Miranda gave Winston his head and hoped he would take them down, but she had a sinking feeling they were still climbing.

Miranda realized they were in the forest, she couldn't see, but felt the density of the trees, she guessed she and Winston were headed to Carmen's Camp and would soon be out of the forest, but she didn't know how far they had come and had no way to estimate when they would reach the safety of the cabin and corral.

"I'm sorry, Winston," Miranda whispered to the gelding, as he slowed to a walk and plodded along. "I promise if we get ourselves out of this, I won't do this ever again."

Suddenly, Miranda heard a crash off to the left, and Winston sprang to the right and into a dead run. Miranda didn't stop him. The horse was probably running on purpose. Whatever spooked him was very real and the safest place for Miranda was with Winston. The race was on again as they streaked through the dark forest. Miranda cursed her irrational behavior and hung on.

Racing through the darkness, she couldn't tell if her eyes were open or shut. Miranda stayed bent low in the saddle, leaned forward over Winston's neck, and kept her face and her fingers buried in his mane, trying to keep from getting swept off his back by low-hanging branches.

Frozen in this position, Miranda was aware of little else except the pounding of hooves, the rocking of Winston's stride, the saddle horn that dug into her belly, causing a burning pain that usurped the pain in her head, face and hand. The horse could have been running for minutes or hours, Miranda lost track. In and out of consciousness, she felt pain in waves, and vomited, and still she hung on. Though she would have been relieved of it all if she could pass out; she fought to stay with the horse.

~****~

Ethan crested the ridge of the little valley where the cabin sat, but saw no light radiating from within. He had ridden for what felt like an eternity, pushing Heart as hard as he dared, but hadn't come across the runaway horse and rider he hoped he was tailing. Where were they? Maybe they had doubled around and were at the house. Maybe Miranda had ridden in another direction, say to the Sunrise Arena, and since returned. Well, no matter what, he had to rest his horse, or he'd soon be walking.

Ethan steered his horse up the path toward the cabin and Heart's pace quickened when he heard a horse nicker. Through the murky blackness, Ethan could see the darker shape of a horse and he dismounted. When Ethan approached the riderless horse, still bridled and saddled, he reached out and touched the dried-on dirt and sweat of caked and matted hair on the horse's neck and shoulders.

It was Winston, but where was Miranda? Had she come off her horse as they ran through the forest? How far had Winston run on without her? As if to answer the questions, Ethan heard a soft murmur from the other side of the horse. His eyes strained to make out the human shaped shadow laying in a heap on the ground. It was Miranda! Winston nuzzled her motionless body as if to say, 'here she is' and Ethan bent down to pick her up. "Good boy," he patted the horse and carried Miranda inside.

In moments, Ethan had the lamp lit, the fire burning, and he had inspected Miranda for more injuries. She couldn't have hit too hard when she fell from the horse, he suspected, because there was no evidence of ground-in dirt or grass stains on her clothing. In the dim light, Ethan noticed the purple and black around Miranda's eye and right cheek, and he gently sponged the area with clean water to remove the slight traces of dirt and sweat.

His anger burned as he held Miranda's hand and noticed her wrist was swollen and blue. "You must have gotten in a swing or two." He was proud of Miranda's tenaciousness to defend herself and held the limp hand to his lips, wishing he'd have pounded Tad further into the ground for what he had done.

Ethan removed Miranda's boots and tucked her under the comforter on the bed before he went out to tend to the horses. After removing the saddles and bridles, he let the horses have a satisfying roll in the scratchy meadow grass before putting on the hobbles and checking the water trough. Next, Ethan texted his father's cell phone to let them know everyone was safe, and they were bunking down at Carmen's.

~****~

Ansel was relieved when he got the text from Ethan and frustrated that he couldn't have more details. There wasn't enough cell service for a conversation, but Ansel, who was coming from the meadow where he had been looking for Randi at Sunrise Arena, was grateful to read the brief words. He texted back to Ethan a response showing he had received the message.

"There's no need for you to worry anymore, Greyson." Vida tried to comfort the high school teacher as she set the teapot to boil. She and Mr. Woods were still waiting for any news regarding Miranda. "They will find her."

"I hope she is alright. I can't believe I let her slip away like that. All I had to do was bring her home safely, and I let her run away. She is in no condition to be out there. She has a concussion. I feel so helpless. If I could ride, I'd be out there looking. As it stands now, I'd be the one needing rescue."

"Ethan will find her," Vida wished she believed her own declaration. It was faith that she relied on now. "It will be fine. Ethan knows every square inch of this ranch, and Ansel is scouring the meadows and the river valley. There is nowhere Miranda can go that they can't find her."

Vida sat down opposite Mr. Woods and poured the steaming water into the kettle, but had forgotten to drop in the infuser.

"These leaves won't steep unless they're in the water." Mr. Woods found momentary relief in teasing Vida. Now he knew she was as worried as he was, and realized none of that would bring everyone home safely. "I'd like to pray."

Vida gladly bowed her head with Mr. Woods. Truth is, she was worried. As experienced as Ethan was at tracking, he did not know which way Miranda had gone. He wouldn't be able to trace her path in the dark. There were bears and mountain lions, and some ranchers had even reported wolves. And those were just the dangers from critters. The horse could stumble or spook and throw the rider. It was dangerous for Miranda and those looking for her. Vida prayed for them all.

Interrupting their prayers, Ansel came banging through the door. "I got a text. They are fine. They are at Carmen's Camp and everyone is safe."

"Hallelujah and Amen," Greyson clasped his hands and looked skyward.

Vida sprang from her chair. "Oh, Ans, I am so relieved." Vida held on to her husband, thankful he, too, was okay.

“Is Miranda okay? Are they staying out there all night? Should we call for rescuers? Shouldn’t we call the police?” Mr. Woods asked.

“Out here, we rescue ourselves.” Ansel sat down with their friend to fill him in on their old-fashioned ways, “It’s being handled.”

Chapter 37

Ansel told Mr. Woods what had taken place out in the parking lot after the teacher left the reception with Miranda.

"Tad had sobered up some, and showed remorse, so Ethan showed him mercy when he doled out a whooping. Tad will feel it tomorrow. There is no need for the law. This punishment was swift and more impactful. Tad will never hit another person, let alone a woman, without remembering the beating he got."

"Ethan hit him pretty good, eh?" Greyson almost smiled, not really proud that it felt good to know Tad was probably still hurting.

"Ethan was so angry, I have never seen him like that. None of us take kindly to men who hit others, especially women. But Ethan unloaded on Tad and Tad never hit back. It was hard to watch. I am glad I was there to stop them."

The weight of responsibility pressed hard on Ansel's senior shoulders. He should have seen this coming, should have insisted Tad leave the reception. If they had all taken a little harder stance on Tad's behavior, if they had seen how inappropriate he was being, they could have prevented this whole thing. "A part of me wanted to take a few licks at Tad, too." Ansel was solemn.

"But you didn't, Ansel, and you stopped Ethan." Vida steadied her husband with her hands on either side of his face when she saw the faraway look in his eyes.

Ansel's glazing eyes focused on his wife's reassuring face. She was a strong and calming influence, but did not know how hard it was sometimes to be a man. With their built-in propensity for violence, in most men, common sense can temper it. Even when provoked, men can learn to control their anger. Seeing Ethan so out of control had been alarming. Could Ethan have stopped himself? Did he have enough control? And what of Tad? Tad hadn't yet learned how to handle the effects alcohol has on a man's better judgement. Had he learned his lesson now?

Maybe Ethan and Tad hadn't had enough opportunity to learn self-control. Who knew? Whatever the reasons, Tad had committed an offense. Adding to it, those around him were also guilty; the bar tender for serving him, his friends for not recognizing the distress, the older adults who lost track of the situation, it was a collection of lapses in responsibility, a group failure.

Among many things, admitting to short comings was hard for any man. "I am very sorry, Vida." Ansel reached for his wife, asking for forgiveness, holding on to her strength of the soul when his own physical strength wasn't enough.

"I know," Vida soothed, not really knowing or fully understanding. "It's no one's fault."

~****~

Miranda came to with a sharp jab of pain in her right eye from squinting to focus in the dim light. *Where am I?* she thought and tried to find something she could recognize through blurry vision. Nothing looked familiar. The last thing she could remember was she and Winston were racing through the dark forest, but she wasn't sure if that had been a dream.

She tried sitting up, hoping a better angle would bring clarity, but her head wouldn't stop spinning. The haziness, she decided, could mean she was dreaming, the slow motion of her perception supported the theory, and feeling too weak to fight it, too weary to care, she settled back down and closed her eyes. In this dream, she felt no danger, there was no sound, she seemed warm and safe; it was best to play the dream out and wait for herself to wake up.

Drifting in and out of the dream, the images kept Miranda vacillating between pleasant dream and nightmare. She was in Connecticut, camping with Amanda. She could smell the campfire and hear the crackling logs. Next, she was cold and scared.

Something was chasing her, but she couldn't see it. She needed to run, but her legs wouldn't move. The chasing stopped and Miranda felt like she was in her daydream again with Ethan in the cabin in the mountains. He was standing over her, touching her forehead and cheek, and she was safe. Relaxing into the peaceful dream, Miranda welcomed the wave of comfort that drifted over her.

In town and far away from his victim, Tad was also struggling, but he wanted to pass out. He hoped he could lose consciousness and never wake up. Laying there on his brother's couch, every bone in his body ached, but he deserved it. He hoped his pain would take away the pain he had caused the one person he wanted to hurt the least. The details of the events that brought him to the present were fuzzy, but the part he remembered best was the part he wanted most to forget.

"Here, drink this," Noah hovered over his broken brother and held a cup of coffee to his swollen and misshapen lips. "Paula, do we have a straw?"

Paula came in from the tiny kitchen in their one-bedroom apartment with a glass of coconut water and a straw, "Here, try this instead of the coffee."

Noah hesitated.

"It's a natural electrolyte replacement drink with antioxidant qualities and supports kidney function." Paula explained. "Trust me."

"Thank you." Noah looked up at his wife and took the glass. The look of concern on her face didn't go unnoticed. He was worried about his twin, too.

"Just leave me be, Noah," Tad groaned and turned his face away from the glass being offered.

Noah stood up and turned to Paula. "Should we have taken him to the hospital?"

Paula hadn't an answer. This whole situation was beyond her experience. She had seen boys fight. In fact, she was sometimes the reason they were fighting, but those were silly little tussles compared to this. From her pocket, her cell phone sounded off, making her jump. She stepped back into the kitchen to answer it.

When she got off the phone, she was glad to see Tad drank a bit of water. "That was Vida. They are handling things up at the ranch, and Mr. Woods is on his way down to help with Tad."

Noah was relieved, but Tad, who had also heard the news, tried to sit up. "I don't want that old man coming here. I don't need his help. He's done enough. It's his fault this whole thing happened."

"What are you talking about, Noah?" Paula couldn't believe her ears.

"Just lay back down. Don't get upset." Noah soothed and when the tension in his brother's body eased, he turned to Paula.

"He is still under the influence, Paula. We don't want to rile him up now."

"He should sleep it off in jail," Paula said. She couldn't keep her emotions down. She was still in shock and conflicted. What Tad had done was so many kinds of wrong. She couldn't forgive his poor decisions, but what Tad was now putting her husband through in the aftermath, as he tended to his brother, just made things worse.

"Are you kidding me, Paula?" Tad rose again from his supine position, then let out a screech like a night owl when his bruised abdominal muscles contracted. He let out a low, grinding moan, then said with a raspy voice, "Ethan is the one who should be in jail."

Noah rushed back to his brother's side when Tad cried out in pain.

"Get away from me, Noah. I don't need you, either." Tad found no comfort from his brother's attention now. Noah hadn't been there to help that evening as Ethan beat him to within an inch of life. Noah had stood by doing nothing when Tad needed him. Why would he need his brother's help now?

"Let's let him be. He needs to sleep it off." Noah felt more assured his sibling didn't need a hospital, he just needed to detox, relax and let his body heal. Noah was certain Tad had sustained no head injuries. Ethan hadn't gone for the face on purpose, other than the first blow, which was only in defense of the strike Tad tried to land initially.

Noah and Paula waited for Mr. Woods, who showed up just in time to help get the inebriated Tad into the bathroom, where he spent the next forty-five minutes emptying his guts from the poisonous effects of the liquor. Paula set up the couch with a sheet and blankets as a makeshift bed for her brother-in-law. When Tad was resting on the couch peacefully this time, Mr. Woods took his leave.

"That's about the most we can do tonight," Noah assured his wife as much as himself. "Things should look better under morning light."

~****~

"Knock, knock?" Paula opened the kitchen door enough to poke her head through and saw Ansel and Vida sitting at the table, silently staring at their coffee cups.

"Morning Paula, come in," Ansel greeted their goddaughter, and Vida stood up to make Paula a cup of tea.

"I'll get it," Paula said, getting a cup from the cabinet. She and Noah had left the apartment early, after a brief night's rest. "Tad was still passed out but resting comfortably. Noah came with me and is taking care of the morning chores."

Ansel stood up, relieved to have Noah's help. "I was just heading out myself."

With the teapot in hand, Paula filled her empty cup and refilled the cup in front of Vida. "Did you hear anything more from Ethan?"

Before they crashed into bed the night before, Vida had notified Noah and Paula of the news that Miranda had fled, Ethan had found her and they were holding up at Carmen's Camp.

"We've heard nothing more since the initial text Ansel got, but cell service is spotty, plus there is no way to charge the phone." Vida knew they wouldn't hear any additional messages other than in person.

Knowing only the surface of Miranda's condition before she took off was a worry, but not knowing if she had suffered any further injury was worse. The text Ansel received was brief. Vida had to assume if there were more, they should know, Ethan would have relayed the information. Was Miranda okay? Did they need additional supplies, first aid? Should Ansel have ridden up last night, too? Not being able to help, unsure if there was anything she should do, Vida felt helpless and uncomfortable. Praying only got her so much solace, and it left her with nothing else to do but worry.

Paula and Noah stayed with the Baldwins, Noah helped with the chores and Paula helped Vida prepare a care package. Ansel prepared the horses he needed for his ride up to Carmen's to deliver the goods. They kept the shelter stocked with essentials, but it would help Randi to have some fresh food, too. Vegetables, fruits and berries, Vida packed mason jars she had canned herself full of all the good things she and Ansel grew right there in their garden.

After breakfast, Ansel prepared to head out. Magic was saddled and ready and they equipped Rowdy with the crossbuck, a saddle for pack horses upon which are fastened panniers that hold food, equipment, tools, camping gear for packing when they went deeper into the backcountry. Noah was filling the panniers with lightweight articles for this trip. Paula had gathered what clothing and toiletries Miranda might need in case she wasn't able to ride for a few days. Everything was in the packs and ready to be taken out to the waiting horses.

"Be careful, Ansel. Let us know how things are going up there as soon as you get there," Vida asked.

"Of course," Ansel bent down to give his wife a goodbye hug. "I will let you know."

"There won't be any need for that." Ethan came flying into the kitchen from the vestibule and surprised the group.

"Ethan!" Vida let go of Ansel and flung her arms around her son. "You guys are alright." She looked behind Ethan. "Where's Randi?"

Though happy to see Ethan, the somber mood in the kitchen didn't lift. Ethan explained in quick detail how he had found Miranda, and the condition she was in. Afraid to leave her side until the wee hours and then, only after she was finally resting peacefully, Ethan had left at dawn to come down and pick up supplies. They needed salves for bruises, and antiseptic for the many cuts and scrapes. Ethan also wanted some of Vida's tinctures for pain. He suspected Miranda was in more discomfort than was clear.

"We have Rowdy packed already. I was just about to head out," said Ansel.

"Great, thanks," Ethan said. "I'll need to switch horses. Heart is spent and we need to hurry." Ethan was worried that Miranda might wake up in distressed confusion. He was also worried she might not wake up at all. She had a concussion; of that he was certain.

"You can't go by yourself without some rest. Let your dad go, Ethan. He'll bring Randi down." Vida tried to be the voice of reason.

"No, Mom." Ethan was firm. "I am going back up there, and Randi is in no condition to travel by horse."

"At least have a meal before you head back up. I'll get something for you." Paula chimed in. "You should go back, but you will need all your strength and a full belly."

"Thank you, Paula." Ethan knew she was right.

Paula quickly went to the refrigerator, jumping at the opportunity to be useful. She remembered that at one time, making a meal for an appreciative Ethan would have been her dream come true. She smiled at the irony.

Noah came in and, in an instant, Ethan saw red. "Easy there, pardner," Noah saw the flash of anger and knew Ethan thought he was seeing his look-alike twin. "Hold your fire. It's me, Ethan."

"Sorry Noah." Ethan let his heart rate return to normal.

Ethan wolfed down the meal Paula had thrown together from leftovers and headed out with Rowdy in tow. Ethan thought Rowdy was the wise choice. If Miranda's condition took a turn for the worst, and she needed to come down the mountain in an emergency, Rowdy was the best option. When pointed in the desired direction and with no further input from his rider, that horse would pack Miranda safely home.

~****~

The light in the room was not so dim anymore. It was morning, but still Miranda slept and still she dreamed. Only the details were clearer. She was at Carmen's Camp in the little cabin. She recognized the stone face of the hearth, the cast-iron cauldron, and the little chest of drawers with the ceramic bowl and pitcher. It all seemed so real.

In her dream, Miranda was cooking dinner in the cauldron, beef and vegetable stew with dumplings, and she could see Ethan squatting and stirring the pot as steam rolled up to the ceiling. As Miranda's eyes followed the rising vapors, in her dream she saw Ethan's face, the lazy grin that got to her every time. She smiled back. She was enjoying the dream, hoped she would not wake up.

"It's good to see you are awake. Are you thirsty?" Ethan said.

Miranda realized she wasn't dreaming. Sitting up in the bed intending to stand, Miranda became dizzy, put a hand to her temple, then leaned back against the wall.

"Easy there. You'd better take it slowly." Ethan sat on the bed beside her, holding a cup of water.

Miranda looked into Ethan's eyes with so many questions on her mind, but answers didn't seem to matter so much. She reached for the glass and put it to her lips. It was the sweetest water she had ever tasted.

"Slow down. Just drink a little at a time," Ethan warned, then stood up from the bed. "Soon as the water settles, and if you don't get sick to your stomach, you can try some food. You must be hungry."

Miranda hadn't thought at all about her stomach. She had too many unanswered questions. "What day is it?" She thought that would be a good place to begin filling in the blanks in her memory. She also wanted to know why was she on the mountain, and how had she gotten there? Why was she in the bed, and why Ethan was there? She blushed a little, wondering, had they been romantic? If so, why couldn't she remember?

The anxiety from the questions had creeped in and gave Miranda a sudden and inexplicable pain in her gut. She held her arms across her stomach with a grimace, and the frown made her face hurt. The pain had a way of clarifying the uncertainty as a flash of memory reminded her Tad had been angrily dragging her off the dance floor and had actually backhanded her across the face. She felt the explosion of pain as if it was happening again.

As the memories flooded in and piled on, Miranda remembered the burning pain as she clung to Winston for dear life. She had hold of the gelding's mane so tightly, his coarse hair had stung her skin as it cut through her fingers. Looking at her hands, she saw the still red bands where the hair had wrapped around. It still swelled the fingers from the lack of circulation.

Miranda sat looking at one hand the way an infant studies his limbs for the first time. Her other hand was still gripped around her middle as the flashes of memory rolled on a screen like a picture show. The saddle horn had dug in as Miranda hunched over the top of the fleeing horse, and she felt again the pain of a thousand gut punches. Ethan was back sitting on the bed holding a small bucket as the water Miranda drank came back up.

The heaving hurt as much as the saddle horn, and when the convulsions stopped, Ethan set aside the tin container she had spat into and let Miranda lean against him. Miranda didn't move away as cool beads of sweat broke out across her forehead. Ethan had a soft, damp cloth ready and wiped her brow. "Just sit for a minute and relax. Don't even try to remember, Miranda. It doesn't matter, anyway. You are safe now."

Miranda did as she was told. She had no other choice. As the acute pain eased to a dull pressure, she slumped into Ethan's chest and drifted back into a dream.

~****~

"You're awake," Noah said when he and Paula got home late in the afternoon to find Tad had gotten off the couch, cleaned himself up, and appeared to be fixing to go.

Tad grunted and asked, "Can I get a ride out to the ranch?"

"You can get a ride to anywhere else, Bro. But not the ranch," Noah said firmly.

Tad lowered his head when he realized, with vague recollection, something had gone down at the Mitchell-Rhodes wedding reception. Waking up in his brother's apartment feeling like he'd slept on the ground under a stampede of hundreds of cattle, Tad figured it wasn't good.

"Si'down, Tad," Noah ordered his twin. "You oughtn't be going anywhere. Best you lie low for a while. The Alma Soñada Ranch is the last place for you to go right now. You are not a favored person among a good deal of townspeople, as well. Do you have any idea what you did?"

The unofficial martial law punishment in Rambletap Springs for Tad was two-fold. He had suffered the beating of one hundred unanswered hits for having violently attacked another human, and now he would have to make amends in the eyes of the town elders and his peers. It was a daunting future.

"I must have blacked out. I don't know what I did. But I suspect it wasn't good," Tad said almost inaudibly. Truth is, he had been getting flashbacks, but the sequence of events wasn't clear. He couldn't be sure which pictures in his mind's eye were real.

He remembered fighting with Ethan, or more like, getting an ass kicking after he swung and missed. He remembered feeling angry and frustrated with Randi and he remembered having a few too many drinks. There was more, of that he was sure, and whether Noah or someone else filled in the blanks, or he continued to regurgitate the memories through flashbacks, it was painful both physically and mentally.

Noah told Tad how it went down as he himself remembered. Like an artist, Noah added details instead of paint until Tad could see the total picture. "Not that it's an excuse, but it is a reason, Tad. You cannot hold your liquor."

"You're right, man. Ohhhh, what have I done?" Tad felt worse and worse with each piece of information his brother added to the story. The anguish oozed from Tad in long, expressive releases of oxygen. "What am I gonna do?"

Noah let his brother wale, maybe it would cleanse his soul like the liver was cleaning the alcohol from his blood. "You can ask, no, beg. If you beg for forgiveness, it is possible the people you have hurt will feel sympathy. You can make a promise to never drink again, for everyone's sake."

"As the Lord is my witness, Brother." He never wanted to see an alcoholic drink for the rest of his life. The ache in Tad's body from the repeated blows, the pounding in his head that made his eyes throb. For Tad, those seemed minor compared to the ache in his heart. He had hurt Randi in a way no one should ever be hurt. The damage he did was irreparable. He wanted to beg for another whooping from Ethan in hopes the other man would kill him. Anything less was more than he deserved.

~****~

Miranda woke up with the strongest need to empty her bladder. She had been dreaming she was searching for a place to go. She was in a public arena or pavilion and couldn't find the restrooms. When she found them, they were not suitable; no paper in the dispenser, used tissue all over the floor. Another toilet was overflowing with wastewater, and a third had no seat. In the dream, Miranda went from stall to stall in that public restroom but couldn't use a single toilet.

Now that she'd woken up and realized she needed a bathroom, Miranda felt confused about which way to go. She stood up as she tried to figure it out. From where he was sitting, Ethan came running across the cabin in two strides and caught Miranda as her unstable legs had no intention of holding her weight.

"Slow down. You don't need to be falling. You've fallen enough lately." Ethan sat down on the bed with Miranda in his arms and didn't let go. Miranda liked the feeling and for a moment, they both held still until her bladder reminded her of its urgency and she tried to break free and stand up.

"Where are you going?" Ethan stayed seated and waited for an answer.

"To see a man about a horse," Miranda said as she made her way to the door on more dependable legs. Her strength was questionable, but the need to go gave her the motivation.

"Got it." Ethan picked up the meaning behind the euphemism. He was about to give Miranda a steadying hand, but thought better of it.

Stepping out the little door, Miranda saw Winston, a horse she thought looked like Rowdy and another horse she didn't recognize all standing in the corral. Was that Sonnet? Why was everything so confusing? Miranda thought she knew just about every horse on the ranch. She and Ethan had spent many hours looking over and evaluating all the horses in the stockyard, paddocks, and barns.

Miranda realized she was obsessing over something inconsequential and she quickly made her way around the back to the little outhouse. No wider than a broom closet with the sign 'privy 'on the door, inside the wooden structure was nothing more than a built-in box with the easily recognizable toilet seat. Miranda had no qualms about using the pit toilet. When she reached down to undo her pants and felt a stab of discomfort in her wrist, she stared at the limb like it didn't belong to her. Miranda studied the bruise, and a memory flashed through.

Miranda saw again Tad's angry face, heard his angry words, felt the crashing of his hand across her face, and it filled her with anguish anew. She remembered feeling embarrassed as Greyson drove her home. Miranda had never been a part of public displays of family drama. She had barely even witnessed such violence except on TV, and though she should have been angry, shame was the emotion she experienced.

After taking care of business, Miranda stepped from the outhouse. Looking out through the same eyes that had wanted nothing more than to flee, Miranda spotted Winston in the corral and went to the fence without thinking. It was then Miranda remembered taking off on Winston and running through the cold, dark forest. So, that's how I ended up here, but did Ethan ride with me? There were still lapses of time unaccounted for.

Miranda was certain Ethan knew what had happened at the wedding dinner, and a wave of embarrassment came over her again along with the question, what she and Ethan were doing up here alone together? The confusion was frightening, there were more unknowns and as fear took hold, flight became the answer.

Climbing into the corral, Miranda caught sight of the saddles and bridles under a little lean-to roof on the opposite side of the gate. Grabbing the equipment from the rack, Miranda went to Winston. She had to get away, but as she stood beside the horse, it reminded her of her promise to make better decisions after the last midnight journey she had embarked upon.

Ethan, who had been watching through the little paned window, stepped out to see what Miranda was going to do. If she was saddling up to take flight, he would follow, but not to stop her. He thought about all that had happened to Miranda practically since she got to Rambletap Springs and he himself, for no reason at all, had treated her like the enemy. Ethan couldn't imagine the uphill battle she had faced in her generous endeavor. She had more than enough money; he thought. She didn't have to do any of this. Miranda had stayed true to herself and her dreams. She was succeeding despite the negative reception.

Then there was Tad's constant pursuit of her attention, culminating in the assault followed by the harrowing ride through the forest thick. Ethan couldn't list all the dangers Miranda faced. The night belonged to the nocturnal. Miranda had stayed with her horse through it all, and based on the bruises and scratches, she must have gotten battered around the entire time. Now Ethan only wanted to give Miranda the space she might need as she figured things out.

In the shadows, Miranda succumbed to her inner sensibility. She returned the riding equipment to its place under the lean-to, then sought the comfort of her horse. Winston stood with patience and understanding as he channeled Miranda's pain away from her and into the atmosphere.

From his vantage point only a few yards away, Ethan could tell Miranda had abandoned the idea of running again, and when he saw her with her face buried in her horse's neck, he moved to her side.

"Come here," Ethan gently guided Miranda to face him and she turned. He could feel her silently weeping. "This is all my fault. I shouldn't have lost sight of Tad that night," Ethan said.

Miranda felt Ethan's arms around her, strong and safe, and though he couldn't understand how Miranda was feeling, she appreciated the try. It was comforting to know Ethan felt responsible, even though he was not. It was a generous thing to share the blame, but he was no more to blame for Tad's actions than she was. Miranda knew she needed to get past it. The more she thought about the crime, the longer she would be victimized by it.

Standing there in the little corral in the expansive valley in the high country, Miranda relaxed. From Ethan's nearness, she allowed herself to draw strength and eased into his arms further.

Ethan felt the tension in Miranda's body ease. He did not move a muscle, just let her be. Right now, Ethan was Miranda's guardian. He would stand there holding her as long as she needed. Without feeling silly, and having no regret, the two people stood in each other's arms as if it was the most normal thing to do.

"Are you hungry? You should try something to eat," Ethan finally spoke when Miranda eased her hold and pulled her head back to look up at him.

Still feeling the confusion from the trauma, Miranda wasn't able to answer the question. The questions in her mind kept her from thinking clearly. Ethan released her from the embrace and, with one arm, supported Miranda as the two walked inside. Miranda wasn't hungry, though she couldn't remember what or when she last ate.

Ethan got Miranda settled on the rocking chair by the hearth while he finished cooking the stew. Vida had sent him up the mountain with all the fixings for beef stew. Everything went into one pot. Ethan was grateful to have some good food to offer Miranda during her convalescence.

"This will be ready shortly." Ethan motioned toward the cauldron, whose contents were heating.

"It was a very kind gesture for Vida to put together a care package for me, and generous of you to bring it here. Thank you." Miranda felt guilty for causing extra work for the people who had so much of their own work to do.

"Out here, we take care of one another, no strings, no questions. When you see a need, you fill it. And you don't procrastinate. If something needs to be done and you wait till later, a bunch of other things needing to be done pile up and your list of things to do just gets larger." Ethan couldn't think of what else to say, but wanted to keep Miranda talking. He didn't want her to get drowsy before she had something to eat.

"I'm afraid this place takes the term rustic to a whole new level." Ethan continued. "I wish I could offer you actual plumbing instead of the pitcher of water with a bowl in which to freshen up. We have not yet built the full bathroom suite." Joking was a good way to keep Miranda's attention.

"The cabin is lovely and has all the essentials of comfort." Miranda looked around and already had an affectionate feeling toward the little dwelling. It was a safe place to hang your hat, a welcome refuge.

"Tomorrow, if you have the strength, I'll help you to the river. You can take a swim. It's cold but refreshing and it can leave you feeling invigorated."

Miranda felt embarrassed, not so much out of modesty, but for being a burden. She understood what Ethan meant by taking a swim, a euphemism for bathing. It seemed prudent a person should stay clean, even in the most remote corners of this earth. Miranda knew it was an imposition for Ethan to be stuck up here taking care of her. He had plenty to do at home.

"As nice as it sounds to bathe in a wild river, I suppose I should make my way back to the ranch. I don't want to take up any more of your time. I will head back first thing in the morning."

"I won't stop you, but it would behoove you to rest a little longer. I don't know if Winston has it in him to rescue you again."

Chapter 38

"What do you mean, rescue me? Winston?" Miranda was having trouble understanding if Ethan was teasing. She felt him watching her and the gentle way his smile lifted the corners of his eyes invited her to listen.

Ethan explained how he had found her that night, laying in a heap on the ground practically under Winston's feet. Miranda had to take Ethan's word for it. She had no recollection of arriving at the cabin, but suddenly a flash of memory made her raise her hand to her ribs and sternum, and the pressure made her cry out in pain.

Ethan's smile evaporated with concern as he moved toward Miranda. With her left hand, Miranda lifted her shirt to reveal the reason for the pain and Ethan gasped before he could temper his reaction.

"What the..." Ethan exclaimed. "How did that happen?"

Miranda shrugged, and then she remembered the searing pain she had felt as Winston raced through the woods. "The saddle horn?" The next flash of memory lashed out in her mind.

"The saddle horn." Ethan repeated, as the picture of Miranda hunched forward and clinging to the racing horse came into his mind.

Miranda remembered, "Something loud came crashing toward us. Winston spooked and took off running. I lost my stirrups but held on. As he dodged through the trees, I leaned forward to avoid being scraped off by a low branch. I felt the horn digging in but didn't dare ease my grip."

Ethan read the pain and fear and anguish written on Miranda's face as she relived the agonizing ride. "Are your ribs broken?" Ethan reached out as if the touch could erase away the signs of injury, but seeing Miranda flinch when he moved his hand was worse than the haunted look in her eyes.

Ethan watched the lines in Miranda's face deepen as a cloud of emotion came over her. She clutched her shirt to her injured abdomen as a reflexive barrier of protection. The helplessness Ethan felt reminded him of the case of animal abuse that had come to the ranch when he was just a teen. He had seen nothing like it before or since. But now he saw in Miranda the same look he saw on one abused animal in particular.

A herd of Arabian horses that were confiscated as evidence against the owners of a ranch accused of animal neglect became wards of the court while the case ran. The horses had been owned by people who hadn't a clue how to run a ranch, let alone breed and raise horses.

The couple lost interest when they realized ranching was a lot of work and they moved to the coast. They hired a caretaker with no qualifications and didn't bother to verify the man knew how to care for animals. Funds for the care and maintenance of the ranch and the animals were sent, but they did not use the money for its intended purpose.

After the trial, they gave all the usable horses to rescue organizations to be placed with new owners. The half dozen young horses that had never been touched came to the Baldwins for gentling and training at Alma Soñada Ranch. While in custody with the courts, five of the horses that had been born on the ranch had been kept in a pasture together, but one horse, a young stallion, had remained isolated. Kept in a pen in the dark barn with only brief interaction with any other beings, the stallion became crazed with fear.

Ethan realized this horse did not know how to communicate, didn't even know how to try. He had never known kindness or a gentle touch, and when the animals were taken into custody, the colt was manhandled, gelded, then forced into a small pen with the other horses. It was all so traumatic for the young horse and he had shut down. His fight-or-flight instinct was all he had and since he couldn't flee, he fought. With only his fear motivating him, it was as if the horse was deaf, mute, and blind. There wasn't a single avenue upon which to establish a path of communication.

Ethan had risen to the challenge and promised this horse he would see it through, but it was an uphill battle with no progress. The horse seemed to get worse the harder Ethan tried, and finally, Ansel, fearing for his son's safety, had put a stop to it. Ethan didn't let it go. He had to try one more thing and, with his father's permission, Ethan attempted to break through this young horse's defenses.

Under supervision, Ansel had watched as Ethan worked on his new idea. Ethan stalked the horse like a predator and when he threw ropes and lassoed the horse's legs so he couldn't kick or strike out, Ansel was concerned. Next,

Ethan pounced like a panther, held onto the horse's head and neck until the thrashing stopped, then tied a blindfold across the eyes.

Ansel had to look away and only heard the noise of the grunting and heaving as the horse struggled to free his legs. Ethan held tight to the head, making sure the horse didn't injure his face, eyes and ears as he ground himself into the dirt in an effort to free himself. Finally, the animal had stopped throwing and thrashing, almost stopped breathing, and lay quivering and rigid, waiting for the death his instinct told him was eminent.

Covered in dirt from head to boots, Ethan was breathing hard, too, but he had stood focused, waiting and watching the puffs of dust as the horse's nostrils breathed into the dry arena ground. It had exhausted Ansel from watching. It felt as though he, too, had been fighting for his life. But then, when Ethan removed the ropes, Ansel had held his breath.

Miraculously, the horse didn't fight, didn't even try to get up. Next, Ethan pulled the blindfold away; the colt rolled off his side and tucked his legs underneath himself, blinked hard as if seeing sunlight for the first time, but still, he didn't stand. Ethan got down on his hands and knees in front of the horse and blew his breath onto the colt's face and into its nostrils. Then when Ethan moved to the horse's side and nudged him in the flank, the horse stood, at first on wobbly legs, then when he was stable, he turned to face Ethan.

It was a moment of truth. Ethan stayed frozen in place. Would the horse charge? Would he still want to fight? If so, Ethan, who was now without a defense, would certainly be hurt, maybe even killed by the potential rage the horse could unleash.

Moving slowly, ears twitching, the stallion took a few steps, stopped and placed his muzzle on Ethan's chest. Ansel, who had been ready to jump into the arena, stood in immobilized shock as Ethan murmured in hushed tones the way a mare would nicker to her foal, and the colt nickered back. From that moment on, that Arabian horse had followed Ethan around like a baby follows his mother.

The whole thing had astonished Ansel. If he hadn't seen it for himself, he wouldn't have believed it and he had many questions for his son, but Ethan had no answers. Not even Ethan knew what he had been doing or if it would work until he did it and he hadn't even thought about it. He figured if the stallion was using his instinct, Ethan had to use his instinct, too.

Miranda's trauma was not unlike what the horse had suffered. Tad's back handed lashing was not the worst thing he did. The mental trauma of the assault was far more damaging. Ethan was glad again to be miles and miles away from civilization, for he was certain he would hunt Tad down, and when he found him, he would make sure Tad felt everything he had caused Miranda to feel in equal measure times ten.

Thinking about the Arabian colt, Ethan compared the two situations and decided instinct had showed him how to help the colt. Maybe it would show him how to heal Miranda as well.

~****~

The sky, at the height of summer that never seems to lose its hue of color except at the deepest point in the night, told Ethan it was late when he went outside to check on the horses. He and Miranda had had a quiet dinner. Miranda ate a little before the effort to be awake was too much. Eating, talking, and remembering had taken its toll. Ethan had given Miranda the change of clothes he had brought up, and she was taking advantage of the privacy while he was out tending to the stock.

I guess we're here for the night, Miranda thought, as she freshened up with the toothbrush given to her. The dim lighting in the room made her grateful when she looked in the mirror above the dresser. She could see the shadow of discolored skin below her right eye and, based on the colors she saw on her ribs, her eye must be a nice match.

Staring at her reflection in the mirror, Miranda spied behind her between the bed and under the window, an old antique trunk and in it were extra blankets. Miranda hadn't considered there was only one tiny bed and two of them, but thinking about it now, she figured they would need extra bedding. She wouldn't mind sleeping on the floor.

While removing the blankets, Miranda came across an Indian gown of soft, white deerskin. The beadwork was exquisite; the dress looked incredibly well preserved. Miranda tucked the gown back in the trunk to ask Ethan about it later.

When Ethan came back to the cabin, Miranda had changed her clothes and was sitting on the rocker waiting to discuss sleeping arrangements. Ethan spied the extra blankets and the pillow.

"I've had the bed since I got here, now it's your turn," Miranda was direct. "I'll sleep on the floor."

"I won't let you do that, Miranda. You shouldn't even think of it that way. I won't be sleeping in the cabin. My bed is outside, around the side of the house." Ethan wanted Miranda to know he had no ill intentions.

To think Miranda wanted to set him straight about sleeping arrangements. Did she think he had ulterior motives? It wasn't actually such a strange thing. With Tad's relentless and uninvited advances, Miranda might think Ethan would behave the same. It all may have been more traumatizing than anyone knew.

Thinking about the young colt as an example, Ethan opted to go back outside before anything more could be said. He had wanted to see that Miranda was comfortable and ready for a good night's sleep, but leaving her alone is what he did instead.

Like how the Arabian colt's actions were based on fear, so Ethan could assume, were Miranda's. Confronting her would only bring out the defenses like how trying to force communications with the abused colt brought out in it the fight.

Left alone in the cabin, Miranda got what she thought she wanted, but not what she needed. With nothing else to do, Miranda blew out the flickering flame of the little hurricane lamp, and laid down on the bed, but didn't go to sleep. When she closed her eyes, it filled her mind with flashes of memory; the dancing at the wedding reception, fighting with Tad, running through the forest, clinging to the side of a fleeing horse. Though she was weary, Miranda couldn't sleep.

"Miranda?"

Through the window, Miranda heard her name.

"Yes?" she answered when she realized Ethan's bed, a hammock strung up between the saplings beside the cabin, was on the outside, while on the inside was the bed upon which she lay.

"I just wanted to check on you." Ethan was just outside the window.

Blindsided by the innocence of the gesture, Miranda's heart warmed. "I can't sleep." She admitted, wishing her earlier message about sleeping arrangements hadn't been so blunt.

"Are you feeling pain? Does your head hurt?"

"Could you just talk to me for a while?" Miranda asked. She couldn't believe she was asking Ethan to tell her a bedtime story.

Without giving it a second thought, Ethan talked. He started by telling Miranda about his father's dog, Quinn. She was due to have puppies. Ethan told Miranda how his father acquired the two dogs he now had after searching for dogs with the qualities he wanted. Ethan explained how half the dogs in the county were related to Ansel's dogs. Everyone in the community, from ranches to families, wanted one of the Baldwin's border collies.

Miranda listened, asked brief questions that kept Ethan talking, and with his words, the tension eased. Going from the subject of border collies to spinning tales that went from legends of the past to the humorous stories of fun times growing up in a small town. Ethan's voice lulled, hypnotized. Like the words Ethan said to the horses through the gentling process, it was not what he said but how he said it. Miranda was falling under his spell. She settled back and let her head sink into the softness of the pillow as the melody of Ethan's voice lulled her deeply into relaxation.

Falling asleep to the sound of Ethan's voice could very well be the best sleep aid Miranda had ever known. If she could bottle it, she could sell it for a fortune. Here in the cozy cabin, Miranda could forget she had appointments, plans and people counting on her out in the real world. She was in the middle of seeing her biggest dreams become her greatest accomplishments, but instead of pounding forward, she was off the grid and thoroughly enjoying a vacation.

Miranda didn't even feel guilty. She was so relaxed and content up there in the valley, under the magnificent peaks that stood and watched the ranch lands below. Miranda hadn't realized how consumed by goals and ambitions she had become. The pressure had grown steadily but too slowly to be noticed. Had it reached an unhealthy level?

Chapter 39

"Good morning," Ethan said as he stood at the edge of the fireplace where the embers from the burning logs crumbled to form a perfect glowing pattern. They provided enough heat to fry bacon and the aroma spread.

"I smell breakfast." Miranda stretched, then caught her breath from the twang of pain because of the stiffness in the healing tissue around her bruised ribs.

Ethan looked up from the sizzling pan he was tending to in time to catch the grimace on Miranda's face. It reminded him how furious he still was at Tad. Ethan squashed the rage and explained, "For breakfast, since we have no refrigeration, we have dry cured bacon and new-laid eggs. Vida prides herself on eating only the foods she makes or grows herself, and even up here, it's her kitchen, her rules."

"Sounds perfect, but how on earth did you get fresh eggs up here without breaking them?" It was rhetorical and Ethan didn't answer.

Miranda enjoyed watching Ethan move about. Ethan looked like he belonged in this tiny mountain home. Miranda thought he looked quite relaxed. Almost sexy. The muscles in his forearm flexed and released as he poked at the strips of sizzling pork. Miranda liked a man who wasn't afraid to show his domesticity.

The coals radiated unregulated heat on the exposed skin on Ethan's arms, and he had to concentrate to evade the spatter of grease from the cast-iron skillet.

Miranda noticed Ethan was focusing too intensely to talk, so she spoke. Remembering how comfortably they had chatted through the window the night before, Miranda decided it was her turn to share a story or two. Miranda's stories took a somber turn when she told Ethan about her childhood as an orphan in foster care.

Miranda told Ethan what she knew about her background story based on the limited information the professionals had. Child protective services personnel concluded there was no physical abuse to baby Miranda when she became a ward of the state. But there was evidence of neglect. They were certain there was trauma, but an infant can't be helped with mental counseling. As she grew, the agencies noted her communication skills failed to develop as those of a normal child. Described as an extremely shy and quiet child, and with a lack of any family history or background story, Miranda appealed to very few parents looking to adopt or foster.

Not the typical subject one would expect to hear while eating breakfast. The sensitive nature of what Miranda relayed hit Ethan hard. He knew Miranda had had a disruptive childhood but hadn't realized the extensive trauma Miranda had been through. When she needed nurturing and comfort the most, there was none available. It touched him deep inside and, with empathy, he felt her pain.

Miranda paused the narrative to evaluate how her story was affecting Ethan. The expression of the sorrow in his eyes reminded her of why she never spoke about her past in such intimate detail. Even people who only knew the surface story became emotional. Miranda never wanted an ounce of pity. When that was the reaction, Miranda always stopped short and let the rest of the story stay squashed below.

But Ethan's response was unique. He showed no discomfort, as most folks did. There was no averting of eye contact. No reaching out a hand, feigning a comforting offer. Ethan was still listening, as if hearing her thoughts. They had both finished eating the eggs and bacon, but stayed at the table and Miranda continued.

She explained how she was instantly at ease with Mr. Gordon Howarth-Dunn the moment they met. Her adoptive father had a kind and quiet soul, generous and giving. He never pressured Miranda with expectations, never put upon her to be normal. Her father celebrated her uniqueness, encouraged her to be an individual. He was demonstrative without demand. She had an undeniable connection with this man. For the first time in her young life, she had a parental figure. In the short time they were a family, Mr. Gordon Howarth-Dunn had given Miranda the gift of an identity.

Under the loving care of her new father, Miranda told Ethan, the social workers were stunned by how quickly she blossomed. She came out of her place of hiding and was now described as socially and communicatively thriving. This made her father's sudden passing all the more devastating. In summation, Miranda chronologically simplified the facts; she went from orphan to adopted, then orphaned again with an attorney assigned to be her guardian.

Ethan noted the shift in Miranda's energy as she spoke. The light in Miranda's eyes when describing her experience as Howarth-Dunn's daughter was extinguished when she stated how her father died. Miranda became devoid of emotion and there the story and the conversation ended.

When Miranda had opened up the conversation over breakfast, she intended to tell Ethan about what spawned her vision of an all-encompassing equine therapy program. She wanted to give Ethan her vision so he might better understand the reasons she was so driven to help others. Somehow, though, Miranda strayed off the topic. Surprised by how easy it was to talk to Ethan, Miranda went deeper than she planned. But Ethan had listened with interest and made appropriate gestures that encouraged her. Miranda had revealed things she had probably not told a soul. Not even her best friend, Amanda.

"Why don't you rest and I'll clean up the breakfast dishes," Ethan offered. He noticed the color had left Miranda's cheeks after all the talking.

Miranda didn't put up a fight. The emotional narrative she shared had zapped her spirit and taken her to a place inside deeper than she realized.

As promised, after breakfast, Ethan brought Miranda to the river's edge, then left her to her privacy. Miranda sat on a smooth and rounded rock by the bank and took in the environment. The path to the bank, overgrown though it was, had brought them to a spot where the water ran still and deep, perfect for swimming and bathing in. Miranda noted the shrubs growing beside the overgrown trial as they passed through. There was Black Choke Berry and Witches Hazel growing in spots in between the White Alder, Birch and Black Willow trees. The over growth of vegetation gave way to the rocky shore and on a sandbar about a third of the way across grew some low, bushy Sandbar Willows.

Miranda removed her boots and sunk her toes into the sand. The scratchiness was pleasing; it was like a natural exfoliation treatment. Not really sure how one goes about bathing in a river, Miranda stepped to the water's edge and went in up to her ankles. The water was shockingly cold, but

Miranda's need to get clean overrode instinct to keep warm. In an instant, she had shed her clothing and was up to her neck in the frigid, flowing river.

It was difficult not to make noises, squeals and gasps. When her bare skin responded to the temperature. Dowsing herself under water, Miranda gave herself a mental cleansing as well. Splashing the parts of her body that needed refreshing, Miranda became playful. She wondered if she looked like the robins and sparrows she used to watch in the birdbaths and fountains of the manicured gardens surrounding the Howarth-Dunn mansion.

Ethan had said a swim in the river would be refreshing and he was not wrong, but what he hadn't mentioned was how she would feel beneath the skin. The penetrating cold had stimulated circulation when her body's instinct was to draw blood away from the surface and extremities. Upon leaving the waters, Miranda's blood returned to the contracted vessels with fresh blood that aided to heal her wounds and bruises.

Wrapped in a towel, Miranda welcomed the tingle of her skin as the shining sun warmed her. She closed her eyes and listened to the chirping of birds, the rustle of the ever quaking aspens, the distant 'awhhhhhh' sound of the waters carried on the breeze from where the river turned rogue.

Feeling very into it all, Miranda got dressed in the white deerskin Indian gown she had brought with her on a whim. The softness of the leather further soothed her broken body. Putting her boots back on, Miranda realized it had felt better to be barefooted, but the stoney path and the harsh meadow grasses would have left her crawling on hands and knees in pain. She was, by the very definition, a tenderfoot.

On the way past the shrubs that lined the river bank, Miranda gathered twigs and bark from the witch's hazel. She would distill the medicinal properties from the bush. Witch Hazel can be extracted by boiling all parts of the bush in water, then the water is used as an antibacterial, astringent, and anti-inflammatory. Miranda was no stranger to the benefits of homeopathic remedies and had built her own home apothecary.

Miranda concentrated as she strolled slowly up the winding path. She didn't want to lose her way to the clearing at the edge of the meadow. She was in no condition to get lost, hadn't the strength to wander around aimlessly until she found her way, and Ethan had made it clear neither he nor Winston were interested in any more rescue adventures.

Arriving to find the cabin was empty, Miranda assumed Ethan may have gone to another section of the river for a private swim of his own. Miranda capitalized on her free time, and after the healing effects of the flowing waters, found she had enough energy to tidy up the place.

First, Miranda set up the witch's hazel distillation process. Breaking up the sticks and sprigs into smaller pieces, she heated some water in the cauldron, but not to a boil, over the still warm embers in the fireplace. Next, Miranda allowed the concoction to simmer while she made the bed, cleaned up the kitchen, and rinsed the pitcher and bowl. Placing the ceramic ware back on the dresser, Miranda spotted her reflection in the mirror. She was grateful the facial contusions were fading, getting lighter purple around the edges, with some yellowing in the middle. Thanks to Vida's arnica tinctures and the body's natural process, she continued to heal.

Tugging at her now wildly unruly hair, Miranda wondered if there was a comb and searched to find a hairbrush. With each stroke, Miranda's long black hair straightened out. Catching sight of the gown she wore, Miranda wondered who had worn it before her and remembered the story of Carmen's mother, Running Fawn. Miranda heard Ethan's footsteps as he came in with an armload of wood. She turned to see his expression of surprise.

"You look like you've seen a ghost." Miranda's face cracked into a smile.

"I take it you enjoyed your swim?" Ethan said. Changing the subject was an easy way to avoid the feelings that stirred when Ethan saw Miranda in the Indian gown. Her black hair hanging loosely down and in contrast with the white deer hide, the intricate beauty of the beadwork on the neckline that paled compared to the striking features of Miranda's face. Keeping his thoughts noble, Ethan concentrated on the conversation.

Feeling foolish, now for wearing the native robe, as she couldn't read Ethan's reaction, Miranda forced herself to think gratitude to Ethan for suggesting she freshen up. "I very much enjoyed the river. Its healing powers are highly beneficial. I also gathered some witch's hazel on the way back here. No home should be without witch hazel extract."

As Miranda moved gracefully about in the deerskin gown tending to her concoction brewing, it enthralled Ethan. Try though he might, Ethan's thoughts wouldn't switch tracks and as Miranda spoke, he couldn't help but stare at the exquisite picture she was unintentionally painting. She looked so comfortable in this environment, being one with nature suited her. In her bare feet wearing that deerskin robe, well, Ethan thought, nothing they sell in a lingerie department could look so good and he doubted that for him anything found at a store could be so effective. His feelings of arousal couldn't be stopped.

"I found this dress in the trunk. I hope it's okay that I'm wearing it." Ethan's stark staring made Miranda uncomfortable. Maybe the dress belonged to a ghost. Maybe it had some sordid back-story. "Do you know who wore this? Did it belong to Carmen? or Running Fawn?"

"I don't think so." Ethan chuckled softly as he stacked the wood.

"I hope it isn't an artifact or something. It looks handmade, but doesn't look old." Miranda probed further when Ethan offered no information. Miranda hadn't seen a label inside and a machine did not do the slightly uneven stitching. "It is not some ceremonial garment worn by the natives, is it?" Miranda joked.

"I have heard my mom and dad talking about the legends and history of this place, but I am unaware of any historical significance to the native dress." Ethan focused on speaking without looking directly at Miranda as her joke flew over his head.

Ethan remembered what the gown was and from where it had come. His mother had given it to Paula. He had come across it the last time he was there. He had wondered if it was to be used in some plan Paula might have schemed up for a romantic getaway when they were to be married. Ethan stayed mum about the providence of the Indian gown.

Miranda sensed there was more he could have said and didn't understand why Ethan held back. She worried he might have a romantic memory of the novelty deerskin dress with another woman wearing it. Suddenly, it embarrassed her, and she regretted having put the leather dress on. Miranda wondered if Ethan, under his tough, cowboy-rough exterior, was a true romantic.

Recalling Ethan's balletic, almost sensual interactions with horses, she could only wonder if it transferred over. Miranda pondered the notion of Ethan romancing her. She remembered their interlude in the stable that night not so long ago. The touch of Ethan's hand on hers started a sequence of reactions. The sensation of his lips on hers fired off sparks she couldn't ignore. But maybe Ethan's intimate energy only connected with horses. Maybe Ethan hadn't felt a thing when he kissed people.

Before her thoughts could go any farther, Ethan was by her side. "You look beautiful in that gown."

Observing Miranda's contemplative mood, Ethan thought he saw disappointment on her face. Ethan felt like Miranda might have been looking for assurance. After the trauma she had gone through, it made sense she needed a boost of confidence. He couldn't stand to discourage her when she was trying to move past her trauma and following instinct, Ethan said, "You are a smart, sensitive woman, wise beyond reason about what matters in life. You are stunning."

Miranda never thought of herself as a person who needed an ego boost. She never fished expeditiously for compliments from men, and under normal circumstances, anyone who handed out a line like the one she just heard would be suspect, but this was different. She felt the honesty, recognized his intentions and hoped she was not reading him wrong.

Looking at Ethan square in the eyes, with complete vulnerability, Miranda leaned into his open arms and let him wrap her with comfort. Still unsure of her place in his heart, she wished to feel warmth from his place in hers. Deep down, she was afraid of what would happen when the blanket of security he offered would eventually be removed. When she was no longer in his arms, wouldn't she be left feeling the cold of the world even more for the contrast of having felt, even temporarily, his warmth? Holding eye contact, Miranda searched for a sign, waited for an answer.

Ethan couldn't hold off his emotions. Instinct had told him to honor Miranda, to hold her in highest regard, and now instinct was telling him to kiss her. He bent forward and captured Miranda's lips in his. He felt a tremble, tasted sorrow and tapped the brakes but Miranda quickened to make up for it. Wrapping her arms tightly around his neck, then sliding her hands forward to touch his face, Miranda kissed Ethan back.

Mindfully aware of the still sensitive right side of her face, Ethan gently kissed Miranda on the left cheek, let his fingers softly run down the discolored right cheek, and gave her a chance to process what was happening. But there was no fear, nor worry. The bruises and the event that lead up to them were a part of the past and quickly fading. Getting the signal he was looking for, Ethan kissed Miranda's mouth again, then her chin, her ear, as his hand moved from her shoulder, over the deerskin garment, down her back and to her waist where he pulled her in, pressing her tighter against him.

Miranda's eyelids dipped as Ethan kissed her and felt the heat of the fire he was drawing with his caressing hands. The taught muscles in Ethan's arms pressed against Miranda and she drew a quick breath. The pressure reminded her of the abdominal contusions, but with Ethan's eager lips on hers, her focus shifted away from any pain. Her legs grew heavy, and Miranda felt Ethan lift and carry her to the bed.

Ethan placed Miranda gently down, watching again to see if there was any change in mood or emotion, but she erased his questions when she pulled him toward her. With his hands and lips, Ethan played with Miranda's senses in sequence as he explored her body through the deerskin gown. With a mutual desire to remove all barriers, Miranda let Ethan help her out of the Indian robe.

As he kissed and caressed, she responded to him like she imagined the young horses did when Ethan began the gentling process. Miranda wasn't sitting jealously on the fence, watching the horses receive their lessons. Ethan worked his magic touch on her. Finally, it was Miranda who was learning to move to Ethan's every cue.

Having lost all sense of time and space, and with nothing to bring in the outside world, Ethan and Miranda reveled in the beauty of closeness between two people as God intended. They rested in each other's arms, peacefully drifting in and out of complete surrender, then as the fires of passion rekindled, matched each other with satisfying ease.

~****~

The sun moved unnoticed across the sky. The daylight hours were slipping by, but it was of no concern. For Ethan and Miranda, they could have been the only two people left on the planet, and couldn't have been happier about it. There was no need for lunch or dinner. The horses didn't need tending to. Miranda had only one thing on her mind as she drifted into a peaceful slumber. Ethan.

Miranda awoke late in the evening with a shiver. She realized she was staring at the dark wall, and the day was gone. Had she been unconscious again? or still? Remembering Ethan, Miranda reached behind for a warm body, but the bed was empty. Had she been dreaming? Miranda rolled over and there was Ethan, placing a log on the kindling he had lain on the almost cold embers.

He was still here, in the cabin with her, and based on what little clothing he wore, she hadn't been dreaming.

There was something very primal in the image, the beautifully sculpted body of a man coaxing flame from the ashes. Miranda drifted back in time and imagined the handsome settler and his maiden, Running Fawn. Had the settler and the Indian maiden made beautiful love in this same valley? Miranda wondered how it would feel to have loved deeply, only to have lost even more deeply when the world moved in and inflicted its insensitive restrictive parameters.

Ethan turned when he felt Mirada's eyes and smiled. "Miranda."

Ethan was the only one at the Alma Soñada Ranch that used her full name, and she liked how he rolled the 'r' off his tongue. Miranda reached out toward Ethan and he rejoined her in bed. She would not think about what waited outside the four walls of this room. They were here now, and she intended to capture every moment. Right now, was the most connected to a fellow human she had ever been in her entire life. She wasn't ready to give it up yet. Let the world force its parameters on someone else. There would be plenty of time for that later. Miranda was going to stay suspended in time for a little while longer.

"You are so beautiful," Ethan studied Miranda's partially uncovered shape supine on the bed.

Propped up with her head on her left wrist, Miranda's hair was still long and loose, cascading down in soft ebony sheets. It seemed to glisten as the logs that had just caught fire cast light on individual strands. The dark shadows emphasized Miranda's features, underlining even more dramatically the eyes and prominent cheekbones. The vision of Miranda earlier in the deerskin gown, which had since been set aside, stuck in Ethan's mind. He imagined how much Miranda might resemble the legendary Indian maiden; tall and graceful with rich, copper toned skin and jet-black hair. No wonder the settler had fallen madly in love.

Ethan slid under the covers and wrapped his arms around Miranda. She let out a sigh of contentment, and Ethan placed a tender kiss on her forehead. "I love you," Miranda thought she heard him say just before she heard the rhythmic breathing of his peaceful slumber.

Chapter 40

The next time Miranda opened her eyes, there was the soft light of dawn showing through the windows. Wrapped tightly in a cocoon of warmth with Ethan on the tiny bed, she took in her surroundings. She was happy to realize, this time upon waking, she knew exactly where she was. Gone was any fuzziness around the edges. This time, she was certain she wasn't dreaming. She hadn't been unconscious; she had imagined nothing. The man lying next to her was very real. They had spent the better part of a day and an entire night together, and it had been wonderful. Everything seemed in place, as if the valley, the forest, the meadow and all who dwell there were whispering their approval. Miranda thought of the handsome trapper and Running Fawn and all the ghosts of lore and decided they, too, were unanimously in favor.

Lying there awake, the security of Ethan's arms was short-lived as old thoughts and insecurities crept in. Was she reading more into this than there was? Were they merely two people passing through the night together because there was little else to do? Remembering what she thought she had heard Ethan say, she wasn't sure if she'd heard correctly. He probably had said nothing at all.

Ethan awoke the next morning and smiled at the first thing he saw, Miranda's sleepy grin and half open lids. For a moment, the interior of the cabin appeared to have more sunshine than what shone from the actual sun. A second later, the light waned when Ethan identified a tinge of fright in Miranda. There was a slight bit of fear, as if waking up beside Ethan was shocking. He moved his elbow under his shoulder to get a clearer look.

Bending forward, Ethan touched his finger to the stray strands of obsidian hair across Miranda's cheek and gently slid it back into place by her ear as his body filled with intention. He kissed Miranda on the forehead as if checking her body temperature. With his mouth still pressed against her head, Ethan said. "Good morning."

Ethan was not expecting what happened next, but quickly realized things were not going as he wished when Miranda disentangled herself from the bedcovers and leaped to her jeans and a sweatshirt. Gone was the confident woman who had been with him yesterday and throughout the night. Lost was the connection he had and pulling away from him was the frightened and confused girl, clutching her arms tightly around herself.

Instinctively, Ethan stood to offer comfort, then reached for a blanket to cover himself when he realized his over exposure. It irritated Ethan when, the next thing he knew, Miranda had fled through the door. He decided not to follow her. When he had a horse that refused to be caught, he would simply ignore the animal and soon its curiosity brought the horse to him.

Ethan tidied up the bed and put on his jeans and his shirt. He stoked the fire, put some water in the kettle and hung it over the flames that were crackling and spitting their way to life. Ethan decided they'd leave after a cup of brew. He wished to take Miranda up to the ridge above the summer valley before leaving the high country. He wanted her to see the sunrise.

"There is hot water on for coffee. Please fill the thermos. I'm gonna saddle up the horses. Get yourself ready to ride." Ethan stepped out of the way when Miranda returned from the outhouse.

"Mm-hmm," Miranda murmured a closed-mouthed response to the orders she was given. Miranda had found the creek behind the latrine to splash in and wash away the sleep. The water was icy, but clarifying. Like the stream behind the outhouse, Ethan's instructions were also cold and clear. Both were an eye-opening experience.

Ethan had gone outside, leaving Miranda alone with her thoughts. "So that was it," Miranda said to herself. "That's all it was?" Miranda surmised Ethan closed the book on the passionate night she and he had spent together. She decided she would act as business-like about it as was Ethan.

Miranda carefully folded the deerskin gown and placed it safely in the trunk, tucked away with the memories of a glorious night that meant a lot to her and was fast becoming more of a dream. She laid the extra bedding, folded and stacked, on top of the native dress. There would be no future need for the Indian robe anymore.

Ethan had resumed the role of guardian. She was his charge. He most likely enjoyed the interlude, but today he needed to get down the mountain and on with his life. Last night hadn't even earned her a decent breakfast, she thought with sorrow, but no use dwelling on it. "It's your own fault," Miranda told herself.

Her head was being logical as she pushed away her bruised heart. She questioned whether she was even feeling anything at all, so accustomed was she to ignoring heartbreak. Had the legends and lore Miranda heard about gotten the better of her imagination? Was she just getting swept up in the moment? Had she focused too much on the romance of Running Fawn? After all, that legend ended in tragedy after a lifetime of yearning. Would Miranda be doomed to spend a lifetime yearning for Ethan?

"Preposterous!" she scolded herself for being so foolish.

Miranda heard the whispers of the trees and the mountains again, but this time they mocked her. She shook the sound from her ears and poured the coffee. May as well get this place ready for the next visitors. Miranda put things away and gave the cabin a once over. As she busied herself, she felt an emotional tug recalling the image of Ethan squatting by the fire, or standing at the kitchen table.

With the water still in the ceramic pitcher, Miranda dowsed the flames of the fire physically and extinguished metaphorically the heat of the images in her mind. She ceremoniously set the pitcher gently back with its partner, the bowl, a matched set. Even the pitcher and bowl knew where they stood with each other. Why did it have to be so vague between herself and Ethan?

Ethan didn't say a word as he held Winston while Miranda mounted, then he climbed on Serenity. With Rowdy still serving as the packhorse in tow behind him, Ethan started up the valley. Miranda wondered why they were heading away from the direction of the ranch. Her abdominal muscles were still tender around the ribs and she focused on relaxing with the movement of the horse.

They caught a trail that led up the eastern side. Ethan hoped to present Miranda with a three hundred sixty-degree view of the mountains, the small valley that cradled the ranch, and the larger valley in the distance where the town of Rambletap Springs lay. The sun would illuminate the entire view rising at their backs.

"Checking on the herd?" Miranda asked, assuming that is why they were riding up the mountain instead of down.

"Among other things," Ethan said, then silence.

"Who is that you are riding?" Miranda drew Ethan out on a safe subject when she realized the horse he rode wasn't Sonnet, as she had previously guessed.

Ethan was relieved when Miranda asked a casual question. He was stewing about how to address Miranda's shift in mood and was glad for a neutral topic upon which to communicate. So badly did he crave interaction of any kind with Miranda. His plan to stay back was drawing her to him. He began telling the story.

"Her name is Serenity. She is Sonnet's dam. She is fourteen... maybe fifteen... I always lose track. She came to the Alma Soñada Ranch at three years old and was labeled a runaway. Her owners wanted us to fix her. They knew my dad was a good hand with rehabilitating runaways. The failed methods to break her used by other trainers did little to help and mostly made things worse. Ansel knew they had badly abused Serenity."

Ethan's face grew long in contemplation as he remembered how senselessly broken at the hands of ignorance the young horse had been.

"I saw in her a deep sensitivity, but fear at the surface was ruling over," Ethan continued the story. "I can't even imagine the brutality with which they had handled her in their previous efforts to train the flight instinct out of her. We got her to a point where she was controllable in an enclosed environment, but soon as she saw an open gate, she would bolt."

"You are riding her out in the open, so obviously your dad could help her." Miranda was invested in a positive outcome to what was so far a solemn tale.

"The owners ran out of patience and came for the filly before we could do anything further. We weren't satisfied and told them she wasn't finished, but they were done paying for her training. They came for her, loaded her into their trailer, and took her away. Three months later and after who knows what else they tried on their own, Serenity came back."

"The cowboys that worked on their ranch had ridden her but realized she was of no use on the range, so when they needed some thrills, they would throw a saddle on her back and whip her into a frenzy. In her fear induced hysteria, she would buck like the dickens. They placed bets on which cowboys she could and couldn't throw. When the owner found out what his cowhands were doing, he put an end to it and told Dad he was going to sell the mare by the pound."

Obviously, the horse hadn't become dog meat, but so engrossed in the story was Miranda. She hung on Ethan's words. "What happened?"

The look of alarm on Miranda's face as she listened showed Ethan her genuine compassion and concern. Her empathy ran deep. "Dad gave the man his money back for the training we'd invested and the owner gave us Serenity. The rest is history."

Ethan looked down at Serenity with pride. She was an example of what can become of a rescued horse, one who no one thought could be gentled with kindness and love. "At first, Serenity was to be a brood mare. She had good bloodlines that complimented the genetic pool of our stallion, Magic. The pair produced a few good foals, then two years in a row, the breeding was mysteriously and heartbreakingly miscarried."

"Having successfully borne and raised the first few foals had changed Serenity and we tried her under the saddle again. She was like a different horse. She had morphed into a solid mount, loyal and dependable. Gone was her need to bolt in fear through any open gate."

"After a few years off, we tried a breeding, and she carried to term. Since then, we have bred her every other year, and each breeding has been a success. Serenity and Magic make quite the pair and produced some of the best offspring on the ranch."

"That is a wonderful story," Miranda shivered with emotion. She gazed into the horse's eye and had a symbiotic feeling. It was a bonding exchange between females who had both experienced abuse while vulnerable. The energy zinging back and forth was full of comfort and understanding.

As they rode on thoughtfully, Ethan considered how much like Serenity was Miranda. Both had been hurt through no fault of their own. Both ran when afraid. Ethan hoped that unlike Serenity, who had endured many violent situations, Miranda would not suffer any more fear or pain.

"We are here." Ethan announced as he stopped and turned Serenity to face the eastern slope, over which the sun was about to rise.

"Where?" Miranda turned Winston to copy Serenity.

"Just in time," Ethan whispered as the first rays shot forth, casting their individual shafts of light over the craggy tips of the peaks. "Behold, the sunrise."

The humans were quiet, as if the sunrise wasn't simply a visual show. It seemed they needed to hear it, too. Sitting quietly in the hush, it reminded Miranda of the moment the audience in the theater or at the symphony knows the show is about to start. Even the horses stood still, as if delighting in the display they were fortunate to witness.

First to cast their beauty, the pinks on the edges of some wispy tendrils of atmospheric disturbances, followed by a splash of orange at the bottoms of the clouds, whose brilliance grew to blazing yellows. Miranda's mouth stuck open in awe as the glorious exhibit unfolded. After what seemed too soon, the colors faded. "And now for a second act in Sunrise Theater." Ethan turned and moved fifty yards across the almost flat ridge to the opposite side, and without her input, Winston followed suit.

The sunlight was touching the top of the dark mountains to the west. The tallest peaks were first to be painted golden browns and oranges. In contrast, were the blues and grays of the part still in the shadows. The unfolding transformations were amazing to watch. Miranda could only stare at the beauty before her. From deep inside, she had a wave of energy that swelled up in her eyes and the emotions came out in tears.

Ethan studied Miranda's changed expression, then bowed his head when he felt he was intruding on her private spiritual moment. Moving into a moment of his own, Ethan dismounted and stepped to the very edge of the ridge and was thrilled when Miranda joined him there. Together, they were taking part in something powerful, moving.

Miranda stood on that ridge and let nature fill her up. She embraced her transcendence and realized the energy was moving Ethan along with her. Standing beside Ethan, Miranda heard the trees whispering again with no condescending undertones. This time they said, "you are home," and suddenly Miranda wanted to be touching Ethan.

As if spontaneously moved by other forces, Ethan and Miranda pushed into each other in a side hug, made more meaningful by the purest of intentions. Watching as the mountain's dark shadows shrank, Miranda felt the light in her heart and when she looked up at Ethan, the emptiness inside her shrank like the sinking umbra of the shadow on the cliffs.

After their eyes locked, next came their lips, touching slowly, gently, savoringly, and with tenderness. From out of nowhere, a wind swept up, swirled about them in a circle, then continued over their heads. Miranda no longer doubted Ethan's feelings for her. Their unspoken declaration of love was as real as the sunrise that had brought them together.

Ethan slowly drifted back and looked into Miranda's eyes. He saw no sign of angst, no more hollowness in the depths. There was peace and tranquility coming not only from within, but from all around them. The two lovers had become one with the harmony of life in the mountains. It was as if their spirits were now joined to be shared with all the spirits beyond the earthly plain.

In the valley below, they could see the cows and calves grazing on the sunlit, dew kissed grass. "Next time we come up here, we'll be driving the cattle home," Ethan declared.

It delighted Miranda to hear Ethan say 'we'. It wasn't often in her life she heard it. "But we will have a few therapy sessions before then," Miranda said, thinking about her program for the first time in days.

"It was your contribution, wasn't it?" Miranda asked the question completely out of context.

"The name for the arena?" Ethan knew what Miranda was asking about without explanation. "Yes, of course." Ethan turned to help Miranda up on her horse. "But it's supposed to be anonymous."

Ethan's signature wink and dangerously appealing grin teased Miranda and left her weak in the knees. She was glad she was already mounted safely on her horse.

Still standing beside Winston, Ethan looked up at his love. Miranda leaned forward toward Ethan then winced when her ribs reminded her of their tender condition. Ethan raised his arm and Miranda pulled his hand up to her lips and planted a kiss. Ethan put the kissed hand to his lips, never loosing eye contact with Miranda.

With matching smiles, they simultaneously started to laugh, unashamed of the silly, tender moment they just had. "It's perfect," Miranda said regarding the name of the arena.

"It will be nice when Sunrise Arena is full of children. And the parents and family members will love to see the Autumnal changing of colors here on the ranch."

Miranda waited for Ethan to mount before they turned in synchronicity and headed for the trail that had brought them up.

"Fall will be my favorite time to bring groups out on the trails." Ethan confessed.

"Fall, alongside winter, spring and summer," Miranda laughed. She noticed Ethan including himself in her program, perhaps as a trail guide and it excited her more.

"Yeah, I guess it's all my favorite, too."

It put Miranda's mind at ease to hear Ethan talk about her therapy program without bristling. She had grown accustomed to bracing for his reaction whenever the subject came up, but that behavior seemed to be gone. Walking down the trail that morning, Miranda and Ethan talked. They each had their plans and ideas, and were surprised to find out how they fit in a complementary way. Ethan wanted to continue running the cattle business, and Miranda needed to provide her clients with a working ranch experience. Miranda needed a string of reliable horses for her therapy children to ride, and Ethan promised to find and train the most suitable stock for the job. Their conversation eventually turned to more intimate subjects.

The circumstances of the trail with just the two of them gave them the uninterrupted opportunity to express to each other freely their hopes and dreams. It pleased them how easy it was to talk about things they hadn't shared with anyone. They both wanted family to be close by so their own kids could grow up with much love and support. It was important to both of them they have a relationship built on consistency, love and respect.

They each longed for an unconditional connection with another human to whom they could commit. On that ambling ride down the trail, they discovered they each had been looking for something they didn't know they didn't have, a soul-mate, a partner, a lover, and a friend.

The trail on which Ethan was taking them home was a part of the ranch Miranda hadn't seen before. It was less of a trail and more of a push through the low branches and undergrowth of the trees that clung to the canyon slopes. They had ridden down the slope on the opposite side of the canyon. With the river on their left, they came upon an outcropping where Ethan stopped, dismounted, and swung Serenity's lead rope over a low-hanging branch. Following his example, Miranda dismounted and secured Winston to another branch.

"There is one more thing I want to show you." Ethan ducked into the shrubs. "Watch your step."

The warning came almost too late as Miranda crashed into Ethan, who had halted on the other side of the wall of vegetation. They had emerged on a ledge that opened up to a perch over the canyon wall.

"Oh my goodness!" Miranda exclaimed. When she thought she knocked Ethan into the abyss, she instinctively reached out and caught him by the arm.

"I gotcha." Ethan closed his hand around Miranda's arm to form a double bridge between them. Neither of them was in danger of losing balance. Ethan squared his shoulders, put his other arm around Miranda, and turned to face the view. "And you got me."

It was then Miranda took in the full vision provided by the granite outcropping. She was staring at cathedral-like columns of stone that seemed to reach higher than the sky scrapers back home. Hearing roaring thunder, her ears told her to look up. Above where they stood were the falls. They were directly below the summer valley's southern edge, the side the river flowed to before disappearing over the rocks and boulders of a vast cliff. The falls began at the valley floor, plummeted and pooled and plummeted nearly three-quarters of a mile down. There were four individual cascades of rushing and tumbling water separated by three pools where the river ran quiet and deep.

"Besides me, you are the only one who knows this place. We are the only two people I know of who have seen the falls from this spot."

Miranda was in awe. Gazing up toward the cascading river, she could see the spectrum of color created by the rays of sun shining through the mist. Across the yawning canyon, the tree branches gently swayed to and fro, set in perpetual motion by the turbulent currents of air. She absorbed the energy from the surroundings. The power of the crashing water energized her, the rustle of the leaves nourished her.

The intermittent spray of mist soothed her. In showing her this place, Ethan was sharing something personal. This was the part of the ranch that Ethan was desperate to protect. It was more private than their conversations. Even more intimate than sharing their bodies, passions and desires of the flesh. This place held the very essence within.

The lovers stood with their arms wrapped around each other, looking out on nature's beauty. The syncopated beating of their hearts turned their two souls into one. Their silhouette embodied the image of another couple whose lives became joined the same way over one hundred years before.

"This will be our spot," Ethan whispered the same words the settler may have said to the Indian maiden.

The simple words floated like the mist and bathed the future with promise. They had a spot. The scars of uncertainty in Miranda's subconscious shifted away from fear and into full healing. For Miranda, it was like the lost and wounded child she kept protected had finally found peace. The emptiness inside was filled as if her soul was now reunited with the parents she never knew.

Subconsciously, Miranda and Ethan had knowledge of the role they played in reconnecting the lost spirits from the past. No longer would the ghosts of Running Fawn and her fur-trapper lover roam the forests and valleys searching. Reunited at last, they could finally rest in tranquility. Carmen's spirit was also healed with her parents' souls now at peace.

"Hmmm," Miranda sighed and leaned closer to Ethan.

Miranda simply and unconditionally loved this ranch, this family, and the man she knew would ride beside her for the rest of her life. Never would she have guessed that by following her dreams of helping others, it would lead her to the place she belonged.

It was no accident she should find herself on a rock ledge, her back to a wall of vegetation, staring into a seemingly bottomless granite abyss with the love of her life by her side. Since before that day in late May, when a random gust of wind blew across their faces, Miranda's and Ethan's fates were written.